PRAISE FOR *AUTHENTICITY*

'This wise, quirky, funny, wholly original book
is an authentic delight. I loved it.'

Tim Harford

author of *How to Make the World Add Up*

'Beautifully written, hugely readable and completely
fascinating – a book for smart thinkers everywhere.'

Mary Ann Sieghart

author of *The Authority Gap*

'Alice Sherwood places "authenticity" in the dock with a
series of brilliantly analysed cases. From soft drinks to
malaria tablets, Andy Warhol to Yves Saint Laurent, they
are unfailingly compelling and often shocking. I found
myself instantly absorbed by a combination of
Sherwood's formidable storytelling powers and her wry
and psychologically penetrating commentaries.'

Philip Mould

presenter of *Fake or Fortune?*

'Perhaps at no point in recent history has "the real"
seemed more elusive than it does now when cons,
counterfeits and camouflage seem to be everywhere.
Deceit is the darker side of intelligence, and this
fascinating and hugely entertaining book is a rich
guide to the many forms it can take.'

Brian Eno

'Alice Sherwood is the real deal when it comes to exploring authenticity. Wielding the weapon of story, usually the preserve of telling tales, she takes the reader on a wonderful rollercoaster of a ride to prepare them to recognise what's real and what's illusion.'

Marcus du Sautoy
Simonyi Professor for the Public Understanding of Science
at the University of Oxford,
and author of *Thinking Better*

'A fascinating and oh-so-cleverly written book about the complexities of creation and creativity, a journey that shifts from Darwin to Warhol in ways you won't expect.'

Dylan Jones
author of *The Wichita Lineman*

'At a moment of shared perplexity, Alice Sherwood's very clever new book puts our counterfeit culture on trial. Misinformation and truthiness jostle for our attention, technology multiplies doubt, and cyber-intangibles are more valuable than solid treasure. With wit, elegance and well-groomed intellect, Sherwood explains how we can try to reclaim reality.'

Stephen Bayley
author of *Design: Intelligence Made Visible*

'*Authenticity* demonstrates that although those who wish to deceive us sometimes seem to have the upper hand, it's down to the individual to fight for authenticity.'

Eliot Higgins
author of *We Are Bellingcat*

AUTHENTICITY

AUTHENTICITY

Reclaiming Reality
in a Counterfeit Culture

ALICE SHERWOOD

MUDLARK

Mudlark
HarperCollins*Publishers*
1 London Bridge Street
London SE1 9GF

www.harpercollins.co.uk

HarperCollins*Publishers*
1st Floor, Watermarque Building, Ringsend Road
Dublin 4, Ireland

First published by Mudlark 2022

1 3 5 7 9 10 8 6 4 2

'Tennessee Homesick Blues' Words and Music by Dolly Parton © 1984.
Reproduced by permission of (Velvet Apple Music/Sony Music Publishing),
London W1T 3LP

A catalogue record of this book is
available from the British Library

HB ISBN 978-0-00-841262-3
PB ISBN 978-0-00-852079-3

Printed and bound in the UK using 100%
renewable electricity at CPI Group (UK) Ltd

MIX
Paper from
responsible sources
FSC™ C007454

This book is produced from independently certified FSC™ paper
to ensure responsible forest management.

For more information visit: www.harpercollins.co.uk/green

To my father, Archie Sherwood.
I wish you'd been here for this.

'It's hard to be a diamond in a rhinestone world.'

Dolly Parton,
'Tennessee Homesick Blues'

'Our degrees of freedom are not zero.'

Charles Taylor,
The Ethics of Authenticity

CONTENTS

ON AVERAGE

On average, you will be lied to three times within the first ten minutes of meeting someone.

When asked by researchers, you will admit to lying one and a half times a day, unless you are the 45th President of the United States, in which case you will lie twenty-one times a day, but not admit to it.

One in ten of you may not have the father you think you have. Best not to give DNA kits as Christmas presents.

In nature, as in life, there are the copiers and the copied. In the struggle for existence, fraud is almost inevitable. 'If you want honesty,' says the biologist, 'try physics instead.'

'There are nine levels of authenticity for an Old Master', according to the auctioneer. Depending on how much of the picture the artist painted, and other factors. But what does it say about authenticity when the Andy Warhol Authentication Board says that a Warhol silkscreen signed, dedicated and dated by him is 'NOT the work of Andy Warhol'?

By this point, on average, 16 per cent of you have started to wonder whether these are facts or wild assertions.

Sources are listed on page 359.

Protestant reformer John Calvin observed that there were enough pieces of the True Cross in existence by 1543 to make 300 crosses.

True Cross relics available on eBay today! Click to view details.

It is said that in some places you will find 99 fake Louis Vuittons for every genuine one sold. The famous design was introduced in 1896 as an anti-counterfeiting measure. In a customs raid in France a hundred years later, police recovered enough fake Louis Vuitton fabric to cover 54 tennis courts.

40 per cent of what doctors prescribe will be placebos. 'Do no harm' is the physician's first injunction. On the other hand, a million people worldwide (including 250,000 children) will die this year because the medicines they take are not what they think they are.

Over two hundred million people – more than the population of Brazil – live, love, do battle, and grow crops in Gielinor, a place that doesn't exist.

Many chatbots are good enough to convince you they are real people. Around 11 million of the 31 million men who signed up for a 'dating' website (tagline: 'Life is short. Have an affair') didn't realise they were chatting to 'fembots', and not to the eager available women they imagined.

Only 1 per cent of you have turned to page 359 so far.

Over 3,500 people come every year from all over the world to Blackpool, Lancashire, to learn to get better at deceiving others. With your patter, sleights of hand, distractions and multiplications, you are my favourite people. You are partly why I started writing this book.

INTRODUCTION

Magicians are the most honest people you'll ever meet. They tell you they are going to deceive you, and then they do.

Perhaps that's why I've always loved them, the paradox of the honest deceiver. Even now, that willing suspension of disbelief returns me to a state of childlike wonder. Magicians take me back to a world wreathed in puffs of smoke, where multi-coloured scarves spiral upwards in defiance of gravity, where coins disappear and then reappear, where pink-nosed rabbits emerge cautiously from empty top hats. A world that I understood, even as a child, was both real and not real.

Magic was my first training in the arts of deception. Conjurers' tricks gave me clues as to what to look for much later in my search for authenticity.* There was *Find the Queen*, a virtuoso display of card-crimping dexterity that I would encounter again when I came to study the workings of street scammers. *Sawing the Lady in Half*, whose false walls and secret compartments turned up as part of the classic 'sting'. *The Ambitious Card*, whose technique of a force and a double lift opened my eyes to the psychology of persuasion. *The Levitating*

---

* Magicians call them *effects*. They're not 'tricks', they say firmly, because they're not actually tricking you.

Lady, whose 'convincer' – the magician running a hoop around the supine, elevated body of his assistant to show that there were no wires holding her up – was a masterclass in how to sell something to an audience that instinctively knows it can't believe what it's seeing. I learned valuable lessons early on. Look behind the façade. Watch the hand that *isn't* holding the coin. Don't believe your eyes: remember you're seeing what you're meant to see, not what's really there. Doubt is the grammar of authenticity.

Not all of us are as honest as magicians. Not all deceit is as delightful as magic. There is something appealing in the joint endeavour of deception between performer and punter, the straight-talking self-knowledge of the magician. At a magic show we lay ourselves open to being taken advantage of, even made a fool of – something we studiously avoid in the rest of life. It is perhaps a uniquely authentic transaction because we know the terms of the engagement, the delimitation of the safe space: inside the House of Fun, if a guy takes your watch you'll get it back; outside it, not so much.

Distinguishing between those who construct alternate realities to delight us and those who deceive for less laudable purposes could not be a more timely and urgent challenge. Two decades into the twenty-first century, there are too many tricksters and too few magicians. We live in a storm of make-believe and deception, from internet phishing to identity theft, fake pharmaceuticals to brand knock-offs. The lines between reality and illusion are increasingly blurred; the need to distinguish between the two is an urgent daily challenge. We are searching for authenticity in a world that is ever more inauthentic.

I first began to think about writing on authenticity some years ago, when I discovered that a close friend of mine was a fantasist and a fraud (his story is told in Chapter 13). Then I began to notice that authenticity was being written and talked about as never before. When I checked on the researcher's favourite, Ngram (type in a word and up pops a graph charting its popularity over the centuries in the 25 million books scanned by Google), it showed a sharp upturn in mentions of 'authentic' and 'authenticity' from the end of the last century and continuing into this one.

Everywhere I turned I heard tales of a decline in authenticity, a modern malaise at once both general and deeply personal. I found physicians worrying about doctored drug trials. Lovelorn Romeos wondering if their Tinder Juliets were what they seemed to be. Employers fretfully sifting out 'diploma mill' candidates. Activists fighting food fakery. Aid agencies and NGOs battling against counterfeit medicines and medical misinformation. No one seemed to have escaped untouched. Advertisers had bots clicking on their ads instead of people. Manufacturers of luxury goods found that although their sales had tripled, sales of counterfeits had increased two-hundredfold.

Digital technologies were raising the stakes even higher. From internet phishing and identity theft to the fabrications of demagogues on social media, technology appeared all too often to be the enemy of authenticity. Some of the problems were common knowledge: the pressure from social media to showcase a pretend perfect life, the reams of unverified digitally-hyped content that take up so much of our attention. Others were less well known. To take just one example, we are spending billions of dollars on virtual goods whose existential and ownership status are, to say the least, unclear; as one in-game retailer said to me, 'We're making a fortune from selling things that don't exist.'

As we head further into the 2020s, many people fear that we may be heading for an irretrievable loss of authenticity. Breakthroughs in artificial intelligence, AI, could make the scale and reach of deception unlike anything we've seen before. Take the AI voice imitator that offers ultra-realistic text-to-speech fakery. Once upon a time, creating a bogus recording of some- one speaking required you to record eight hours of them talking, and then to cut and paste each individual word or phrase of the phoney soundtrack. Now all you need is to sample a couple of minutes of their speech and your (easily available) deepfake software can create a voiceprint. Then you just type in what you want them to 'say', and out it comes in their voice. When one reporter tried it, the software rang his mother and convinced her that she was talking to her son.

What is it exactly that we're so worried about losing? And what do we mean by 'authenticity' anyway? It's a word that takes some pinning down. For a start, the two main ways in which we use the word have almost completely opposite meanings.

The original, and – until relatively recently – primary, sense of authenticity is of verisimilitude. An authentic account of an event is an account that represents the event honestly and accurately. An authentic account of a president's inauguration gives the number of people who were actually there, as opposed to the number of people that the president would have liked to be there. This is a kind of authenticity that is outwardly-focused, objective, evidence-based, and, above all, public. The great advantage of this sense is that claims as to fact can be argued over. They can be examined, checked, verified, until you come to a conclusion that is (to use one of the earliest senses of 'authentic') *authoritative*. This is the version of authenticity that makes our everyday lives reliable and predictable, that gives us the sense that what we see is very likely to be what we get. And it's what we lose if depictions of the world fuelled by dis- and misinformation start to outnumber more accurate representations of reality.

If that were the only concept of authenticity, this book would have been about fake-spotting and fact-checking. But authenticity has acquired a second, more recent, meaning, to do with a kind of authenticity that is more subjective and fluid than the fact-based variety – a *personal* authenticity. A child of the Romantic period, born of our impulse for self-discovery and self-creation, personal authenticity is about being true, not to external reality, but to your own, internal sense of self. Looking to feelings rather than facts, answering only to the voice within, this newer kind of authenticity is subjective, inwardly focused, and most of all private.

The concept of personal authenticity may be relatively recent, but it has become very significant. For the generations living at the tail-end of the twentieth century and the beginning of the twenty-first, the promise of our age is authenticity as self-fulfilment. The quest for personal authenticity is often a driving force, a force that affects not just how we see ourselves, but our patterns of consumption, our job choices, how we relate to the world and its problems.

These two meanings of 'authenticity' could hardly be more different. One a matter of science and statistics, verification and falsification. The other, by contrast, aspirational and self-actualising (know yourself, follow your dream), non-conformist (resist the pressures of society), privileging the natural and untouched over the polished and artificial. But although these two main ways in which we talk about authenticity have such very different meanings, they do have something important in common. In each case, authenticity requires a match between the story being told and the reality – outer or inner – that lies behind it. A factual description is authentic when what is described matches reality. A person is authentic when the person they are inwardly matches the person they are able to be outwardly. What the two meanings share is that the pursuit of authenticity is also a search for harmony and unity in our lives. If inauthenticity is that familiar head-scratching 'does not compute' moment – the improbable boasts (or are they lies?) you hear the first time you meet someone, the disconnect of the politician's oh-so-scripted ad lib, the art expert's blink of intuition that a painting's brushstrokes don't mesh with the signature in the corner, the 'designer' bag you bought that all of a sudden looks flimsy and tawdry, or the uncomfortable moment when social expectations make you act in a way you know is not really 'you' – then authenticity is consistency and congruity. No wonder we're keen on it.

So keen, indeed, that we have come to apply the label 'authentic' to almost anything that we value – to the point where the word can mean whatever we want it to. We talk about an 'authentic' Rembrandt (meaning painted by the master himself), for instance, or an 'authentic' Italian pasta sauce recipe ('just like Nonna used to make!') – even though it's hard to see what the two might have in common. We do the same with 'real': I might say I'll order the apple pie, but only if it comes with 'real' cream, and in the next breath say proudly that I'm wearing a 'real' Ralph Lauren polo shirt. Not much in common there either. By 'real' cream, I mean cream that is not processed, or heat treated, or squirted out of an aerosol tube. A 'real' designer shirt is not one made by Ralph himself (unlike an 'authentic' Rembrandt), but one that is not an unofficial copy.

The philosopher J L Austin pointed out that 'real' is a word that is best understood by considering its negative use.* Like 'real', 'authentic' and 'authenticity' are best explored by looking at their opposites. If you want to know what makes a particular painting or recipe (or shirt, or type of cream) 'authentic', the trick is to ask, 'As opposed to what?' An authentic Rembrandt is one painted by Rembrandt *as opposed to* somebody else. Authentic recipes have a provenance traceable to a person, place, or culture, *as opposed to* ones that have just been invented for a supermarket magazine. The real job of the authenticator is to decide what to exclude.

At the heart of this book is the belief that the best way to understand what is authentic is to look first at what is not. This was the lesson that I learned as a magic-obsessed child. The opposite of illusion was not disillusion, but illumination. You can get to the real by way of the make-believe.

The more I saw how important authenticity is to us, the more I wanted to understand why we're so bad at it. Just what is it that stops us being more authentic? To answer that question we need to look not just at our social and psychological make-up, but also at the most fundamental forces of evolution and economics – and, indeed, to explore the connections between them. We need to think across boundaries: to make links between areas as diverse as history, biology, economics, art, fashion, marketing, and tech.

To give structure and shape to a potentially vast and unwieldy subject, what I've done in this book is to look at the forces that

---

* Actually, what Austin (1911–1960) said is that 'real' is a 'trouser-word', that is, one whose negative use 'wears the trousers', to which I can only say that, although a brilliant philosopher, he was very much a man of his time.

favour fakery – psychological, biological, economic – and suggest ways in which we can reclaim authenticity in the face of them. The book is divided into five parts. The stories in Part 1, *Basic Instincts*, explore human impulses towards fakery in chapters titled 'Aspiration', 'Deception', and 'Complicity'. In Part 2, *Natural-Born Fakers*, chapters on 'Mimics', 'Free Riders', and 'Competitors' tell the tales of other living creatures who seem to be biologically wired for deception, and ask what clues they might give as to our own impostor impulses. Part 3, *On the Authenticity of Things*, looks at why we label some things as authentic and others as counterfeit, why we punish some 'Multipliers' and 'Attention Seekers' and reward others, and the problems for authenticity posed by a world of increasing material 'Abundance'. With stories from the worlds of luxury goods ('Intangibles'), soft drinks ('Mythmakers'), and pharmaceuticals ('Externalities'), Part 4, *Selling Authenticity*, investigates how authenticity has become intertwined with consumer culture. Companies have moved into the business of selling authenticity, linking their goods to inspiration and self-fulfilment – in ways that have led to own goals for them and, at times, serious and far-reaching consequences for the rest of us.

Each of these chapters tells stories from our counterfeit culture, using them to make wider points about what we can do to reclaim reality. Why stories? Partly because I love stories, but mostly because I think they're the best way to explore serious issues.* So you'll find here a whole range of them – about the world's greatest impostor, a human chameleon who finally became what he pretended to be; about the art forger whose

---

* The word 'story' can mean both a narrative and a lie. Every successful deceiver is aware of the power of a well-told tale; I like the idea that I'm using their weapons against them.

fakes fooled a nation into rewriting its own history; about the birds engaged in an unrelenting egg race; about the elks who can't put their hooves down, and their hunters, who could but won't; about the painter who encouraged his friends to fake his work; about the two famous fashion designers who alighted on the same concept for a dress; about the 'all natural' drink that was anything but. The book looks back to a time when to be a counterfeiter meant an agonising death, and forward to a time when state-sponsored counterfeiters are bringing death to hundreds of thousands of others. Rather than point the finger at all-too-obvious villains, I have sought throughout to explore biological wiring, tectonic shifts and ethical conundrums.* At each point, I've tried to illustrate which aspects of inauthenticity are evolutionary and inevitable, and which aspects humans have created for themselves – and can do something about if they choose to.

In the final part of the book, *A View From Now*, I look at technology, often seen as the most powerful of all the enemies of authenticity. A line often trotted out is that twenty-first-century digital technologies have been an unalloyed disaster for authenticity; that speed, connectivity, the ability to make perfect, instantaneous, and virtually unlimited copies, and the opportunity to hide behind a social-media persona have led to a world full of people and products who are not what they seem to be. A lie can find its way into a million social-media feeds before the truth has got its boots on.

Technology can indeed be harnessed to amplify the forces of fakery, but it seems to me a counsel of despair to suggest that we

---

* Which is why – and it is a small matter of pride – the 45th President of the United States rates a namecheck only once in this book, and that in a footnote.

cannot fight back. Contrary to the claims of the 'cyber-miserabilists', technology has the potential to become reality's greatest friend, enabling and empowering those who are trying to turn the tide. More and more people are using the potential of the internet as a force for authenticity, and the book ends on a note of fierce optimism. The penultimate chapter, 'Real Lives', tells the stories of people using the virtual corridors of cyber-space – places where no one is an impostor, because imposture is understood as a precondition of entry – to explore new and unexpected ways to live more authentically, and to become the authors of their own lives. And in the final chapter, 'Reclaiming Reality', I meet some of the ever-increasing number of armies of truth who are busily engaged in taking down the conspiracies and the cons. Amateur cybersleuths are 'fact-shaming' state propagandists. Instagrammers are calling out fast-fashion knockoffs. Professional fact-checking networks are working side by side with amateur keyboard warriors. There are fake-brand hunters, scam-spotting dating site entrepreneurs, internet-savvy school kids exposing online fraud. And there are the journalists and the open-source intelligence professionals, whose work I'm lucky enough to know at first hand. All of them doing something to combat inauthenticity, all of them inviting you to join in.

Authenticity is worth fighting for. But our quest for authenticity mustn't blind us to the pleasures of make-believe. Like children watching a magic show, we need to be able to lose ourselves in wonderment even though we know that what we are seeing is not real. We shouldn't lose our pleasure in honest deception. Nor should we make gods out of facts.

A truly authentic life is one where we can have reality when we want it and are able to suspend disbelief when we don't.

Where we can delight in deceit that we know to be deceit. We demand authenticity both public and private, but we demand the right to the fruits of our imagination too. The right to invent, to create, to be someone different or better is an essential part of what it means to be human. Alternative facts may be insignificant in the long run, but to be able to imagine alternative worlds is an imperative. Uniquely among animals, we are able to imagine the world not as it is, but as it might be.*

Magicians understand the paradox that to create illusion you have first to create a context of reality. But they also understand the need for wonder, that to kindle a willing suspension of disbelief we have to regard the illusion, however temporarily, as more exciting or important than the reality. Above all, magicians know, better than anyone, the precariousness of pretence. The art of the pretender lies in the alchemical mix of setting and patter: the enchantment of the theatrical spell; the rapt attention of the audience; the love affair between the spell-caster and the spell-bound. So, I'll start the book with one of the masters of the art: the supreme role-player of the twentieth century and certainly my favourite impostor.

---

* 'Imagine the world' is a slogan borrowed from the Hay Festival, the best festival of storytelling – in the good sense of 'story' – in the world.

PART 1
BASIC INSTINCTS

1

ASPIRATION

The Impostor Who Became What
He Pretended to Be

'One man's life is a boring thing.
I've lived many lives. I'm never bored.'
Stanley Clifford Weyman

Aspiration is a uniquely human quality. We are the only animals that can choose to pretend to be something other than what we are. To be human is to be able to imagine yourself as someone different, to picture yourself living a life more exciting than the one you were born to, to fashion yourself into the person of your choosing. But is it possible to aspire to glory without some degree of imposture? Can we ever make it without to some extent faking it?

Stanley Clifford Weyman* was the ultimate self-made man. A charming and successful serial impostor, he made a career of pretending to be people other than himself. Flitting easily between re-inventions, he was at different times: a series of high-ranking officers in the US Navy; an officer in the French Navy; an officer in the British Army; a psychiatrist; a lawyer; Peruvian ambassador to the USA; a high-ranking official in the US State Department. He was a medical officer turned sanitation

---

* The name he eventually settled on in middle age.

expert in Lima, where he was renowned for throwing lavish parties, and later a lecturer in medicine and representative of the New York Lunacy Commission. In 1920 he played the part of Consul General for Romania; when he visited a naval dockyard, attired in top hat, tailed morning coat and striped trousers, and inspected the USS *Wyoming*, a 21-gun salute was fired in his honour. More than once, Stanley played two parts simultaneously: he was the Serbian military attaché and a lieutenant in the US Navy, who helpfully wrote references for each other; he was personal physician to a Hollywood star grieving the premature death of her lover, and at the same time the public relations impresario organising the lover's funeral. Eventually he became a successful and accredited journalist and broadcaster specialising in Balkan and Far Eastern affairs, spending two years in Washington and at the United Nations, and mixing daily with leading statesmen of the time.

Stanley's deceptions were journeys of self-exploration and self-expression, the trying on of new skins in the hope of finding one that fitted best. He slipped easily from being S Clifford Weinberg to being Ethan Allen Weinberg, Rodney S Wyman, Sterling C Wyman, Allen Stanley Weyman, C Sterling Weinberg, Stanley C Weyman; the pseudonyms he chose rendered him so readily identifiable that they could scarcely count as conceal-ment. The greatest impostor of the twentieth century was a man whose life's work was self-discovery and self-creation – what we would see today as the hallmarks of a search for personal authenticity.

We are perhaps more tolerant than previous generations. We make allowances for individual aspiration and re-invention. We understand that sometimes you need to revise your past in order to devise your future, that being true to yourself may not always mean being true to the world. In a sense, Stanley's was a very modern condition. Unwilling to stick with the cards he had been dealt, he was determined to live life not at the periphery, but at the centre of things. Wherever there was excitement and fun, a newsworthy event or the popping of flashbulbs, that was where you would find Stanley Weyman.

Stars of the Silver Screen

Perhaps his greatest triumph was in 1926. Already ten years into his career as an impostor, Stanley propelled himself into the epicentre of the most exhilaratingly newsworthy event of the year, the death and lying-in-state of Rudolph Valentino, silent-film star and legendary silver-screen lover.*

In the summer of 1926, Valentino had fallen suddenly and violently ill. His devoted fans were treated to daily bedside bulletins. He died on 23 August, aged 31, leaving two ex-wives and a current lover, the sultry Hollywood star Pola Negri. Stanley the impostor rose magnificently to the occasion. He appointed himself not only Miss Negri's personal physician, Dr Sterling C Wyman of Flower Hospital ('Rudy would have wanted me to take care of you, my dear'), but also, with a different name and persona, public relations adviser to the dead star's manager, George Ullman. More or less single-handedly, Stanley seems to have taken charge of the arrangements for Valentino's funeral in New York. Always at home in the eye of a news storm, he proved invaluable in the mayhem, soothing distraught

---

* Valentino exuded a powerful magnetism in all his incarnations. He brought a flutter to a million bosoms as a desert Arab in the hot-sands epic *The Sheik*, and as a tango-dancing Latino in *The Four Horsemen of the Apocalypse*. Men were not immune to his spell either. Would-be Valentinos who mimicked his patent-leather hair were known as 'Vaselinos'.

fans, speaking to reporters, and issuing daily bulletins to the press.

When Valentino's body was laid out in the Gold Room of Campbell's Funeral Parlor on Broadway and 66th Street, over 30,000 mourners converged on the building to pay their final respects to the Sheik. It was an extraordinary outpouring of public emotion for a man who had done nothing more than make a career out of playing people other than himself.* Breaking through the plate-glass window, the crowd surged into the room, nearly knocking over the casket, and the corpse was hastily transferred to a more robust coffin. Mounted police charged to stop the mob from overrunning the building, injuring more than a hundred mourners in the process. Fortunately, Dr Sterling Wyman of Flower Hospital was on hand to set up a temporary infirmary to take care of the injured and overemotional fans.

If Dr Wyman was not entirely the genuine article, nor were many others in the media circus surrounding Valentino's death. Although it took place almost a century ago, the fake news, PR fabrications and celebrity stunts lend the story a curiously contemporary feel. Frustrated by the absence of any photograph of Valentino's corpse, the *New York Evening Graphic* pasted up shots of an empty coffin with a photo of the star's head superimposed. Even before Valentino's body had reached the funeral parlour, the paper ran a front page 'composograph' – that is, a photomontaged image – of the Great Lover lying in state. (Later,

---

* Valentino himself recognised that he was a construct. 'Women', he said, 'do not become infatuated with Rudolph Valentino. They do not love him … they become infatuated with what he stands for. They love the man they imagine he represents.' After his death, his brother Alberto tried to replicate the construct, undergoing seven plastic-surgery operations in order to look like Rudy.

Fig. 1.1. Composograph by the *New York Evening Graphic* of Valentino in heaven with Enrico Caruso.

the *Graphic* was to excel itself with a further composograph, this one showing Valentino in heaven with his fellow Italian, the operatic tenor Enrico Caruso.)

Four uniformed and black-shirted 'Fascisti' stood guard over the body – a tribute to Valentino's home country supposedly sent 'on orders from Rome' – and among the rows of floral tributes was a wreath marked 'From Benito'. But Mussolini cabled to deny any involvement, and the guards were most likely actors hired by Campbell's Funeral Parlor. A distraught and tearful Pola Negri flew in from California to be beside the casket. She knelt by the body for fifteen minutes, collapsed, then

23

held back her tears just long enough to murmur, 'It is true; we were engaged to be married!' before swooning again.

It was towards the end of Valentino's lying-in-state, as mourners rioted, that the newspapers discovered Stanley's double imposture. Stanley, in his medical ducks as Dr Wyman, was ministering to a fainting female fan and yelling 'Stand back and give this woman some air!' when a reporter recognised him from earlier impersonations. The game was up. Although Valentino's manager, George Ullman, rapidly disowned him, Pola Negri did not; she was reported to say that Stanley was the best doctor she had ever had.

The papers were initially reluctant to expose the man whose announcements they had recently been printing so avidly. But within a few days, the *New York World* decided that the story was just too good not to print. A veritable avalanche of exposure followed, as journalists competed to uncover Stanley's spectacular history of imposture. There were days when his press coverage exceeded Valentino's.

Most impostors fear exposure: the cold sweat as chance discovery walks past, the relief when it passes by. But when the *New York Journal-American* interviewed Stanley at his home in Brooklyn, they found him open and unrepentant. 'What is the sense in all these exposés?', Stanley asked. 'I wish you would let me alone. I am not doing anything wrong.' He went on to explain his credo: he deceived to achieve. He did not act out of malice; he simply claimed the right to reinvent himself whenever the opportunity presented itself. This, combined with an honest pursuit of fame, was Stanley's version of the American Dream.

I am an American boy, one hundred percent, born in Brooklyn. From my earliest days as a kid, I have been imbued with the go get 'em spirit. Now one of the things that an ambitious lad learns is that every opportunity for increasing his fame must be taken advantage of. Take off your coat, jump right in when you see the advantageous gulf at your feet. And if the opportunities don't materialize spontaneously, there is just one thing to be done and that's to create them. That's been my motto all along and people who have made up their minds that I'm cracked or have some sinister motive are simply deluding themselves.

Stanley was an impostor, not a conman. His career was one of aspiration, not deception. The impostor only wants to change himself – for him the imposture *is* the achievement. By contrast, the conman's imposture is a means to an end: he will change himself, his surroundings, his relationships, deceive whoever he needs or is able to in pursuit of some other goal – most often money but sometimes revenge for actual or imagined slights. And unlike a conman, Stanley was open and honest. He was remarkably frank about his life, including his mental illness – what today we would call bipolar disorder – and the many spells in prison he underwent as a result of trying on new identities and new skins.*

The authorities seemed baffled by this impostor without criminal intent. Stanley was always in plain sight, never left Brooklyn, never hid from the police even when he knew there was a warrant out for his arrest. In time, the police found it easier not to go to Brooklyn at all when they wanted to pick him up, but simply to turn up at the most newsworthy event of the day. If Stanley wasn't orchestrating it, he would at least be

---

* Some of Stanley's convictions were the consequence of his impostures – impersonating a US naval officer or an attorney, for example, were criminal offences – but many others were for breaches of parole. Stanley could seldom bear to set aside a new and exciting adventure for the time it took to check in at the parole office.

likely to be taking part. And it was always easy to recognise him: despite his fondness for dressing whatever part he was playing, he never shaved off his 1920s-style pencil moustache.

The Power of Context

'How do they get away with it so easily?' is the question people often ask about impostors. Part of the answer is that we use just a few indicators when making our initial judgements of people. We identify a person by appearance and job description – 'the blonde lawyer', 'the good-looking window-cleaner' – and by voice, body language, and manner. And in the moment of judgement we assume identity is singular. We forget that we are all able to present different faces in different places; that we all change our clothes, our voices, our personae to suit different situations; that we become someone else when we change our job, or our hairstyle, or even our mood. When making a judgement, it's easier and quicker to prioritise the surface textures of life, the exterior and the immediate. We don't stop to check that every doorman is a real doorman, that the policeman in the street is a real policeman, that the pilot making his way through the cabin with a broad smile is a real pilot. We rely on probability to tell us that the man in a blue uniform with a peaked cap, striding from First to Economy and glad-handing the passengers, is what he appears to be. Above all, we rely on context. As Sarah Burton points out in *Impostors: Six Kinds of Liar* (2000), in a hospital setting, the masked man holding a knife over an unconscious naked body is likely to be a surgeon; in a horror film, we can safely assume that he is a homicidal maniac.

It's easy to underestimate the power of context in everyday life. For instance, I bear a very passing resemblance to the glamorous wife of a friend who used to be the editor-in-chief of a major newspaper. Every year at the paper's summer party, at least half a dozen people I'd never met before would advance on me with outstretched arms and broad smiles. Because of my resemblance to Fiona (as I'll call her), I moved up in status from just another guest to the one you flash your most ingratiating smile at and pay court to. I'd get a small thrill at being mistaken for someone prettier, younger, and richer, but an even bigger thrill at passing for someone else, living someone else's life, for one evening at least. People *expected* to see Fiona at the party; they may not have known her all that well, the lights were dim, and, if in doubt, it was clearly in their interest to err on the side of being nice to the editor's wife. In that context, even people I know used to mistake me for Fiona. But no one has ever mistaken me for her in any other setting.

The syntax of social situations permits an almost infinite variety of readings. The grammar of life is expansive. People, and the settings in which you come across them, are the building blocks of everyday life, and the impostor equation is the meaning you derive from the two combined – what you project upon what you see.

Stanley Clifford Weyman was born Stanley Jacob Weinberg in Brooklyn on 25 November 1890. He was the oldest, brightest, and most talented of the four Weinberg children. Good-looking, eloquent, and with charming manners, he was indulged by parents who envisaged a dazzling future for their son. To be a parent is in many ways to encourage imposture. We congratulate our children on their ambition and indulge their aspiration. Alert for the slightest precocious talent, we find reasons to cheer them on. If a child argues back, why surely they have a future as a barrister! A great bedside manner presages a career in medicine. So it was with the Weinbergs. The young Stanley's orations had his mother declaring he was a born lawyer. If he wanted more praise and attention, he would play doctor. Once he found red spots on his youngest brother and told the family it was chickenpox, a judgement that proved to be correct. His family, delighted with his medical prowess, declared they had a doctor in the making – a diagnosis not uncommon in Jewish families.

Stanley told his parents that he planned three careers for himself: as a diplomat, a doctor, and a lawyer. His father, a real-estate broker who had never been to college, was broadly supportive. He offered to help with the cost of college, provided Stanley limited himself to studying for just one of his potential careers. But Stanley was impatient; as a judge was later to observe, he said to himself at an early age, 'If I can't climb the ladder, I'll jump it.' Rather than go to college, he began to make his first appearances on the stage of imposture. In 1910, aged 20, he turned up as US Consul General at Algiers (a wise choice, given that few Americans of the time would have been able to pick out Algeria on a map), and proceeded to entertain the great and the good of the diplomatic and social worlds at a consular banquet. Unable to pay the bill, Stanley found himself charged with fraud and sentenced to do time in a correctional institution. When he was released in 1911, his father dispatched him to River Crest Sanitarium, a mental hospital in Queens. He underwent a course of treatment intended to help him understand his impostor urges; if the treatment worked, it certainly didn't cure him of them.

A typical escapade occurred in 1917 when he was 26 years old. In the words of St Clair McKelway, chronicler of the New York of the 1920s and 1930s:

On that day, nothing much was going on in Manhattan, but there was a military shindig in progress at an armory in Brooklyn ... [Stanley] was in the dress uniform of a rear admiral of the United States Navy – a striking outfit, with a high-crowned cap, epaulets, flotillas of brass buttons, and garlands of gold braid. It was the sort of naval uniform that is never seen anymore except in movies or on the covers of historical novels. After returning the salute that the Army sentries at the entrance to the armory gave him, Weyman sailed inside, received and returned a salute from the major general in charge, and told the general that, as a gesture of interservice courtesy, he had come to inspect the troops.

Unfortunately, Detective Francis X Sullivan of the Delancey Street police station in Manhattan was lying in wait. Just as the troop inspection began, Sullivan leaped out and handcuffed Stanley, putting paid to the 'rear admiral's' otherwise harmless afternoon of fun. Stanley was imprisoned for impersonation of a naval officer and not released for the best part of three years.

Having tried diplomacy and the military, Stanley still craved a medical career. Shortly after being released on parole in 1920, he answered an advertisement seeking a young doctor willing to go to Lima, Peru. The final shortlist of candidates was assessed by an eminent professor at Columbia Medical School. Like so many, he was impressed by Stanley's manner and charm. In fact, the professor felt sure that he recognised Stanley from somewhere. He must be a former pupil. Which in a way he was. Some years earlier, Stanley had shown up at Columbia posing as a student, attending classes and clinics and picking up useful medical jargon. Stanley got the job in Lima, and by all accounts performed as well as could possibly be expected of a wholly untrained and unqualified doctor. It took almost a full year for his imposture to be detected, and when it was, his employers declined to prosecute him. Stanley returned to New York a free man.

To the White House

It was in February 1921 that Stanley first tasted real glory, as the man who introduced a princess to a president. Following the Third Anglo-Afghan War, Afghanistan had become a fully sovereign state in 1919. However, President Warren G Harding had been strongly advised by the State Department that the sensitivity of the USA's British ally, who still regarded the country very much as their backyard, meant that it would be unwise to have any relations with anyone from the newly independent kingdom. When the Amir of Afghanistan sent a delegation to Washington, declaring his 'sincere wish to establish a permanent friendly relation between the two nations', Harding ignored it.

In the same month as the Amir's emissaries, there appeared in New York a princess from Afghanistan called Fatima. New Yorkers, in love with the exotic and the unfamiliar, revelled in her arrival. Fatima and her three teenage sons, Ashin, Azic, and Akber, were the subject of unceasing press attention. According to one reporter, Fatima was festooned with jewels and feathers and wore a large sapphire in her left nostril (although it has to be said that the glories of her dress were somewhat at odds with her corpulent, square-jawed appearance). The princess declared that she was in America for two reasons: she wished to be introduced to 'that handsome man' President Harding at the White House, and she hoped to dispose of the enormous diamond that she had brought with her, the Darya-i-Noor. The Amir also wanted to meet the President, but his official delegation never even got close to it. But then, they didn't have Stanley Clifford Weyman on their side.

Sitting at home in Brooklyn, reading the newspaper accounts of Princess Fatima's arrival, Stanley resolved that he was the man to take her and her sons to the White House. The way to do this was to assume the role of State Department Naval Liaison Officer. That there was no such position did not deter Stanley. From his wardrobe,* he took a white dress uniform, suitably naval in appearance, and a white dress hat with gold braid running along the peak. That this was in fact the uniform of an officer in the United States Junior Naval Reserves, what McKelway calls 'a kind of sea-going Boy Scout affair', proved to present no obstacle. By 11 a.m. that day he was at the Waldorf-Astoria, assuring Princess Fatima that her trip to Washington was imminent. A few days later, the Third Assistant Secretary of State, one Robert Woods Bliss, was called by the State Department Naval Liaison Officer, one Commander Rodney Sterling Wyman. Commander Wyman had the honour to report that Princess Fatima of Afghanistan was agreeable to seeing President and Mrs Harding on or about 25 July. As State Department Liaison Officer, he would communicate directly with the White House about making the necessary arrangements for the visit. Aware of the State Department's advice that the President should not receive anyone from Afghanistan, Bliss decided that Wyman's call must mean that State had been over-ruled by the White House.

---

* Stanley's wardrobe needed to be, and was, impressively capacious. In 1951, *Life* magazine reported that an FBI raid of his apartment had uncovered '43 assorted pairs of shoes as well as 25 suits, 28 jackets and 130 ties', together with an outstanding selection of both military and civilian headwear.

President Harding's meeting with Princess Fatima and her three sons on 25 July 1921 was a sensation. As the *Washington Post* breathlessly reported, 'Royalty touched hands with Democracy at the White House yesterday when Princess Fatima, Sultana of Afghanistan, and her three sons were received by [the] President.' Seldom, the report continued, had the President received a more exotic troop:

> The costume of the princess was of deep pink satin heavily embroidered in Egyptian designs in gold and black. The coat-like bodice was high at the neck and had loose sleeves which revealed many bracelets when she moved her arms ... A huge 50 carat diamond, enormous diamond pendant earrings, many chains of pearls and other jewels, a jewelled girdle about her waist, and a long veil caught about her head by a close-fitting bandeau of green ostrich feathers and twined about her waist completed the costume.

During the visit, Stanley's skills as a quick-change artist came to the fore. At some point, possibly as he was walking into the White House, Stanley decided that his useful life as Commander Rodney Sterling Wyman of the US Naval Militia had come to an end. He promptly informed Princess Fatima that the State Department had given him leave of absence, so that he was now free to act as her personal advisor, interpreter, and physician. We can only speculate as to what brought about this sudden change, but there are two photographs taken at the White House on that momentous day. In one, Princess Fatima and her sons are posing together on the lawn, flanked by Commander Wyman on one side and a mysterious character by the name of Prince Zerdecheno on the other. Stanley is wearing a jacket with naval epaulettes bearing a star and three bars. In the second

Fig. 1.2. Stanley on the White House lawn (far left), with Princess Fatima, her sons, and the mysterious Prince Zerdecheno.

photograph, the Afghan royal party, minus Stanley, are leaving the White House. They are led by an impressive-looking naval figure sporting a generous sprinkling of decorations as well as aiguillettes, a quantity of ornamental braided cord looping from his left shoulder to his collarbone. Had Stanley perhaps decided that the presence of the genuine article made it wiser to dispense with his naval persona? Whether his change in role from US official to personal adviser to Princess Fatima was a matter of necessary discretion we will never know. What we do know is that the princess spoke perfect English; for her to communicate with the President via an 'interpreter' was nothing but pure theatre on her part.

On 4 April 1922, Stanley was tried in the Brooklyn Federal Court on a charge of impersonating a United States naval officer. His defence was that he had not impersonated an officer in the

Fig. 1.3. The group leaving the White House with Princess
Fatima on the same day. Stanley is absent, and they are
escorted by a man with a great quantity of ornamental braid
looped from his shoulder.

Navy; the uniform he had worn was that of the Junior Naval
Reserves, of which he was a member. It carried no weight with
the judge; Stanley was sentenced to two years in the Atlanta
Federal Penitentiary. He put his time in the pen to good use. He
studied law and proceeded to pass the bar examination, becoming an accredited attorney under the laws of the State of Georgia
– a state broad-minded enough not to exclude a man from a
legal career simply because he had been convicted of a felony or
two.

The Self-Made Man

What is it to want to assume a life that is not yours, to dress in borrowed finery and take on another's trappings? In 1968, some forty years after Stanley's greatest performances, he was the subject of two long articles by St Clair McKelway in the *New Yorker* – appropriately enough, as New York was always the stage for Stanley's artistry. As I leaf through the magazine, I am struck by how many of the advertisements urge you to do exactly what Stanley did: lift yourself out of the rut, live someone else's life, *become* somebody else. Although 1968 was the year of war in Vietnam, of civil rights protests and student riots in Paris, of Black Power and free love, of *Hair* and Valerie Solanas shooting Andy Warhol, you wouldn't guess it from the adverts. Rather than stir up readers to fight the system, advertisers showed them how to jump the rungs of the ladder. For men, naval style – Stanley's go-to status indicator – is still a mark of distinction: Higbee's of Cleveland offers a Pierre Cardin blazer 'with sophisticated flair'. To complete the naval look, why not buy a $95 boxed set of Fourteen Karat [*sic*] Gold Buttons from F R Tripler and Co. of Madison Avenue? Want to be a Consul General? Tripler's 'The Ambassador' range of sleepwear, with its contrasting colour robe and pyjama sets, will enhance your diplomatic potential. Royalty still has its particular mystique: aspirant Princess Fatimas are offered 'Royal Robes' (nylon 'V'Allure' quilted floor-length dressing gowns in red, turquoise, emerald, and primrose pink), while from Evelyn Pearson Inc. comes the 'Rajah look' (boudoir coats in 'easycare fleece … opulently enhanced with glittering gilt embroidery'). The most blatant invitation to imposture comes from a brand called Countess Mara, whose ties, so the Countess claims, will endow you instantly with 'Elegance. Distinction. Authority.' These remarkable strips of cloth 'define the aura that superiority radiates'. The reader is urged to 'take note of the men who wear them', for they are 'ties for one man in a million'. All that from a necktie. Just imagine how you would feel in a full uniform! 'Buy me! Buy me!' say the advertisements. 'I will lift you out of the commonplace. I promise you diplomatic privilege, royal secrets, a life less ordinary.' Just like Stanley's dressing-up box, they conspire to make a little man feel big. The only difference is that these ambassador and princess fantasies are to be played out in the privacy of our bedrooms, rather than in the public gaze and the national press.

In 1943, after living a quiet life with his wife and daughter for almost a decade, Stanley was charged by the FBI with teaching would-be draft dodgers how to fake the symptoms of insanity. He pleaded guilty, telling the judge: 'In none of my acts has there ever been an intentional turpitude. All were committed in a phase or cycle or period of recurrent manic depression, to which the doctors found I was subject.' Mental illness cut no ice in federal court in wartime: Stanley was sentenced to seven years.

When he came out of prison, Stanley, himself the subject of so many headlines, became a journalist. It was an inspired choice of career. You can participate in a great many lives as a news reporter, albeit at second-hand. Journalism offers the opportunity to be at the centre of newsworthy events. For two years Stanley worked for the Erwin News Agency in Washington and at Lake Success, temporary home of the United Nations. It proved to be one of his most successful and extended impostures. He also acted as master of ceremonies for a weekly programme on Balkan and Far Eastern affairs on radio station WFDR-FM, interviewing many diplomats and politicians, by whom he was regarded as an informed and intelligent observer of the political landscape. He became friendly with leading statesmen and Cold War players, including Andrei Gromyko, the Soviet Foreign Secretary, and Warren Austin, the US Ambassador to the UN. He was where he had always sought to be, close to the centre of affairs, but no longer as an impostor. The pretend PR man had become a real journalist. He may have flown false colours to get the job in the first place, but they became real enough. Then he applied to become press officer to the Thai delegation to the UN. The State Department conducted a routine vetting, and Stanley's past came to light. The Erwin Agency felt compelled to fire him, but his boss put on record that 'Weyman had done a splendid job in every way, and had never shown any sign of being anything except a competent journalist and a talented master of ceremonies on the radio program'.

At his last federal court appearance in 1954, Stanley was officially certified as legally sane. A friend who saw him at around this time described him as calm, untroubled, and happy in his own skin. He was over 60 by now, still living with his wife in Brooklyn. He took a job as night manager at the Dunwoodie Motel on Yonkers Avenue, saying he wanted more time to think.

You don't always know the full story until the final reel. Only time can tell who or what a person really is; if we pause the film of their life too soon we may never find out. Valentino's life was cut short at 31, and we will never know whether the public adulation he received for his personas and performances would finally have made him content. Just before he died, the star had dinner with H L Mencken; in an article published after his funeral, the great columnist wrote that Valentino had seemed 'precisely as happy as a small boy being kissed by two hundred fat aunts'.

Stanley's final chapter suggests that he did in some way become what he had so long pretended to be. On 27 August 1960, about a year after he had begun working at the Dunwoodie Motel, Stanley was working the night shift. He was alone at the front desk when two men walked in. Holding him at gunpoint, they demanded that he hand over the motel's money. Then several shots rang out, waking motel guests, one of whom called the police. When the patrolman arrived, he found Stanley lying dead – not behind the reception desk, but on the floor of the room, towards the door through which the gunmen had entered. The cashbox, still locked, was on the floor behind the counter.

The police later deduced what must have happened. 'Weyman had taken the cashbox from behind the counter as though he was about to hand it over to the gunmen', said one of the detectives.

He must have thrown the cashbox over his head and onto the floor to distract them and leaped over the counter, going after the armed men bare handed. It took the agility of a young man to leap over that counter. But he must have leaped over it after he threw the cashbox over his head because if he had simply *climbed* over it, they would have shot him while he was doing it. As it was, they must have shot him just before he got to them, because his body was about seven feet beyond the counter. I've known about the man's past record for years. He did a lot of things in the course of his life, but what he did this time was brave.

Stanley died with the courage that might have been expected of one of the senior naval officers he had so often impersonated. In the end, he became what he pretended to be. There is no knowing what Stanley's life might have been if he had been born in different circumstances, if he had had the means to pursue the triple career in diplomacy, law, and medicine of which he dreamed. But we know what he did become: not only an accomplished and popular impostor who achieved more than his fifteen minutes of fame, but also a well-respected journalist and broadcaster, as well as holding down other jobs – in medicine, in law – for which he had no formal qualifications. He had more than a few run-ins with the law, but he was no swindler or crook. On the contrary, he was a magician – a conjurer of delight. He enjoyed his successes. Always generous, he was, in St Clair McKelway's words, 'in the habit of showering newly hired stenographers with rich gifts, such as orchids and imported bonbons, and asking nothing of them in return except their astonished gasps'.*

Most of us have imagined ourselves as someone taller, better, prettier, more successful. Only a handful of us go the whole way and pretend to be someone completely different. For Stanley, every imposture was a reinvention, an attempt to become someone or something better. Perhaps a little bit of dissimulation is necessary for all of us as we change shape, change job, change our way of living. The human spirit encompasses both aspiration and deception. Not for nothing is that feeling of not-yet-deserved success called 'impostor syndrome'.

It is the mutability, that protean quality of impostors like Stanley, that intrigues me. The fluttering of their butterfly souls,

---

* Although Woody Allen has never admitted as much, it's hard to imagine that his film *Zelig*, which charts the rise of a Jewish human chameleon, a fame-hungry New Yorker whose fragile psyche and ego-hunger propel him centre stage to the most newsworthy events of the day, is not to some extent based on Weyman.

their dreams of glory, their refusal to remain in the niche they were born into. Plain white butterflies longing for the glorious wings of scarlet, ochre, and black flaunted by butterflies of greater substance. What must it be like, I wonder, to live life unafraid? Among the milk-whites destined to flutter and shiver at the margins, a few are born with the biochemistry of change, able to take advantage of their passing resemblance to more glorious creatures. Is that what Stanley Weyman thought? Did he suppose that naval officers, doctors, diplomats do not suffer as ordinary mortals do? That rank, position and uniforms offer protection against the everyday dangers of life? Exposed to every vicissitude of fate, is it any wonder that our milky impostors are tempted to display the false colours of more successful species?

But perhaps I shouldn't be misled by the soft sepia tones and the quaint stories. Not every imitation is as unconscious as a butterfly's; not all impostures are as benign as Stanley's. I need to spend some time in the company of quite different tricksters, ones who reveal us in our true colours while hiding their own.

2

DECEPTION

The Anatomy of a Con

'They wanted something for nothing.
I gave them nothing for something.'

Joseph 'Yellow Kid' Weil,
The Autobiography of America's
Master Swindler

On average, around 10 per cent of you will fall victim to a fraud, scam, or con every year. Over half of you will receive a credible but fraudulent telephone call. Few of you will realise that you've been conned, and even fewer will report it. The older you are, the more embarrassed you're likely to feel at having been duped.

Conmen know that the best people to target are those of us who think ourselves especially clever (the 65 per cent of high school students who describe themselves as 'above average', for instance, or the 94 per cent of college professors who lay claim to 'above average work'), those sporting souls who can't resist a gamble, and, perhaps more unexpectedly, those who've been conned before. Why that last should be true is unclear. Perhaps it's the desire to recoup our losses – what behavioural psychologists call loss aversion – that leads us to throw good money after bad instead of just seeing the loss as a sunk cost.

Or perhaps it's just that some of us never learn.

The sheer variety of con tricks is a testament to human ingenuity. At their simplest, they range from the Gold Brick Scam (a gold 'ingot' that is, in reality, a gold-plated lead bar) to the Pigeon Drop or Switch (the trickster swaps a package containing real money for a bundle of counterfeit notes) and Vanity Listings (charging prestige prices for an entry in a low-rent, no-status publication). At their most choreographed, they include the horseracing 'Wire' cons of a hundred years ago. At their most profitable, they take in financial scams such as Bernie Madoff's Ponzi scheme – the largest in world history – which netted $64 billion from its hapless investors. Cons can be as hoary as the classics you still find on street corners today (Three-Card Monte, the White Van Scam), or as surreal as the 'God Bless America' orchestra swindle (the ensemble played a 54-city concert tour and a PBS Special, but the musicians were miming to recordings).

All cons are frauds, but not all frauds are cons. Something of a snob, the classic conman recognises only a few felonies as worthy of his artistry and skill. It is a point of pride with him never to resort to violence, or to pick on the vulnerable. His grift has a gentle touch; his trade is superior to the 'heavy rackets' of safe blowers and armed raiders and the faceless indiscriminacies of burglary and bank-robbing. But what really sets the con apart from other deceptions is not so much that it is elite, but that it is participatory. Whereas most crimes are done *to* you, the con is a crime done *with* you.

White Van Man

As I walk down one of London's busiest shopping streets, I wonder if there is a collective noun for deceivers. A *dissimulation* of impersonators? A *pretension* of charlatans? In the shadow of a department store, vendors are laying out scarves, hats, and T-shirts that are approximate copies of the real brands inside. A *rookery* of conmen? On my right is a narrow alley with a 'No Entry' sign and a loading bay. A white van is parked with its back door open and a pile of boxes on the ground. A man in a shiny ill-fitting nylon uniform is chatting to the driver. He beckons me over.

'Wanna buy a home cinema system?' he calls. 'Brand new. Still in its box.'

The logos on the boxes look familiar but not altogether right. 'B&O', but not quite the Bang & Olufsen 'B&O'. I walk towards him.

'What's in there?'

A tumble of words pours out of him. 'Sophisticated surround sound system … high-performance drivers … components, speakers, amplifiers … polycarbon enclosure, titanium tweeter, aluminum woofer, low-distortion bass performance …' I raise an eyebrow, but he continues unabashed, building to the climax: 'Small speakers, Missus. But a big sound. And all in one box!' And with a wink, 'It's an absolute steal.'

'Is it?' I ask. 'A steal?'

He looks offended and, drawing himself up with some dignity, adds, 'They're overstocks. The factory asked me to take care of them.' He comes closer. I can smell the nylon sweat on him, as he whispers: 'I've got to shift 'em soon. Tell you what. I'll knock off 30 per cent for a quick sale.'

If the merchandise is what he says it is, my new friend – 'the speakerman' as he is known in the trade, on account of his bootlegged loudspeakers and audio systems – is showing me an easy win. For a moment I'm tempted, but he's not offering the boxes up for inspection. No checking before sale. I wonder what's inside them. If it's a pile of bricks, it's the old 'Rocks in a Box' scam. More likely it will be audio equipment, but probably not the high-end merchandise he's promising. I find myself weighing up the chance of the sound systems being the real deal rather than rocks or substandard counterfeits. The 'B&O' packaging, the warehouse uniform, and some glossy brochures I glimpse in the van make his offer seem somewhat more convincing. Later I find his website. It trumpets 'bargain prices for excess stock', which adds credibility. There's even a link to another website with full-price merchandise for any 'compare the market' wise guys who want to check out his prices. I'm not quite sure what I have in mind when I go past there the following day, but the cul-de-sac is empty. The speakerman, the driver, his van and the boxes have gone. I had almost fallen for one of the many small here-today-gone-tomorrow scams known in the language of the grift as 'short cons', all offering you a 'great deal' that probably isn't.

That's the collective noun for them: a *great deal* of white van men.

The term 'confidence man' was first used in 1849 in connection with a certain William Thompson. Described as 'a man of genteel appearance', Thompson would accost strangers in the street, engage them in polite conversation, and, after a short while, ask them if they had sufficient confidence in him to entrust their watches to him until the following day. A surprising number did so, thus demonstrating the admirable human propensity to trust other humans. It was a trick doomed to fail: it could only be a matter of time before one of the growing number of indignant watchless men on the streets of New York spotted Thompson and alerted a nearby police officer. According to the *New York Herald*, Thompson was a 'graduate of the college at Sing Sing'; he was back in prison almost immediately.

Since then, conmen have become both more ingenious and more subtle. They have learned that they need to gain your confidence while at the same time making you party to something morally questionable. W C Fields got it absolutely right: 'You can't cheat an honest man.' Most of us have at least a little larceny in our hearts, and the conman's skill is to find it, excite it, and amplify it. My White Van Man made it pretty clear to me that he had acquired the music systems by dubious means; he also made it clear that if I only trusted him, I could share in the proceeds. He was inviting me to join in his duplicitous world, to become his accomplice in deceit. He wanted me to believe that he was not simply dishonest, but *honestly* dishonest. The successful conman or woman makes their duplicity contagious; they infect you with their inauthenticity.

What is remarkable is how throughout history we have fallen for the same cons over and over again. Though they appear in different guises, the White Van Scam has much in common with the sixteenth-century 'Pig in a Poke'. Today's Tinder Romeo hustlers follow in the footsteps of the eighteenth-century Gypsy Sweethearts as they extract money from the lovelorn and the lonely. The nineteenth-century Spanish Prisoner swindle (wealthy individual imprisoned in Spain sends a letter asking for help to get his money out of the country) has its modern counterpart in the Nigerian Money Transfer scam whose emails litter so many of our inboxes. There is a *Groundhog Day* feel to these cons. Their consistencies of script and shape carry across the centuries, never-changing scams in an ever-changing world.

Blood and the Wire

What if the resemblances were more than coincidental? What if every con followed the same basic pattern, shared the same universal anatomy, from which we could recognise the stages of deceit? I'm struck by the parallels between the most ingenious 'long con' of a century ago, the racing scam known as the Wire,* and one of the biggest business frauds of recent years, the Theranos blood-testing scandal. On the face of it, an unlikely comparison; but the similarities of motivation and execution, of style as well as substance, and the congruencies of their charismatic leads are striking. The swindler 'Yellow Kid' Weil and the tech billionaire CEO Elizabeth Holmes could have been using the same playbook.

The first four decades of the twentieth century were the Golden Age of the conman. The exploits of the tricksters chronicled in the 1940 classic *The Big Con: The Story of the Confidence Man and the Confidence Trick* are bathed in a sepia glow of historical romance that our present-day identity thieves and internet phishing fraudsters have yet to achieve. Even the back-cover blurb on my paperback reissue of *The Big Con* has me tightening the belt on my trench coat and tipping my fedora over my eyes:

---

* Immortalised and impossibly romanticised in the movie *The Sting*: Henry Gondorff, played by Paul Newman, and his sidekick 'Hooker', played by Robert Redford, are both so *handsome* in their spats and hats.

Once upon a time these conmen could be found in every hotel lobby, on every cruise liner, in every Pullman car. They were looking for the rich, the greedy and the vain ... They were the master criminals and the greatest actors of their age. They played their lines to perfection, enlisting hundreds of extras to lull their marks: their sets were elaborately constructed betting shops, their plot the subtle mechanics of the wire, the payoff and the rag.

The Big Con was no pulp thriller. Its author, David W Maurer, the grifter's Boswell, was a professor of linguistics specialising in the argot of the underworld, who interviewed hundreds of conmen throughout the 1930s.* Maurer codified the confidence games, showing how the tricks follow a formal sequence of acts and actions to which individuals added their own flair and flourishes. I imagine a silent movie, title cards captioned for the audience but invisible to those on screen. I hear the faintest tinkling of a piano playing a Scott Joplin rag in the background as the screen flickers into life. The **Roper** lures the unsuspecting victim, or **Mark**,† into the scam. The **Shills** (plants or stooges secretly in league with the gang) give their support as necessary, assisting with both the **Convincer** (satisfying the mark that he's going to make money) and the **Take** or **Touch** (relieving the mark of his money). The **Blow-Off** (getting rid of the mark after

---

* Most books and films about the era draw heavily on his work, some of them acknowledging it more openly than others. I couldn't help noticing that the stage directions in the script of *The Sting* reprised Maurer's book almost verbatim. Maurer noticed it too, and filed a $10 million lawsuit against the film's producers.

† 'Mark' is a 'carny' (carnival or fairground) slang term for the victim of a con. The name derives from the chalk mark surreptitiously placed on the back of someone seen as an easy target, or thought to be carrying a lot of cash.

he has been fleeced) and the **Fix** (bribing or otherwise dealing with the authorities) are applied as and when necessary. How the working parts fit together hardly varies; there are only so many ways to rook the mark. The anatomy of the con is always the same because human nature is always the same.

Many of the sepia-toned swindlers died penniless. Others made millions. Perhaps none did better than Joseph 'Yellow Kid' Weil, estimated to have stolen $8 million in the course of his stellar criminal career.* Weil claimed to have invented the Wire scam. Though whether we should believe someone who liked to describe himself as 'America's most notorious swindler' is a moot point.

The Yellow Kid's Story

Around 1903 or 1904, bored with selling 'patent medicines' to farmers' wives, and wanting to test out an idea for a new racing scam, Weil put a notice in the paper:

> WANTED – MAN TO INVEST $2,500. OPPORTUNITY TO
> PARTICIPATE IN VERY PROFITABLE VENTURE. MUST BE
> RELIABLE. CONFIDENTIAL, BOX W-62.

One reply in particular intrigued him. It was from a Chicago theatre owner and businessman called Marcus Macallister.† 'He not only had money', wrote Weil, 'he was a plunger.' The Kid had found his mark.

---

* Infuriatingly for moralists, Weil lived to enjoy his ill-gotten gains; he was 100 years old when he died in 1975.

† At least, that was the pseudonym Weil gave him in his autobiography.

Fig. 2.1. The nattily attired Joseph 'Yellow Kid' Weil, who made millions of dollars as an international swindler.

Weil's idea was simple. In those days, all racing news travelled by telegraph. The 'gold wire' carried results from the New York race tracks to Western Union offices across the country, from where operators relayed them to local poolroom betting shops. Weil explained to Macallister that if you could intercept the results before they got to the poolroom, you would be able to bet on a race that had already been won. Macallister's eyes widened as Weil outlined the scheme. A cousin of Weil's named Billy worked at Western Union. In exchange for a share of the jackpot, Billy would hold back the race results long enough for Macallister to head to the nearest poolroom and place a bet on a horse he already knew to be a sure thing.

In the jargon of the con, the **Telling of the Tale** is the opening act, the inciting incident, the first domino fall in a carefully pre-set sequence. It's the hook that excites the imagination and cupidity of the victim. In Weil's account, he first takes Macallister to meet his cousin Billy, an anxious, green-visored figure, in a corridor of the Western Union office. In a hurried and whispered conversation, Billy agrees to hold back the results from the sixth race run at Saratoga the following day and to tip off Macallister with the name of the winning horse in exchange for a share of the proceeds. Then, waving apologetically to a fellow worker, Billy rushes back to work. Macallister, too excited to think straight, is already dreaming of betting on a horse called Foregone Conclusion. He doesn't notice that Weil and his 'cousin' are simply using the Western Union building as a back-drop to tell their story. Nor does he detect that Billy's wave to a 'co-worker' is a little bit of actorly business, a nod to a complete stranger done to make it look as though Billy actually works there.

The next stage, the 'convincer', called for the more elaborate artifice of the **Big Store**. The Kid took Macallister to a poolroom that 'had been arranged for his special benefit'.

> We had rented the banquet hall of the old Briggs House and outfitted it fully with equipment … rented for the occasion. Of course, the telegraph instrument was not connected with Western Union, as Macallister believed. It received messages from another instrument which we had installed in a room of the Briggs House.

Weil had arranged all the props and people that Macallister would expect to find in a bookmaking establishment. As well as the telegraph machine, there were a cashier's cage, tables and chairs, a large board, a clock (set a few minutes slow, so that the mark would not realise that the race must already be over) – and the **Boost**: not only Weil's shills, but also a hundred innocent actors who had been told that they were auditioning for roles as extras in a poolroom scene.

The following day, the tip-off comes from Billy that Colorado is the horse to bet on in the sixth at Saratoga. Weil quickly steers Macallister to the poolroom. As they enter, the telegraph machine is chattering furiously. A man is rubbing out odds and chalking up new ones on an enormous board as new bets are placed by others. Over the tannoy comes the race-caller announcing the start of the sixth race. Macallister is steered past the throng to join the line of betters snaking towards the cashier. Money-fever is in the air. This is an establishment for high rollers, and the cast are nattily turned out: sober-suited bankers barely concealing their anticipation, blazer-clad sporting types affecting casual bar-room stances. Money is everywhere, some of it almost under Macallister's nose. A waistcoated financier casually lays a $20,000 bet; a sportsman peels off his stake from a bulging roll and slides it through the window. The cashier adds it to one of the toppling piles of bills which form an enticing chequerboard of green and white on his shelf. Behind him is a safe from which he periodically withdraws securely rolled wads of cash. Macallister is transfixed by this apparent wall of money. He does not know that the safe has a false back and that as quickly as money is taken out, it is restocked by unseen hands from behind a partition. Even less does he realise that the crisp wads of cash are that staple of the conman's toolkit known as 'mish rolls', stacks of cut newspaper tightly rolled inside an outer coat of genuine notes. If Macallister feels any guilt about betting on a sure thing, he doesn't show it. He can see his future unrolling before him:

more tip-offs, more dashes to the poolroom, a future carpeted with green and white bills.

Having convinced the mark there is money to be made, the conman can let him have a small but easy win. Alternatively, if the mark is not plunging quite as high or as hard as he could, he can be given the **Shut Out**. Weil has shrewdly decided on the latter. Macallister takes out the $2,500 he plans to bet on Colorado. At odds of 4 to 1, he feels assured of a $10,000 win. But as he makes his way towards the cashier, he finds his route blocked by several men in a violent argument. He tries to get past, but he can't. The altercation is still in progress when the flash comes: '*And … they're off!*' Macallister is forced to listen impotently, his stake burning a hole in his pocket, as his horse romps home in first place. As soon as Weil has left the room with a despondent Macallister, the clatter abruptly ceases. The whirring and the hubbub die away, the gang drop their accents, loosen their ties, rip off their scratchy false beards, pull over some chairs and put their feet up. Its work done, the Big Store shuts up shop.

FOMO, fear of missing out, is one of the most powerful weapons in the conman's armoury. The 'shut out' fuels desire, and, done well, closes the door to reason. The Kid tells Macallister that there has been a visit from suspicious Western Union inspectors, and that trips to the poolroom are too risky for the time being. He promises to be in touch as soon as the coast is clear. A fundamentally decent man, Macallister pays Billy and Weil their pre-agreed cut, despite having no winnings to pay them out of. As Weil later wrote: 'Our dilatory tactics served only to whet his appetite and ripen him for a bigger killing.'

Surprising as it may seem, Macallister was no more than averagely gullible. Conmen have always been instinctive manipulators of the human psyche. Recent studies of cognitive biases, the systematic quirks or errors in our modes of thought that make us act less than rationally, suggest that they have been pushing at an open door. If we want to believe something, we will select information that supports our existing beliefs (Confirmation Bias). We have an inbuilt tendency to focus on optimistic rather than realistic outcomes (Positivity Bias or the Pollyanna Principle). We justify, change, or ignore beliefs or behaviours that make us uncomfortable (Cognitive Dissonance). Once set on a path, we resist changes of direction or speed (a psychological Newtonism known as Momentum Theory). Above all, our propensity to *trust*, a heuristic (rule of thumb) which humans have evolved to make their lives predictable and society functional, makes it easier rather than harder for us to be deceived. These traits have not emerged accidentally. Evolution favours reciprocity and likeability. Progress is made easier by consistency and consensus. Our instincts for herd behaviour and our fear of scarcity, hard won by natural selection, have served us well. But the skill of the conman is to turn our strengths into vulnerabilities, and, like a seasoned judoka, to use them against us.

The Magic Machine

Some months after giving him the shut out, the Kid dangled a new baited hook in front of Macallister: a magic machine. He showed him a secluded spot, not far from a genuine poolroom, where telegraph cables ran overhead. Weil explained that with a special transformer they could tap into the wire; then Macallister would be able to intercept the results to the poolroom himself and delay them until he had placed a bet on the winning horse.

The only thing he would need was a skilled telegraph operator to work the machine. Macallister took the bait. He and Weil paid a visit to Moffatt's Electrical Shop, an electrical equipment store that dealt exclusively with conmen, conjuring up a variety of phoney devices for them to sell to their marks. Macallister was shown a box about three feet square and eighteen inches deep, with a reassuring heft. It was intricately wired, festooned with trailing cables and fancy switches. This, he was told, was a special transformer, 'one of the most intricate mechanisms ever constructed'. Delighted, Macallister agreed to pay $12,000 for it. Later that night Weil, Macallister, and the 'telegraph operator' headed for the out-of-the-way spot where they planned to intercept the telegraph wires. As they prepared to hook up the magic machine, a voice came out of the darkness. 'Up with your hands!' They could see not only the outline of a gun, but also the policeman holding it. Weil realised that the cop must have been tipped off by a rival who knew what was going on. It was time for a 'fix'.* Coolly, Weil pointed out to the policeman that he would get $20 for turning them in and $250 if he didn't, and he was easily persuaded to relent.

After this unexpected setback, they tried again. By pure chance, the 'telegraph operator' identified a horse for Macallister to bet on that actually won its race.† Elated by success, Macallister was keen to continue; Weil, well able to calculate the odds of lightning striking twice, claimed that the magic

---

* In later life Weil would become notorious for his fixes, and for his skill in nobbling juries. On one occasion, when facing trial, he 'fixed' (that is to say selected) his own jury. When they decided in his favour, he refused to pay his lawyer on the grounds that he had won the case for himself.

† Even if the magic box had been capable of intercepting signals on the wire, it wouldn't have done so: Weil's accomplice, reluctant to electrocute himself, had hooked it up to the insulators of the telegraph pole.

machine needed repairs – which cost Macallister a further $7,800.

An Irresistible Tale

A hundred years later, a Silicon Valley start-up called Theranos also had a magic machine. One that would revolutionise blood testing and transform public health by detecting illnesses from HIV to cancer with just a finger-prick, according to the company's charismatic founder Elizabeth Holmes.

Holmes told a mesmerising story of money *and* the moral high ground. She touted technology that would yield a quantum leap in public health as well as extraordinary shareholder returns. The icing on the cake: a cool Silicon Valley vibe, with a newsworthy and saintly kale-smoothie-sipping CEO. Too good to be true? You might have thought so. You might have been a little bit sceptical. And yet, and yet ... Such was the Pollyanna-ish enthusiasm for Theranos that for over a decade and a half almost every observer failed to notice that the magic machine was not delivering, that the explanations of how it worked were constantly changing, that the blood test results seemed no more accurate than guesswork. Dazzled by valuations that at their peak reckoned the company to be worth $9 billion (nine Unicorns, in Standard Silicon Valley Units), no one called out its fantastical financial projections. It is estimated that, to date, Theranos has taken its marks – sorry, *investors* – for more than $600 million.

How did it happen? What ingenious sleight of hand could catch so many unawares? What alchemical mix of deception and collusion made it possible? Although the story of this quintessentially twenty-first century business (biotech, disintermediating, disruptive) may seem to have little in common with the cons of 'Yellow Kid' Weil and his ilk anatomised by D W Maurer, look a bit closer and it turns out that Theranos could have been following their playbook to the letter.

Theranos began as a summer project. The preternaturally self-possessed daughter of ambitious parents, Holmes was brought up to believe that life should be both purposeful and successful. In 2002, she went to Stanford to study chemical engineering. In the summer vacation of her freshman year, she took a job in a lab testing patient specimens for SARS (a forerunner of COVID-19) using blood samples drawn from patients' veins. Struck by how protracted and frightening the tests were (Holmes had had a mortal fear of needles since childhood), she had the idea of creating a quick, cheap, and painless alternative.

Having taken a seminar on controlled drug-delivery devices, she first planned to develop an advanced therapeutic patch, similar to a nicotine patch, that would not only take the blood samples needed for diagnosis, but could also be used to administer treatment. The technologies were not new, but combining them in this way was a novel and exciting proposition. That at least one aspect of it – the miniaturisation of diagnostic equipment – was widely regarded as the Holy Grail of medical engineering did not deter Holmes. Nor did the fact that she was wholly lacking in relevant qualifications. Her innovation would make it easier for people to come and be tested. Those with a fear of needles would no longer be put off. Diseases would be diagnosed earlier and people treated more quickly. The company would be called Theranos, from a combination of the words 'therapy' and 'diagnosis'.

Holmes lost no time in locating a well-to-do investor. With $1 million in initial funding from the father of a family friend, taken by her enthusiasm and vision, she dropped out of Stanford. Theranos was off to a running start.

It was not long before the therapeutic patch proved unworkable. The focus switched to a different technology. Holmes had become obsessed with self-administered finger-prick tests as an alternative to the venous blood draws that had to be carried out with a needle and syringe by a medical professional. This was ambitious. Although some blood tests (for blood glucose levels, or clotting factors) need only a droplet of blood, and can be done quickly and even at home, others call for a syringe-full, followed by complex analysis in a laboratory. But Holmes was undaunted. Theranos created a sleek credit card-sized cartridge that was inserted into a larger machine called a reader. The system fulfilled her specifications: it was small enough to sit in a corner of a drugstore or pharmacy, or to be used at home. There was just one problem – it didn't work.

In any speculative or R&D-based business, it can be difficult to know where to draw the line between anticipation and reality. It's not clear at what point Holmes moved from sharing a vision she believed in to peddling something she knew to be fantasy. By all accounts she was a spellbinding saleswoman. In *Bad Blood: Secrets and Lies in a Silicon Valley Startup* (2018), his gripping investigation into Theranos's 15-year ride, John Carreyrou writes of Holmes wielding 'both engineering and laboratory lingo effortlessly', showing 'seemingly heartfelt emotion when she spoke of sparing babies in NICU* from blood transfusions'. As Carreyrou puts it, 'Like her idol Steve Jobs, she emitted a reality distortion field that forced people to momentarily suspend disbelief.'

---

* Neo-natal Intensive Care Units.

Enter the Edison

Abandoning the failed cartridge system, Theranos decided to switch to more established technologies. By 2008, Holmes was proudly pitching a new magic machine, the Edison, named after the great inventor. The Edison was a semi-portable box, its cover opaque to hide the fact that the much-touted 'miracle' technology was nothing more than an imperfectly automated lab test. Holmes's claims for the Edison would become increasingly improbable over time. She maintained that it could handle 192 key blood tests (it could only do half that number), that it contained ground-breaking proprietary technology (it consisted of a standard-issue robot arm, designed for dispensing glue, bought for $3,000 from a company in New Jersey). More worryingly, she presented the Edison as though it were the finished and tested article, rather than a prototype. In John Carreyrou's words, 'It was as if Boeing built one plane, and without doing a single flight test, told airline passengers "hop aboard".'

But the Edison machine *looked* the business. Just as the 'special transformer' from Moffatt's Electrical Shop, with its reassuring heft, its trailing cables and fancy switches, was the embodiment of up-to-the-minute turn-of-the-century telegraphy, so the Edison, with its sleekly minimalist look, Yves Béhar-designed black and white case with a diagonal slash, and stylish iPhone-style touch-screen, epitomised the Silicon Valley start-up aesthetic. By now, Holmes herself had taken on the guise of a tech-sector innovator, wearing black polo necks in emulation of Apple's Steve Jobs.*

---

* Rather unnervingly for Theranos's employees, she had also dropped her voice in order to sound more like a man (Margaret Thatcher had done the same in her heyday) – though it would rise several octaves at moments of excitement.

58

Like the 'Yellow Kid', she instinctively understood the importance of dressing the part. Just as Weil affected a pearl tiepin and a diamond horseshoe locket on his watch-chain, Holmes's minimalist geek-chic was the signal she needed to send. In any era, the confidence man or woman needs to sport the uniform of success if investors are to be convinced to part with their money.

Theranos was on a roll. Successive fundraising rounds brought in ever increasing sums, first $25 million, then another $32 million. Although it was not in fact a technology company – biomedical engineering is very different to software development – Theranos had cannily located itself in Silicon Valley. The company's assumed link to the super-successful tech disruptors attracted increasingly inflated valuations. By 2010, a Silicon Valley gold rush was gathering pace. Speculative investors circled like sharks around anything that might be the next big win, their lust for profit almost palpable. The air of California was thick with money even as the rest of the country remained sunk in economic gloom.

In a series of steps, Holmes built up a compliant and increasingly well-connected Theranos board. By 2013, it included such luminaries as Henry Kissinger, former Secretary of State George Shultz, and Commander of the Joint Forces Command and future Secretary of Defense James Mattis.* It's difficult to overstate the boost that this kind of star power can bestow on a company. Holmes flattered and cajoled her board, rewarding them with grants of ever more valuable company stock. She seems to have had a special affinity with much older powerful men, and they with her, and their advice and contacts

---

* When it became clear how far from the truth many of Theranos's claims were, these eminences left the board to form what Carreyrou describes as 'a new ceremonial body called "a board of counsellors"'.

were invaluable. When Shultz tipped off the *Wall Street Journal* about a company that was going to transform healthcare, the paper published a favourable article, handily timed to coincide with the launch of Theranos's blood test and diagnosis service.

Both Walgreens and Safeway were keen to acquire some of the Theranos stardust, vying with each other to put its low-cost blood-testing services into their pharmacies and supermarkets. In normal times, each of these retail rivals would have insisted on an exclusive contract; such was their fear of missing out on a golden opportunity that they tamely agreed to share access to the technology. Waiving the investigations and assessments that would normally be required before making a major investment, Walgreens signed a contract to pilot Theranos's blood tests in exchange for a $100 million 'innovation' fee plus a $40 million loan to the start-up. Steve Burd, the CEO of Safeway, who had wooed Holmes with presents and flattery,* committed to spending a total of $450 million to create dedicated 'Wellness Centers' to house the miracle machines. Once again, FOMO was closing the doors to reason. Neither company asked for proof that Theranos's machines could in fact do what it was claimed they could. On the contrary: Walgreens signed a non-disclosure agreement whereby it undertook not to tamper with or even look inside the Edison. Here were major corporations spending hundreds of millions of dollars, signing multi-year contracts with a commercial tiddler, and yet *they never looked inside the*

---

* On one occasion Burd sent Holmes white orchids; on another, a model of a private jet with the message 'Next time it's a real one'. It didn't save him from the 'blow-off', though: having been one of Theranos's most loyal supporters, Burd found that as soon as he stepped down from being CEO, Holmes no longer returned his calls.

*box.** What might pass as carelessness when taking up a White Van Man's 'unmissable' offer looks like astonishing negligence from these two business giants.

Theranos launched a pilot scheme in Walgreens and Safeway stores in Arizona.† Almost immediately, it proved unable to carry out the promised volume of in-store testing and analyses.‡ It resorted to carrying out the tests in store and FedExing the blood samples back to its labs in Palo Alto, some 700 miles away. A few finger-prick samples were analysed on the Edison, with highly erratic results; others had to be diluted (to obtain a sufficient quantity of blood), before being analysed on Siemens equipment that Theranos had bought and secretly installed in a second lab that visitors were never shown.

---

* Here Theranos was applying the same principle as the 'Pig in a Poke' scam that has been operating for at least five centuries. Not looking in the box is what keeps the White Van Man street scam going, and it's what kept Theranos going for at least five years longer than it should have done. As the name suggests, it's appropriate to sign an NDA if you're a potential investor or business partner asked not to reveal the details of commercially sensitive technology to a third party; it is emphatically not appropriate to agree not to be given those details in the first place.

† In an impressively upscale demonstration of the 'fix', the company got the Arizona state legislature to enact a law (said to have been co-authored by Theranos) permitting its citizens to have their blood tested without the need for a prior doctor's request. In 2017, Theranos agreed to pay $4.65 million to cover refunds for the 175,000 Arizonans who had paid for the company's blood tests since 2013.

‡ The Edison could only do immunoassays, a type of test that uses antibodies to measure substances in the blood. Theranos's other great innovation, the miniLab, was a miniaturised laboratory small enough to fit on a shelf. It supposedly contained the equipment to carry out all the other sorts of tests required. It never worked at all.

Betting Fever in Silicon Valley

This should have been the point at which Theranos came unstuck. But it was 2013, and money was pouring into Silicon Valley. Estimates of the value of Theranos exceeded those of both Uber and Spotify. A slew of high-profile articles propelled Holmes to instant celebrity. *Fortune*: 'This CEO is out for Blood'; *WIRED*: 'This Woman Invented a Way to Run 30 Lab Tests on Only One Drop of Blood'.

Understandably nervous about revealing its secrets to the world, Theranos carefully stage-managed any visits to its labs. An investor or journalist would be shown around, offered a finger-prick blood test, and allowed to stay just long enough to see their sample placed in a Theranos miniLab machine. As soon as they left, the sample would be removed and rushed down for analysis on one of the commercial Siemens machines concealed in the secret lab. For its most high-profile event, the visit of then Vice President Joe Biden, Theranos created its own 'Big Store' – an entirely fake laboratory. A suitable space was commandeered, the staff ordered to repaint it and stack miniLab machines along the walls to 'dress the set'. The press stood in rapt attention as Holmes showed Biden around the phoney lab, piled high with non-functioning machines. Then Biden, along with Holmes's 'boost' – a group of senior healthcare officials no more aware of what was going on than Weil's auditioning actors – joined Holmes for a roundtable discussion on preventative healthcare. I like to imagine that when Biden had gone, telling the assembled press that he had just seen 'the laboratory of the future', the Theranos team could finally relax, loosen their ties, and put their feet up on the tables – just as the 'shills' had done in the Briggs House a hundred years before.

Fig. 2.2. Elizabeth Holmes, in her trademark
black polo neck, holds a pinprick-sized vial
of blood.

How much thought did Holmes ever give to others? It was a
point of pride with Weil only to pick on people who could
afford to lose the money they willingly thrust into his hands.
While Theranos's investors were well able to take the financial
hit, there is no record of Holmes showing compassion or
remorse for the real victims of her con. The level of heartlessness
is quite staggering. By the end, Theranos had voided over a
million tests carried out in California and Arizona. That's up to
a million people who might have been told they were cancer-
free when they weren't. Or told they were HIV-positive when
they weren't. Or wrongly diagnosed as free from an infectious
disease such as hepatitis C or herpes, which they then passed on
to others. You don't have to have lived through a pandemic to
appreciate the importance of accurate medical testing. It takes a
special kind of sociopathy to build a business that falsely claims

to deliver that accuracy while being totally indifferent to the outcomes for patients.

What You Most Desire

The power of the great confidence trickster derives from the psychological skill with which they intuit and speak directly to what each mark most desires. In a 1956 profile of the 'Yellow Kid', the Nobel Prize-winning author Saul Bellow wrote that, while it was never easy to know if his subject was telling the truth – 'long practice in insincerity gives him an advantage' – at one point Weil did seem to speak from the heart. 'I was a psychologist', Weil told Bellow. 'My domain was the human mind ... With this understanding, I entered the lives of my dupes ... When they looked at me they saw themselves. I only showed them their own purpose.'

Weil was the secret wish, the face in the mirror. To businessmen like Marcus Macallister, he was a fellow speculator, looking for a quick win. To wealthy spinsters, he was the suitor yearning for matrimony. The little tricks and touches that make for easy friendship and engender reciprocity – the generous dinners, the gift of perfume for the mark's wife – were second nature to him. Elizabeth Holmes had the same uncanny ability to sense what would resonate with a particular audience at a particular moment. To investors, she represented the chance to profit hugely from a tech start-up's conversion of vision into riches. To George Shultz, who believed in the power of science to save the world from pandemics, she was going to make the world a better place. To the *Wall Street Journal*, her company was a disruptor poised to shake up a somnolent healthcare sector.

Holmes was also delivering another, equally effective message. She was routinely proclaimed as the 'first tech start-up female billionaire CEO'. If you read that sentence again, you will see that of its six words, only three are true: 'start-up', 'female', and 'CEO'.* What made this message so resonant is that the number of 'hero' businesswomen can be counted on the fingers of two hands, if not one. At the time of Holmes's dizzy ascent, there were more CEOs called John than female CEOs,† and the very few high-profile women in tech, such as Sheryl Sandberg of Facebook, Meg Whitman of eBay and Hewlett Packard, and Marissa Mayer of Yahoo, were not founders of the companies they led, unlike Zuckerberg, Ellison, or Gates. So there was good reason for Barack Obama (who appointed her US ambassador for global entrepreneurship), the Clintons (for whom she hosted a fundraising gala), and *Fortune* magazine (who did the maths that valued Theranos at $9 billion and Holmes's share of it at somewhere north of $4.5 billion), along with any number of television shows and business publications, to celebrate the self-styled First Lady of Tech. Theranos's spectacular success was not just because Holmes told the tale that people wanted to hear, but because for many Holmes *was* the tale they wanted to hear.

Holmes was not, of course, what she pretended to be. She was acting a part, she was a pretender as well as a trickster. As an

---

* Even though Holmes was never the 'first tech start-up female billionaire CEO' of the headlines, she has achieved a 'female first' of sorts. She can lay claim to the dubious accolade of having carried out the biggest female-led confidence trick of all time. (Though she may not hold on to her crown for long. Another contender for the title has cropped up. So-called Cryptoqueen Ruja Ignatova has to date managed to scam $4 billion out of luckless Bitcoin investors.)

† Also David.

entrepreneur she was a failure, but as an impostor she is rather unusual. Like the top echelons of the professions, the annals of professional imposture exhibit a marked shortage of women.* Bram Stoker's (yes, the *Dracula* one) 1910 *Famous Impostors* includes just two out of a total of around twenty: a bogus princess (Olive) and an avaricious spiritualist-witch (La Voisin).†

This is not, I suspect, because women are necessarily nicer or more honest than men, but because, until now, imposture has never remotely been an equal opportunity employer.‡ Until women could in real life occupy the roles that impostors typically choose to personate – doctor, lawyer, airline pilot, businessman – there was no possibility of a woman pretending to be one. Historically, there were only two roles that female impostors could play. Either they could claim to be a princess, or they could pretend to spiritual powers: think of all the fortune-telling fraudsters, crystal-ball readers, and psychics who claim to commune with the other side.§ If Holmes is unusual in

---

* As do the annals of the grift: D W Maurer's definitive account of it features only one woman, Lily the Roper, and then only very briefly.

† Stoker's collection of impostors is broad and eclectic. He features 5 pretenders, 3 magicians, 1 wandering Jew, 1 faux financier – the founder of the South Sea Company, 6 witches, 1 claimant, 4 women-as-men, and 1 cross-dressing spy.

‡ Only relatively recently have figures for what is rather charmingly known as 'pink-collar' crime begun to edge upwards.

§ A very few particularly enterprising women have done both. Ann O'Delia Diss Debar started her career as the 'daughter' of Ludwig I of Bavaria and his mistress Lola Montez, and ended her (very lucrative) days playing a succession of bogus spiritualists, including one named Swami Laura Horos. The great magician Houdini, who knew all too well how she did her tricks, described Debar as 'one of the most extraordinary fake mediums and mystery swindlers the world has ever known'.

her imposture, it is because it is only now that a woman could credibly impersonate a titan of the business world.

The aftermath of a con can be messy. In 2016, Holmes was banned from operating a lab and Theranos's blood-testing licence was revoked. Walgreens terminated its partnership with the company and closed all forty Wellness Centers; its claim for breach of contract was settled for an undisclosed sum. Theranos was also sued by patient groups and some investors, even though the company had no assets; other investors were able to write their losses off against tax. Holmes herself was charged with numerous counts of fraud, as was her former business (and romantic) partner. It may be that Holmes will at some point tell (or sell) her story and attempt a rehabilitation. This is a well-trodden path: 'Yellow Kid' Weil, having bilked millions of dollars from his marks over the course of a long career, produced a ghost-written autobiography in which he claimed that he was a changed man.

So what conclusions can we draw? Any reader hoping to hold on to their life savings should remember a few simple maxims:

No good story is ever quite true.

It takes more muscles to doubt than it does to believe.

Belief has no place in a business proposition.

Always look inside the box.

If you are offered something for nothing, you will get nothing for something.

Perhaps most important of all: there is no con without complicity. No grift without a gull. You can't cheat an honest man.

The classic confidence trick is essentially a one-to-one affair. No matter how big the cast or elaborate the setting, the deception is always a matter of individuals. But what does it take to

achieve deception on a mass scale? How do you deceive someone you've never met? Change a human phenomenon to a
cultural one? Can you deceive a town? A country? Can you
make a country deceive itself, and come together in one big lie?

3

COMPLICITY

Lothar and the Turkeys

On the eve of Palm Sunday 1942, a full moon in a clear night sky made Lübeck easy to find for the first wave of RAF pilots. Later raiders were able to see the glow of the inferno from over a hundred miles away. A series of firestorms ignited thousands of blazes, devastating the historic centre of the city, and the thirteenth-century Marienkirche was almost completely burnt out. In the church's bell tower, the fires produced fierce draughts that caused the great bells to ring out a final time before they crashed to the ground.

Arthur 'Bomber' Harris had chosen the German city as his first experiment in incendiary bombing because of its many medieval timbered buildings. His aim was not so much to demolish Germany's military targets as to bombard its industrial base and undermine the morale of its civilian population.* 'The damage is really enormous', wrote Joseph Goebbels, the Nazi Minister of Propaganda, after seeing a newsreel of the destruction. 'It is horrible. One can well imagine how such a bombardment affects the population.'

---

* This was a miscalculation. In the period of the most intense saturation bombing, German industrial production went up rather than down.

The Miracle of Lübeck

More than a thousand people died in Lübeck as a result of that night, and fifteen thousand lost their homes, so it was some time before the town could attend to the firebombed church. When they got there, the repair crews found that the heat of the fire had caused whitewash to peel from some of the internal walls. To their amazement, fragments of brightly coloured frescoes had appeared beneath. As they chipped away, they began to uncover the outlines of angels and saints, some of them gigantic figures over ten feet high. As in many other churches, the murals had been whitewashed over at the time of the Reformation. The citizens of Lübeck could thank their iconoclastic fifteenth-century ancestors for the miraculous preservation of the frescoes.

Given that few Gothic wall paintings were still in existence, the delighted town elders knew they had a major artistic find on their hands. But restoration work could not begin until the war was over and money could be raised. By 1948, the town was able to engage Professor Ernst Fey, his son Dietrich, and their team, who had worked on many churches in northern Germany. The restoration took place amid some secrecy; three years later it was unveiled to great acclaim across the world. Thanks to the whitewash, said *TIME* magazine in 1951, 'the interior of the Marienkirche looks more as its original decorators intended than it has for 500 years ... The colours, brilliant reds, blues, greens and yellows, were still unfaded.' Germany was in urgent need of good news, and people flocked to view the murals.

The frescoes along the walls of the nave were in full Gothic style. Individual saints were portrayed alongside group scenes of the Annunciation, Crucifixion, and Resurrection, together with lively medieval street scenes and vignettes from the Bible and

Aesop's fables. One remarkable assembly consisted of an angel flanked by a haloed pilgrim on either side. Each holy traveller was carrying a staff and wearing a hat with a low crown and straight brim, reminiscent of a priest's bowler-style hat. There were saintly maidens with pulpy mouths and eyes as dark as caviar, and fantastical animals: lobsters, doves, a wolf in monk's robes accompanied by a goat and a calf.

In the choir, giant figures contained echoes of an earlier style. As a treatise on the murals published around the time of their unveiling noted, 'Above the high altar is a portrayal of the Virgin together with St Anne and St John, the two co-patrons of the church, and in other parts of the choir are triple groups of Apostles, patriarchs and monks. These exhibit a severe style, Byzantine-influenced and still almost Romanesque, and undoubtedly originated a few years earlier than the figures in the main aisle.' The learned author highlighted the German preference for the Gothic manner over the Byzantine, describing the nave friezes as 'more animated, softer, entirely Gothic', adding that 'done with a coarse brush, the painting was probably carried out in a very short time'.

The official re-opening of the Marienkirche took place in September 1951, the 700th anniversary of its first construction. The occasion was as much a celebration of the murals as of the church, with local worthies, church dignitaries, diplomats, academics, and ambassadors all present. West Germany's Chancellor, Konrad Adenauer, stood in the nave during the ceremony. 'This, gentlemen,' he declared, gazing upwards towards the choir at the twenty-one giant figures of saints in glowing colours, 'is uplifting!'

The townspeople spoke of the 'miracle of Lübeck'. They told how the precious frescoes had been peeled out of the old mortar with the aid of a wonder fixative, leaving them looking as fresh

Fig. 3.1. A stamp issued to celebrate the
700th anniversary of the Marienkirche,
featuring two bowler-hatted pilgrims
and an angel.

as the day they were painted. The Federal Post Office printed
two million special anniversary stamps featuring the angel
between two bowler-hatted pilgrims. Restorer Dietrich Fey was
awarded the Bundesverdienstkreuz, the Order of Merit of the
Federal Republic, and an additional 150,000 marks in restoration money. Dr Adenauer asked to be shown the 'unique
frescoes' and marvelled at their lustrous colours and clear bold
outlines. In the months that followed the anniversary, over
100,000 people visited the church – a welcome boost for
Lübeck's fragile post-war economy.

Lothar's Story

Just over a year later, an anxious-looking man marched into the office of the public prosecutor for Lübeck and told a story that made his audience gasp. His name was Lothar Malskat. He was an artist, one of the restorers working on the Marienkirche murals. He wanted to confess that he and his boss had forged all the frescoes. Malskat was furious that the Feys had taken all the glory for the work. The anniversary celebrations in particular had rankled. While Dietrich Fey was accepting his decoration, said Malskat bitterly, 'I, the man who had done all the work, was sitting in the backroom where I had been given a bottle of beer.'

The prosecutor refused to believe the story of the forged frescoes. The local newspapers derided Malskat as 'crazy'. Then he showed them diaries he had kept and photographs he had taken during the restoration work, and began to tell of the many other fakes – paintings as well as frescoes – that he had done for Dietrich Fey. The two of them, he said, had been up to their tricks for years. Malskat did all the work, creating imitations of the works of great artists: Renoir, Chagall, Degas, Corot, Gauguin, Rousseau, Munch, Utrillo, and many more. Fey would sign the pictures and sell them to dealers, collectors, and museums. Malskat had become so good at the French Impressionists that they sometimes took him less than an hour. He directed a disbelieving police force to Fey's apartment, where they found seven paintings and twenty-one drawings in the style of well-known masters. Fey was arrested immediately, and a commission of experts set up to investigate the forgeries.*

---

* Malskat's fakes were so numerous that the commission's report eventually ran to 43,000 pages.

Fig. 3.2. Lothar Malskat and some of his
works.

To accommodate the many spectators, the trial of Dietrich
Fey and Lothar Malskat had to be held in the Atlantic, Lübeck's
biggest dancehall, a place more accustomed to the sounds of
polkas and folk dancing than legal proceedings. A cloth was
thrown decorously over the bar area. Loudspeakers were placed
outside for the ever-increasing crowds. With his winning wide-
mouthed smile, long nose, and eyebrows permanently arched in
what looked like amusement, Lothar Malskat was the undis-
puted star of the show. He readily confessed that he and Fey had
forged the murals in the Marienkirche. The full details emerged
as he gave his evidence.

As a young man, Lothar had attended art school. His professors were quick to recognise his talent, one mentioning the

young man's 'extraordinary, almost uncanny productivity and versatility'. He had dreams of becoming an artist on his own account, but just after the war he was struggling to feed his family. He ran into Dietrich Fey, who suggested that there might be more money in Malskat fakes than Malskat originals. Fey set him to work creating reproductions and works 'in the style of the great artists of the past and present'. When Fey got the job of restoring the Marienkirche, said Lothar, 'I was allowed to stop fabricating French Impressionists. Fey had a better job for me: I had to go back to the Middle Ages.'

The plan was for the restorers first to clean the frescoes, so as to remove the remaining whitewash, then to 'fix' them so that they stuck firmly to the walls, prior to restoration. Perched on top of a 90-foot scaffold, however, Lothar soon realised that the years after the bombing, when the frescoes had been exposed to the elements, had left only scattered patches of the original paint – and 'even that turned to dust when I blew on it'. Faced with near-blank walls, he decided to use what fragments he could, and to fill the rest with paintings of apostles and monks, saints and pilgrims, using features taken from his sister, schoolmates, local labourers, and historical figures. The audience in the court-room gasped as Lothar admitted that he had even modelled figures of the Virgin on photographs of Austrian movie queen Hansi Knoteck.

'I learned a lot of things about my art', said Lothar. When visiting experts pointed to 'the magic eye of yonder prophet', he refrained from pointing out that 'yonder prophet' was his father, a second-hand clothing dealer in Königsberg. He had watched visitors gaze in rapt concentration at 'the peaceful lines in the face of the old Gothic King', unaware that they were actually looking at Malskat's portrait of Rasputin. He even claimed to have painted Genghis Kahn with a halo.

Fig. 3.3. A Malskat Madonna and Lothar's inspiration, the
Austrian movie queen Hansi Knoteck.

Lothar's sketchy technique enabled him to work at high
speed: 'one saint during breakfast'. With a year still to go before
the 700th anniversary, he found that he was ahead of schedule
and had time on his hands. It was at this point that Fey 'proposed
that [I] discover an additional cycle of murals in the choir',
where not even fragments of fresco remained. Lothar set about
the task, taking as his model photographs of mosaics from the
church of Sant'Apollinare Nuovo in Ravenna – which did at
least explain the 'Byzantine' influence experts had noticed.

It was hard for the art historians who had been so enthusiastic about the Marienkirche murals, citing them as evidence of a
hitherto unrecognised 'Lübeck School' of Gothic art, to accept
that they dated not from 1280 but from 1950. When the forgeries were revealed, one PhD student who had written that 'the
splendid figure of Mary bears the brush marks of Gothic genius'

indignantly pointed out that the paintings were remarkably similar to the Gothic murals to be found in the Heilig-Geist-Hospital, the Holy Ghost Hospital, in the town. 'I also painted those', explained Lothar.

The Importance of Being Gothic

Before the truth came out, at least one art expert had noted the striking similarities between the Lübeck murals and the famous frescoes in the cathedral at Schleswig, about 75 miles to the north-west. As they put it, 'the Lübeck murals ... express a certain Nordic boldness, which may be sought in vain in other High Gothic murals, excepting those of Schleswig Cathedral, where the nose formation of the Salvator Mundi and of the figures on certain of the buttresses suggest the studio of the master of the Lübeck nave and choir must here too have been at work.'

The expert was more perceptive than they realised. Lothar Malskat and the Feys had indeed worked on the Schleswig murals in 1937, some years before they came to Lübeck. Cleaning away an unfortunate earlier nineteenth-century restoration of the late-thirteenth-century works, they had found that only the barest traces remained – most of which they managed to obliterate as well. Aghast at the newly blank walls, Lothar had had to fill the gaps with figures of his own invention.

To all who saw them after their restoration in 1937, the Schleswig frescoes were outstanding examples of medieval German Gothic art. Particularly celebrated were the saints, kings, and knights, with their strong-willed Aryan gaze, long noses, and distinctly Nordic chins. Under the Nazi regime, these murals were so important to the idea of national identity that a copy of a book about them by Alfred Stange, professor of art history at the University of Bonn and an expert on German Gothic, was sent to every school. Heinrich Himmler had them photographed and sent on tour as part of the propaganda war effort.

Regarded as an authentic and enduring thread that ran through German art, the Gothic style was energetically promoted by the Nazi propaganda machine to help foster a myth of national rebirth. Inspired by reconstructed traditions of the Ancient Germans, the belief in the superiority of all things Gothic, from art to typography, became an article of faith. The pointed arches of Gothic architecture were said to echo the shape of the huts that Germanic forest dwellers had formed by bending trees together. The link between Germany's Gothic past and its National Socialist future was symbolised by the magnificent medieval Gothic city of Nuremberg, where the movement held its rallies and passed its race laws. Even calligraphy was part of the great synchronisation (*Gleichschaltung*) and Nazification of the state and German society: the use of the characteristic blackletter Fraktur font was mandatory for all official documents, and citizens were instructed to use exclusively Gothic typefaces.*

If it was important to the Nazis that German art should be Gothic, it was even more important that German heroes should be Nordic. Many of the racial theories enthusiastically adopted by the regime had been developed elsewhere at the end of the nineteenth century by the likes of the American writer Madison

---

* Or at least they were until concerns that Gothic type was proving a challenge for readers of Goebbels's foreign propaganda brought about a reversal. In 1941 Hitler's deputy, Martin Bormann, issued a declaration that henceforth Antiqua, a Roman font, was to be used instead.

Grant, one of Adolf Hitler's favourite authors.* Their dismal –
and, it should be said, utterly unscientific – hierarchies ranked
the white races above all others, with Jews and blacks regarded
as degenerate and inferior respectively. Of the three Caucasian
races (white-skinned, of European origin) in their eugenicist
pecking order, they deemed the Nordics (light hair and skin, a
longer head, blue eyes and a narrow nose, tall of stature with a
slender body type) to be superior to both the Mediterranean
(swarthy complexioned, dark eyes and hair, short-to-moderate
stature) and the Alpine (rounder head, darker complexioned,
shorter in stature). As Madison Grant put it, the Nordics were
'a race of soldiers, sailors, adventurers, and explorers, but above
all, of rulers, organizers, and aristocrats'. Nordicism, still the
dog-whistle of white nationalism, infected every part of life.
Married members of the SS were urged to spread their Aryan
seed, in or out of wedlock, as part of Himmler's *Lebensborn*
programme. Hitler too was what has since been called a 'gene
believer'.† 'I shall have no peace of mind', he said privately,
'until I have planted a seed of Nordic blood wherever the popu-
lations stand in need of regeneration.'

---

* Grant's *The Passing of the Great Race* (1916) was lauded by Hitler, who
wrote a fan letter to Grant in the early 1930s in which he called the book 'my
Bible'. Grant's work was embraced by proponents of the National Socialist
movement in Germany and was the first non-German book reprinted by the
Nazis when they took power.

† As is the 45th President of the United States, who has described himself as
such. Donald Trump endorsed a garbled version of eugenics (without appear-
ing able to recall the word), when he explained in a 2010 interview with
CNN, 'Well, I think I was born with the drive for success because I have a
certain gene. I'm a gene believer.'

Rewriting History

As he worked away on his 'restoration' of the murals at Schleswig Cathedral, Lothar began to let his imagination run away with him. Along with the Nordic saints, renditions of the Holy Virgin, and a medieval bestiary including stags, cocks, griffons, and mountain goats, he devised a frieze of eight medallions as a border to his Massacre of the Innocents in the cathedral's cloister, and in them he painted images that were plainly recognisable as turkeys.

This posed a problem for historians of the Nordic School of Art. The turkey is a New World bird; it could not have been known in Europe at the time of the Schleswig murals in 1280. The decidedly non-Nordic Christopher Columbus – an Italian sailing under a Spanish flag – would only reach the shores of America in 1492, two centuries later. And the first turkeys were brought by Spaniards to Germany some sixty or so years after that. If the status of the Schleswig Cathedral frescoes as a triumph of Teutonic civilisation was to be maintained, the experts were going to have to rewrite history.

I am holding a little bit of that rewritten history in my hand: Alfred Stange's 1940 book *Der Schleswiger Dom und seine Wandmalereien* (*Schleswig Cathedral and its Murals*). Copies are not hard to come by, no doubt because every school library had one. The thick cream paper is spotted with age stains the colour of well-brewed tea. The book is printed in a blackletter Gothic font that is impenetrable to me, but the pictures speak for themselves. The frescoes are almost cartoon-like, a medieval comic strip. In one, a naked witch on a feather-duster broomstick flies up into the vaulting. In others there are female figures with retroussé noses, almond-shaped movie-star eyes, and bee-stung lips as popularised by Hollywood actresses of the 1920s and 1930s.

And then there are the turkeys. Stange wrote that the painter, whom he identified as having worked in Schleswig circa 1280, at the time of the Hohenstaufen emperors, had 'with astonishing powers of discernment ... observed and reproduced the creatures' individuality and smallest idiosyncrasies. The portrayals are not, as so often, borrowed from reference books, but are based on a high degree of personal observation.' In other words, the painter was drawing from life. It followed that there must have been turkeys in Germany by 1280. Stange was giving his art historical support to the theory that, long before Columbus, America had been discovered by bold blond Vikings.

I find it hard to imagine what made the author of the definitive work on German Gothic Art write this. Surely he must have known that the frescoes couldn't possibly be the work of a thirteenth-century artist. How could he bring himself to authenticate what was so patently inauthentic? Stange was a member of the NSDAP (Nazi Party) and the SA (the brown-shirted precursor of the SS), and an employee of the Ahnenerbe, Himmler's cultural propaganda unit. Was he afraid that he would lose his job if perceived to be insufficiently dedicated to the cause? Or was it simply a matter of careerist calculation, that his interests were best served by giving the appearance of belief in the thousand-year Reich? Or maybe he didn't know after all. Maybe, in a phrase that became current many decades later, he had simply drunk the Kool-Aid.

In his apocalyptic 1986 novel *Die Rättin* (*The Rat*), the German novelist Günter Grass uses Malskat's forgeries as a metaphor for the troubled wartime German psyche, describing satirically how Lothar's turkeys clinched the pro-Nordic faction's view of German supremacy. 'At last, what had hitherto

Fig. 3.4. One of the anachronistic turkeys
Lothar Malskat included in his Schleswig
Cathedral frescoes, which caused the revision
of so much history.

been no more than a dubious presumption, often ridiculed as nationalistic fantasy, was established. Thanks to Malskat, historical truth came to light. For this early Gothic painting proved that not the wop Columbus, but the Vikings, Germanic Norsemen with long noses and jutting chins, had brought that undeniably American bird to Europe.' History was rewritten on the basis of Lothar Malskat's turkeys.

A Wider Complicity

Forgers' most useful allies are not their fellow criminals, but those innocents who fervently want to believe in the deception. 'It takes a village' was a phrase that came to prominence in the 1990s through a book of the same name. The premise, purportedly taken from an African proverb, was that 'it takes a village to raise a child' meaning that a child is not just the product of its parenting but of all the people, the community, and the prevailing culture and expectations surrounding it.

Just how many people does it take to rewrite history? To become complicit in a national lie? It took more than just a single talented painter to perpetrate the Great Gothic Art Swindle. It took a town bombed into splinters and near submission, restorers with an eye for the main chance, dishonest architects, collusive art experts and church authorities, supine municipal leaders, negligent federal organisations, and a national and international press all too keen to rush into print. Wittingly or unwittingly, all were complicit in the forgeries – even those who merely turned a blind eye or failed to ask the right questions. Each colluding, for his or her own reasons, in a single morale-boosting, face-saving lie.

Plenty of people knew at the time of the restoration that there were no longer any frescoes in the Marienkirche to restore, that there was no 'wonder fixative'. The church commission had been warned repeatedly about the Feys' earlier work at Schleswig Cathedral. Some tried to speak up. The Inspector of Ancient Monuments had specified that he only wanted existing fragments to be restored; missing parts were not to be recreated. He made thirty-six visits to the site over a period of three years and sent his report to a slew of departments: the public records office, the church authorities, the Ministry of Culture at Kiel, the municipal Board of Works, the West German Association for the Preservation of Ancient Monuments, and the administrators of Lübeck Museum. Had any of them paid attention, there would have been no invented saints or made-up Madonnas. But the Lübeck authorities did not want scraps of restored frescoes: they wanted whole, unblemished paintings that would beautify their church, rather than a museum of bits and pieces.

Malskat's forgeries had infected a population desperate for uplifting stories, so bombarded with propaganda that it had lost the ability to see the truth, with an epidemic of self-deception. As Günter Grass noted, it was not just paintings that were inauthentic, but the entire country. 'Malskat's gift for being authentically Gothic ... was timely, falling in with a basic need, a general forgery-mindedness', he wrote, adding that, 'You had to lie to hold your head high ... lies were not lame; they strode sturdily in those days.'

Spiritually Starved

The stated policy of the Allies after the war was to de-Nazify Germany and return it to the international fold. In the summer of 1945, the poet Stephen Spender was sent to the country on an official mission to discover what remained of intellectual life. In Cologne, bombed barely two months after Lübeck, he found the ruin of the city 'reflected in the internal ruin of its inhabitants who, instead of living lives that can form a scar over the city's wounds, are parasites sucking at a dead carcass, digging among the ruins for hidden food'. Spender also interviewed Konrad Adenauer, then Mayor of Cologne, who as Chancellor of West Germany would be present at the celebrations in Lübeck six years later. 'The German people are spiritually starved,' Adenauer told him, 'the imagination has to be provided for.'

Indeed it does, and it was Lothar Malskat's paintings which, however briefly, provided for the imagination of a nation that had lost its way. The people of Lübeck may have lied to hold their heads high, in the words of Günter Grass, but these were people whose lives were fractured and who wanted to make them whole. They were harking back to a distant past at a time when recent history was too painful to contemplate, clinging to a narrative that united them when all around was falling to pieces. Falling for the big lie that makes us all feel better about ourselves, the seductive propaganda that something, or somebody, can make our country great again.

What remains of this brief forging of national pride, this mass-willed delusion? Lothar's once-celebrated murals were rapidly whitewashed over and the two great melted and broken bells of the Marienkirche were left as a memorial where they had fallen on the night of the Palm Sunday bombing.

Dietrich Fey was sentenced to twenty months' imprisonment, Lothar Malskat to eighteen. The superintendent of the Marienkirche asked to retire. Lübeck's art director suddenly decided to move to East Germany; his assistant was abruptly pensioned off. The architect of the restoration lost his job. Alfred Stange had spent much of the war in occupied France attempting to coerce art historians there into admitting the superiority of German Gothic over the French version. After the war, he too lost his job. Günter Grass, a fierce critic of Germany's Nazi past, determined that Germany should never again be strong enough to dominate Europe, campaigned against the reunification of East and West Germany. In 1999 he won the Nobel Prize for Literature. In 2006, forty years after the end of the war, he revealed that he had been a member of the Waffen-SS.

Malskat was released before he had served his full sentence. For the first time in his life, he was in demand as an artist under his own name. He found work in Sweden, painting pictures for the Tre Kronor Inn in Stockholm 'in the style of the fourteenth century'. For the entrance doors of the Royal Tennis Courts he painted a turkey – just like the ones in Schleswig Cathedral. Whereas in earlier times he had denied that he was a forger, he was now known to sign paintings as 'Lothar Malskat, Forger and Artist'.* You can still buy works by Malskat on a number of German internet sites today.

Malskat also appears as a character in several thrillers set in the murky period towards the end of the war, cropping up fleetingly to illustrate the corruption and decadence of the Reich. Otherwise his story has been written out of German history – an example, perhaps, of what the German writer W G Sebald called 'the extraordinary faculty for self-anaesthesia shown by a community that seemed to have emerged from a war of annihilation without any signs of psychological impairment'. Perhaps self-anaesthesia, painting over the past and the part so many had played in it, was the only possible response to complicity in a dreadful episode in a nation's history.

---

* At his trial, Malskat's story had been that he merely painted pictures and that the forgery lay in the labels Dietrich Fey put on them.

PART 2
NATURAL-BORN FAKERS

4

MIMICS

Nature's Impostors

'The mysteries of mimicry had a special attraction for me. Its phenomena showed an artistic perfection usually associated with man-wrought things ... When a butterfly had to look like a leaf, not only were all the details of a leaf beautifully rendered but markings mimicking grub-bored holes were generously thrown in ... I discovered in nature the nonutilitarian delights that I sought in art. Both were a form of magic; both were a game of intricate enchantment and deception.'

Vladimir Nabokov, *Speak, Memory:*
An Autobiography Revisited

For the past few days there's been an impostor in my bath-room. Perched at the top of the blind, it looked like a withered autumn leaf, and I kept meaning to get a broom handle to get rid of it. By today, it had slipped down to the windowsill just above the bath. Autumnal reds and golds faded, it was now the colour of crinkled cigar leaves.

I look closer. And then in astonishment.

Not a leaf, but a butterfly, its wings folded, perfectly mimicking a leaf. I'd thought imposture such a uniquely human habit that it was both shocking and thrilling to find it so perfectly fashioned in nature. We think of our skills of imitation – turning paint and canvas into likenesses, sculpting clay and marble into lifelike figures – as talents so rare and prized that the results belong in museums and galleries. And yet here was artistic perfection wasting its days away on my windowsill.

A few minutes on the internet and I've identified it as a 'Comma' butterfly – so called for the little white punctuation mark on its underwings. This unassuming insect is a master of deception and surprise. At every stage of its life, it pretends to be something it's not. Its pale green eggs are such a perfect colour match for the leaves on which they are laid that they disappear from view. The brown caterpillars that hatch develop a distinctive white stripe on their backs, giving them an unmistakable resemblance to bird droppings: a useful trick to discourage predators. With its wings shut, the adult mimics the scalloped and withered surface of a dead leaf so perfectly that it can hide in plain sight – or in my bathroom. But the Comma butterfly has another trick up its sleeve. Should its disguise be rumbled, it opens its wings suddenly, flashing upper sides of brilliant orange mottled with dark brown and sunlight-yellow patches, startling its predators and giving it the chance to make its escape.

My only other encounter with nature's impostors was in primary school. In a lesson I'm sure was intended to teach us the details of the butterfly lifecycle, what caught my attention was that the butterfly on display, a glorious orange-and-black creature called a Monarch, had an imitator named – the verbal pun following the visual – a Viceroy (see Plates 1 and 2).

I found them impossible to tell apart, and it turns out I was not the only one. Every year, millions of these 'wingéd tigers', as they were called by Mexican poet Homero Aridjis, fly south from the USA and Canada, a tidal wave of orange and black, to overwinter in warmer climes. In 2004, the Mexican government

Fig. 4.1. The Mexican government finally gets its butterflies right. A 2012 50-peso note.

decided to feature the Monarch butterfly on its 50-peso note. Or what they thought was the Monarch. Eight years later, they reissued the note, this time with the correct butterfly.

What, if anything, do these enchanting imitation games tell us? Might they tell us anything about the forces that shape inauthenticity? In particular, what insights into our world might these insect impersonations give us? Might we even find clues to our own impostor impulses?

It was Henry Walter Bates who first uncovered and explained this curious and unconscious imposture in nature. A keen amateur naturalist with a passion for insects, Bates was rescued from an unpromising career as a clerk in a brewery by the unsung hero of evolution, Alfred Russel Wallace, who suggested they embark together on a voyage of discovery. In 1848 they sailed to the Amazon rainforest, planning to study the birds and insects, and to support themselves by sending specimens back to London.

Ill-health forced Wallace to return to England before long, but Bates was to remain in the Amazon for eleven years, collecting over 14,000 specimens and keeping detailed diaries (see Plate 3). A particular delight were the fat-billed toucans. Bates recounts their nesting and feeding habits, speculates on the reasons for their enormous bills, informs readers how and when to eat them ('at their best stewed or roasted ... and in months of June and July, the birds being then very fat, and the meat exceedingly sweet and tender'), later describing how he kept one as 'one of the most amusing pets imaginable'. There were privations too: giant leaf-cutter ants pilfered his provisions; when blows from wooden clogs failed to disperse them, he resorted to blowing up their trails with gunpowder. At one stage, his clothes in rags, robbed of his money, and about to give up on his Amazon adventure, only a providential bout of yellow fever kept Bates from sailing for home.

The Amazon was an insect lover's paradise. Bates became fascinated by a particular family of butterflies, the Heliconidae, whose best-known members are known colloquially as 'Passion Vines'. These long-winged dazzlers were gorgeous creatures, their black wings splashed with patterns of red, yellow, and white. Bates was struck by how they behaved as a kind of privileged elite with no apparent fear of predators. 'The fine showy Heliconii often assemble in small parties, by twos and threes, apparently to sport together or perform a kind of dance', he wrote, remarking on their exuberant colours, their slow and carefree flight, and their fondness for roosting in open view on the ends of branches rather than hiding among the leaves. However languorous their flight, Bates noted that he 'never saw the flocks of slow-flying Heliconidae in the woods persecuted by birds or Dragon-flies, to which they would have been easy prey; nor, when at rest on leaves, did they appear to be molested by

Lizards or the predacious Flies of the family Asilidae, which were very often seen pouncing on Butterflies of other families'. Predatory birds left heaps of half-eaten butterfly wings on the forest floor; but even on the rare occasions that remains of Heliconidae were found at all, their wings had been left mysteriously untouched. Knowing that other insects, including beetles, built up their defences using 'fetid liquids or gases', Bates concluded that the Heliconidae must in some way be similarly unpalatable to their enemies.

Bates had discovered what the butterflies' predators already knew. These brightly coloured insects can afford to be nonchalant; their dazzling colours serve as a warning that they are unpleasant to eat. The Passion Vine butterfly is so called because its caterpillars feed exclusively on a single variety of the passion-flower plant. Although the flowers contain poisonous cyanide-generating compounds, the caterpillars absorb these with no harm to themselves and then reuse the toxins for their own defence as adults. They metamorphose into butterflies who can afford to be 'gay, eye-catching and self-advertising', because their warning signals are known not to be a bluff.* A young and inexperienced bird might choose to ignore the signals, and try to snack on one. It would spit the butterfly out, and never do so again.

---

* The passionflower is itself evolving furiously in order to avoid being eaten by the butterflies. As well as the poisons which the plant uses to defend itself against its predators, it too uses mimicry. The plants have recently (in evolutionary terms) developed little pale green circular markings on their leaves, which, from a distance, simulate a butterfly's eggs already laid on them. A Passion Vine butterfly circling above will lay her eggs elsewhere, rather than risk her offspring having to compete with another brood.

A Most Remarkable Case of Mimicry

Bates noticed something else, however. Many times when he looked in his net after capturing what he took to be one of the Heliconidae,* he found to his amazement that it was a member of a quite different family that was *mimicking* one or other of the Heliconidae. Every time it happened, he said, 'I could scarcely restrain an exclamation of surprise.' The impostors were Leptalides,† members of a quite separate species of predominantly *white*-winged butterflies – indeed, Leptalides are Amazonian cousins of our own Cabbage Whites. But here they were flaunting the dazzling colours of the Heliconidae with – remarkably – splashes of red, yellow, white, and black in exactly the right places, the impersonation perfectly rendered. A resemblance of appearance, shape, and colour between members of widely distinct families that was, Bates remarked, as unlikely as a pigeon taking on the appearance and plumage of a hawk.

That one butterfly could impersonate another so exactly and precisely perplexed and delighted Bates. He called the phenomenon 'mimicry', from the Greek word *mimesis* – imitation. Imitation and imposture were familiar human traits, but to find them in nature was as exhilarating as it was unexpected.

---

* Specifically, an Ithomia. Confusingly, Ithomiae and Heliconii are no longer considered to be genera of a family called Heliconidae – indeed, there no longer is a family called Heliconidae. Ithomiae are now a genus of the Danainae sub-family of Nymphalidae, and Heliconii are a genus of the Heliconiinae sub-family of Nymphalidae. The fact that Ithomiae and Heliconii closely resemble each other is now understood to be the result not of close kinship, but of Müllerian mimicry, which we will come to shortly.

† Leptalides are now known as Pieridae: Dismorphiinae after another classificatory dust-up.

It was not just the butterflies. The Amazon jungle was awash with imitators. Bates found flies that mimicked bees and beetles, and moths that imitated wasps.* There was a buff-tip moth that he described, with wonderful specificity, as looking like a broken piece of a lichen-covered branch; other moths were said, with rather less wonderful specificity, to look just like birds' excrement on leaves.† Cassidae (tortoise and leaf-mining beetles) resembled 'glittering drops of dew on the tips of leaves owing to their burnished pearly gold colour'. Some crickets even mimicked their own predators. Mimicry seemed to be the rule rather than the exception. One of the most astonishing impostors was the viper-mimicking caterpillar (see Plate 4). We don't know for sure which species Bates amused himself with, but you can sense the schoolboyish glee (he was only 23 years old when he set off for the Amazon) with which he used it to prank the locals.

The most extraordinary instance of imitation I ever met with was that of a very large Caterpillar, which stretched itself from amidst the foliage of a tree which I was one day examining, and startled me by its resemblance to a small Snake. The first three segments behind the head were dilatable at the will of the insect, and had on each side a large black pupillated spot, which resembled the eye of the reptile: it was a poisonous or

---

* Though there is no need to go all the way to the Amazon to see this type of mimicry. Over a hundred species of hoverfly disguise themselves with wasp-and-bee-like yellow-and-black stripes in order to trick predators into thinking they are more dangerous than they really are. How to tell them apart: bees and wasps have two pairs of wings, hoverflies only one pair. Oh, and they hover.

† There are at least fifty species of British moths and butterflies that resemble inanimate objects at some point in their lifecycle.

viperine species mimicked ... this was proved by the imitation of keeled scales on the crown, which was produced by the recumbent feet, as the Caterpillar threw itself backwards ... I carried off the Caterpillar, and alarmed everyone in the village where I was then living, to whom I showed it. It unfortunately died before reaching the adult state.

Nature is forever trying on new clothes in the hope of attracting a mate or fooling a predator. It doesn't have to be a perfect disguise: any characteristic that increases an individual's attractiveness, or reduces its chances of being eaten, however slightly, is a useful survival device. If a Cabbage White butterfly happens to have a patch of colour on its wings that makes it look a bit more like a poisonous Passion Vine than other Cabbage Whites, then it is less likely to be eaten, and more likely to survive and have offspring who will in turn inherit the useful splodge of colour.* Any further descendants with variations in colour or pattern that make them look even more like poisonous butterflies will, in turn, survive longer and breed more than their less successful siblings. Within a matter of generations, you will have a Cabbage White butterfly that looks very like a Passion Vine. Bates's beautiful butterflies were not just unconscious impostors, they were survival machines.

Bates could now account for his observations: over succeeding generations numerous small, incremental, and successful variations had accumulated to create the startlingly perfect

---

* Remember: you don't have to be a perfect impostor to succeed, you just need to be more convincing or better adapted than others around you. In the same way, the cheetah, which can accelerate from nought to sixty miles per hour in three seconds, poses a lethal danger to the antelope. But the antelope doesn't need to be faster than the cheetah to survive; it only needs to be faster than other antelopes.

96

mimicry he had observed. It had long been known that you could selectively breed animals or flowers for certain characteristics, or to look a certain way.* The insights that were to astound the world, changing how we think for ever, were that nature itself could play the role of selecting agent, and that life is not directed but supremely opportunistic. No butterfly chooses or intends to become a mimic, but if chance hands them a useful way to survive in an unfriendly world, natural selection will ensure that they do so.

A Beautiful Proof

After eleven long, hard years in the jungle, Bates returned to England shortly after the century's most seismic scientific event. The year 1859 was when Charles Darwin's sensational *On the Origin of Species by Means of Natural Selection* was published. Darwin's theory of natural selection explained nature's astonishing variety as the product of an inevitable mechanism rather than as the handiwork of God. It suggested that designs as extraordinary as the elephant's trunk or the giraffe's neck were the product of nature working over time rather than the creation of a divine being on the sixth day.†

Darwin had been wrestling privately for twenty years with his big idea, one he knew would be regarded by many as dangerous and radical, and supporting evidence from the tropics was very welcome indeed. Bates wrote excitedly to the famous naturalist of his findings among the Amazonian butterflies. 'I think',

---

* Darwin used the example of breeding pigeons – a popular mid-nineteenth-century pastime. We might think of dog-breeders at Crufts.

† Or the divine being's twentieth-century incarnation, the Intelligent Designer.

he said, 'I have got a glimpse into the laboratory where Nature manufactures her new species.'

Bates's association with Darwin catapulted him into the scientific firmament. As he said in a lecture to the prestigious Linnaean Society, his butterflies offered 'a most beautiful proof of the truth of the theory of Natural Selection'. The theory explained how unadorned Leptalides had come to imitate patterned and coloured butterflies so perfectly. It explained moths imitating wasps, caterpillars' rear parts resembling vipers, and Comma butterflies mimicking dead leaves in my bathroom. This type of impersonation – where there is a mimic and a model – was named Batesian mimicry in honour of its discoverer. Bates's findings boosted Darwin's ideas and vice versa. Bates needed a theory to explain the predilection for copying that he had observed in Amazonian butterflies; Darwin needed examples to illustrate his new and controversial theory of natural selection. It was a most happy mutualism.

But there was a further puzzle. Bates had noticed that his dazzlers were frequently found in the same areas as other, unrelated species of butterfly – and even some species of moth – all of which appeared to have converged on a similar design. These 'rings', sometimes of six or even more species, all sported similar wing patterns and colours, and were all to some extent unpalatable to predators. This didn't at all fit the Batesian pattern of a noxious model and a harmless mimic.

Some twenty years later, the mystery was solved by Fritz Müller, a Prussian zoologist who had also decamped to South America. The various butterfly species shared a common problem: the need to train their predators to associate their crimson, black, and gold patterns with the unpleasant meal that would follow if they were eaten. Müller theorised that by resembling each other, the butterflies magnified the warning effect and minimised the number of individuals lost to hungry birds – a co-operative and risk-sharing arrangement later dubbed Müllerian mimicry. If they joined forces and sported similar colours, patterns, and behaviours, their predators would have to learn only a single warning pattern; a predator who had a bad experience with one butterfly would avoid all others that looked the same. There was strength in numbers. The mimicry rings were a self-preservation society formed by species who shared a common interest in not being eaten.*

Sending the Right Signals

Insect mimicry by bluff (Batesian) and by pooling of warning colours (Müllerian) both have counterparts in our world. As Edward Poulton, one of the pioneers of evolutionary biology and author of *The Colours of Animals* (1890), noted: 'A Batesian mimic may be compared to an unscrupulous tradesman who copies the advertisement of a successful firm; Müllerian mimicry to a combination between firms to adopt a common advertisement and save expense.' ('Advertisement' is being used here in its original sense of a notification to the public.) We might characterise Batesian mimics as knock-off merchants and Müllerian mimics as business cartels. In both the natural and man-made worlds there are a vast number of advertisements. We are all constantly transmitting, endlessly signalling, sending messages in sound, smell, and pattern that carry detailed information intended for interception.

---

* You'll want to know that it has recently been discovered that the Monarch and Viceroy butterflies we met earlier, long thought to be an example of Batesian mimicry, are in fact both poisonous Müllerian mimics.

In nature, there are two types of 'advertisement', the negative and the positive. A 'negative' advertisement is one that signals danger or issues a warning. Passion Vine butterflies, venomous snakes, wasps and their imitators, all make use of bright colours and striking designs to ward off attacks. We use the same techniques (see Plate 5). Often we even use the same colours and patterns, ones that stand out equally well against the green of the rainforest canopy and the grey of an urban landscape.

'Advertisement' can also be positive, which is the sense in which we most commonly use it today. Whereas the animal imitators we've met so far aim to deter, floral mimicry almost always aims to attract and invite. Unlike animals, plants spend their lives rooted to one spot. Needing to entice insects, birds, and other pollinators, they have developed some of the finest advertising in the natural world: flowers. More than 90 per cent of the largest group of green plants produce flowers, many with vivid colours, bespoke shapes, and alluring scents that signal the rewards available to any pollinator who cares to drop by. Floral signals are mainly positive ('come hither'), truthful (there *is* a nectar reward at the end of it), and conspicuous (for obvious reasons). Like Müllerian mimicry rings, they often converge around a common set of signals that are well understood by potential pollinators. Blue and purple flowers tend to attract bees, white and yellow blossoms are preferred by ants and wasps. Red blossoms are the hallmark of a bird-pollinated flower, because insects, whose vision is at the ultraviolet end of the spectrum, cannot see red.

We are equally familiar with the notion of attracting consumers by using a common set of signals. Tom Sherratt, a professor of evolutionary ecology whose specialties include mimicry and signalling, notes that in his native Britain the packaging designs of potato crisps have converged to such an extent that the leading supermarkets (Sainsbury's, Tesco, Asda, Waitrose) all sell their own-brand 'Ready Salted', 'Salt & Vinegar', and 'Cheese & Onion' crisps in similarly coloured (red, blue, or green) packets.* By resembling each other, the crisp packets magnify their signalling effect. The colourways signal not just the crisps, but the *correct flavour* of crisps, and minimise the number of individual customers lost. As Sherratt says, 'The chances of these competing supermarkets independently arriving at the same colour classification for these products is extremely small, and it is much more likely that different varieties have been given common appearances so as to visually inform busy shoppers of their contents.'

As for busy bees, so for busy shoppers? It's interesting that a bona fide biologist is entertaining these parallels, and there are similarities. But there is of course a critical difference between insects and humans: intention. Müllerian convergence is the outcome of unconscious evolutionary adaptation; crisp-packet convergence is the result of deliberate marketing decisions. It was a huge leap for Bates and Darwin to explain the origin of animal species without reference to a Creator; even a century and a half later, I'm not sure that I'm ready to dispense wholesale with human spirit and agency, or to characterise us as robot products of natural selection.

I had learned a lot from the encounter with the impostor in my bathroom. I'd learned that my withered leaf was no leaf. That mimicry occurs when it helps an individual to survive. That creatures seek defence in disguise and share common

---

* There is a similar convergence for milk packaging. Almost everywhere you will find that full-fat bottletops are blue, semi-skimmed are green, and skimmed are red.

advertisements and warning signals. I'd learned that those who fail to fake it, seldom make it. I'd found, to my surprise, that insects, in their systems and structures, can be impostors just like us. Or at least they would be, if they were acting intentionally, rather than being unconsciously moulded and coloured by the silent hand of evolution. And my investigation of analogies between impostors and insects had illuminated something that had long puzzled me. I was perplexed by one of the photos of my favourite impostor, Stanley Weyman, at the White House in 1921. It was obvious why Princess Fatima and her three sons were in the picture with Stanley. But who on earth was the moustachioed and morning-suited Fifth Man?

I look again at the picture. On the left is Stanley, in his peaked naval-style cap; I marvel that such a makeshift disguise even got him through the door. On the right, the other side of the exotic princess who so wanted to meet President Harding, is the gent in the silk hat and overconfident grin: Prince Zerdecheno.

Zerdecheno was described in some of the newspapers of the day as the heir apparent to the throne of Turkestan.* He claimed that he had been raised in a private palace of white marble that boasted 350 rooms and a courtyard of 20 acres; that his stables housed 600 camels and 600 horses; that his servants numbered 400. New York society was entranced by this exotic figure, listening avidly to his accounts of his princely lifestyle. He never dressed in any cloth but white satin: 'My favourite robe, I remember, was made of twenty yards. Thirty men were killed in a battle as they brought it in a caravan over the hills from Paris … In my hat was a ring of diamonds supporting six ostrich plumes. And the hilt of my sword was one huge emerald.' Alas,

---

* Or sometimes as the 'Emir of Kurdistan'. Or, from time to time, as the 'Crown Prince of Egypt'.

someone did their homework. Turkestan had no regional government, no king, and certainly no Crown Prince. Zerdecheno was simply another impostor who had ingratiated himself with Princess Fatima and come to hover in her orbit. Notwithstanding his voluminous robes of white satin, he had at some point stolen an overcoat, for which he was in due course deported. Eventually the French took him in; five years later we come across him as 'Prince Zerdecheno, who these days presses pants in a Paris Hotel', still clinging doggedly to his claims of royalty. Thereafter, he disappears from view.

Not much is known about Princess Fatima either. It was claimed that she had been receiving funds from the British government for herself and her sons to live on. Despite that, though, she was also trying to sell a diamond, the Darya-i-Noor, which she claimed was worth half a million dollars (around six million dollars in today's money). There is indeed a splendid diamond of that name, but it is part of the Iranian crown jewels, and has been safely in their collection since 1739. Princess Fatima's diamond was finally sold for just four thousand dollars, so perhaps there is a sense that, like Stanley Weyman, neither she nor her diamond were quite all they claimed to be. As for Fatima herself, she was last heard of being persuaded to board the steamship *Lahore*, sailing from New York for India on 16 March 1922. But when the ship left, neither the princess nor her sons were on board. At that point, Princess Fatima disappears from view too.

I found myself not only entranced by imposture and mimicry, but astonished that there was so much of it about. Stanley's story has three impostors where I had thought there was only one. It contains a cartel, a company – whatever the collective noun for impostors is – of charlatans. The faded photograph of our three chancers, Stanley, Fatima, and Zerdecheno, shows not only that impostors are social animals, but that the collective – the sum of the parts – achieves a greater whole. Because Fatima played the princess, Stanley got to the White House; because Stanley played his parts – naval liaison officer, personal inter-preter – Fatima and even Zerdecheno got there too. The mimicry ring, self-preservation society, impostor cartel – call it what you will – is a powerfully protective arrangement. Three flashy social butterflies wearing the same colours, sending the same signals, and sharing the same risk.

Nature got to imposture and mimicry a long time before us. We are told that we share a common ancestor with every animal and plant, so perhaps there is a thread that ties butterflies to bogus princesses, a sense in which we too are linked to insects. But imposture, or mimicry, is just one tool in the deceiver's tool-box, and the question becomes: What other deceptions might nature have up her sleeve? How many other forms of fakery and anti-social behaviour has she contrived to shape? Are there natural-born con artists? Counterfeiters? Criminals? Racketeers?

We've seen nature on the defensive. What does she look like on the offensive?

5

FREE RIDERS

The Great Egg Race

'Thou mordrer of the heysugge on the braunche
That broghte thee forth, thou rewthelees glotoun!'
('You murderer of the hedge-sparrow on the branch
The one who brought you up, you ruthless glutton!')

Geoffrey Chaucer describes the cuckoo
in *The Parliament of Fowls*

'There's no shame in being a parasite. We join a
venerable guild that has been on this planet since
its infancy and has become the most successful
form of life on the planet.'

Carl Zimmer, *Parasite Rex*

In 2004 a young zoologist, Claire Spottiswoode,* travelled to Choma in Zambia to investigate a curious case of counterfeiting.

On reading her subsequent papers, I found them full of characters you might expect to find in a classic detective novel – if, that is, you are, like me, a devotee of lowbrow crime fiction –

---

* Now a professor at the University of Cape Town and a lecturer at the University of Cambridge.

rather than in the pages of *American Naturalist* or *Proceedings of the Royal Society*. Set under the beating African sun, Claire's stories featured a couple of determined sleuths, a feckless and elusive villain responsible for a series of mysterious forgeries, and a plucky heroine who finds a way to outwit the forgers. They were all straight out of central casting. They even included that staple of the mid-twentieth-century Agatha Christie mystery, the irascible major. It can be hard to tell stories about animals without slipping into stereotypes, casting some of them as doughty heroes and others as lowlifes and reprobates. But zoologists, thankfully, are a calmer breed, and eschew winsome animal tales – except when explaining things to the rest of us.

What had brought Claire to Choma was a pocket-sized African warbler, the tawny-flanked prinia. The prinia, a charming and hard-working bird, weaves her nest high in the long grass to keep her eggs safe from passing predators, and uses her beak as a needle to painstakingly stitch the nest to the leaves of neighbouring shrubs.

But the tiny African bird has one big problem: the cuckoo finch. Like their cuckoo namesakes, cuckoo finches are shockingly neglectful parents.* The male is a puffed-up, yellow-breasted bird, but it is the female, drabber and dun-coloured, who is the real villain of the piece. Rather than trouble to build her own nest, she lays her eggs in those of other birds, including the prinia, hoping to dupe the unwitting host into incubating, hatching, and feeding her chicks. Having

---

* Namesake, but no relation. Cuckoo finches – from the family Viduidae – are not technically cuckoos – Cuculidae – being more closely related to whydahs and indigobirds, but the cuckoo finch is every bit as deadbeat a parent as its namesake, since both birds share what Darwin called a 'strange and odious instinct' to leave their offspring in other birds' nests rather than do their own parenting.

palmed off their parenting duties onto the hapless prinia, the cuckoo finches head off to mate again and to lay yet more eggs in the nests of their unwilling hosts.*

The Life and Hard Times of a Tawny Prinia Chick

If the prinia chicks' mother has failed to identify and summarily eject any impostor cuckoo finch eggs from the nest, a bleak future awaits her offspring. Like most parasitic nestlings, cuckoo finch chicks are rapid developers, and will hatch a day or two before the prinia chicks. With their bigger gape (mouth), the cuckoo finch chicks will corner more than their share of the food brought back by foraging parents. Infuriatingly for the prinia chicks, their mother won't notice that while her own flesh and blood have pinkish mouths, the alien chicks have great big yellow maws with two black spots on the underside, and she will carry on feeding the impostors regardless. All the prinia chicks can do is beg for food, and watch helplessly as the brutish cuckoo finch chicks outgrow and outcompete them. Most of the prinia chicks will shrivel and die from starvation. By the time they leave the nest, the changeling chicks are twice the weight of the prinia mother bird. I can imagine her advice to those few fledgelings who manage to make it out of the nest.

---

* Animals who palm off parenting onto others are known as brood or nest parasites. Those who have even forgotten how to nest, incubate, and hatch their own eggs – like the cuckoo finch – are known as 'obligate' brood parasites.

Dearest Chicks,

I know it's been tough in the nest, but well done for surviving so far. Sorry to have to tell you this, but once you've left home and set up on your own, your horrid foster siblings will no doubt return and lay their foul alien eggs in your nest too. I'm sorry, but that's just life. Hope you are better at spotting the fake eggs than your parents were.

Love, Mother

Egg-spotting

About one time in three, the prinia mother bird fails to spot the impostor eggs.* Among Claire Spottiswoode's films is one that captures the moment of maternal decision. The little prinia is cocking her head from side to side like an art expert in front of a picture of dubious provenance. Once she has decided that she has an interloper on her hands, she spears the counterfeit egg with her beak and heaves it over the side of the nest. If she picks the wrong egg, she will tip her own chick onto the ground, where it will most likely be eaten by a passing snake. If she fails to get rid of the cuckoo finch eggs, the prinia will find herself raising giant interloper chicks instead of her own. What's the

---

* Possibly the most poignant part of the tawny prinia's story, to me at least, is that its pattern recognition skills are simultaneously expert and surprisingly limited. Great discernment in one part of life can be matched by complete gullibility elsewhere. As a result, the prinia mother bird makes what seem to us absurd mistakes. She is an excellent fake-spotter when it comes to eggs, but almost completely blind to the impostor chicks emerging from them, still feeding them when they are almost twice her size. Birds respond to signals and patterns with curious specificity. Researchers have put cardboard cut-outs of parent birds in nests, and the chicks were unable to tell them from the real thing.

poor bird to do? She can't, of course, write a letter to future generations. Nor does she know that natural selection will favour two groups of her descendants: those who are better fake-spotters, and those who produce eggs more easily identifiable as their own.

Claire Spottiswoode and her colleague Mike Stevens, an expert in bird vision, began to study nests full of prinia eggs, measuring and analysing the eggs' colours and markings as they would appear to birds.* Prinias produce eggs that feature colours and markings which vary over time – like the designs that make banknotes harder to counterfeit.

What fascinated Claire and her colleagues was that the eggs produced by these little birds were probably the most diverse of any bird species. Not just the range of ever-evolving patterns, but the astonishing assortment of colours. Most birds' eggs come in the colours you might expect to see on your breakfast table: shades of white, or buff, or brown.† But prinia eggs come in a range of tints, from exquisite sugar pink to delicate eau-de-nil blue, creamy ivory, and, most recently, palest olive green. Combined with the squiggles and scribbles, filigree patterns, mottled splodges, and Pollock-y drips and splashes, this yields an astonishing range of different designs. Whereas most birds of a species lay eggs of similar design, every prinia's eggs are slightly different to every other prinia's. Each bird's egg design is as unique as a human signature, a

---

* A bird's eye view is wider and, in many ways, much better than ours. A human eye has just three light-sensitive cones, so we can only register red, green, and blue light, but birds have a fourth cone that can detect ultra-violet rays, making their blue eggs even more dazzling to them than they are to us.

† Or the pale blue eggs you find on the menu at hipster foodie joints and in the more expensive aisles of the supermarket.

'signed special edition' with its own combination of tints and markings.

Claire – a passionate birdwatcher since her childhood in South Africa – was intrigued. In terms of energy and nutrients expended, it costs a mother bird dearly to produce this extraordinary and varied range of eggs, so it was amazing to see the tiny prinia produce such a costly pattern book of different designs in different colourways.

Was the prinia mother bird unconsciously crafting the changing designs in order to detect the eggs that interlopers slipped into her nest? Assembling a constantly evolving armoury of designer-edition eggs to fight back against the counterfeiters? Claire and Mike were sure that they were. But how to prove it? They could make inferences about the evidence they had gathered, hypothesise about the future, and watch how the colour and pattern battle between prinia and cuckoo finch panned out – but it would be a long haul.

Or they could look into the past.

The Irascible Major

When she first arrived in Zambia, Claire had paid a visit to an eccentric former major in the King's African Rifles turned tobacco farmer. According to his friends, John Colebrook-Robjent could be bombastic and arrogant, but he was also a talented amateur ornithologist, who amassed a vast and varied collection of birds' eggs (and came within a whisker of being imprisoned for his egg-snatching habits). A photograph taken towards the end of his life shows a wild-eyed and stick-thin gent in a loud check jacket, pink shirt, and spotted red pocket-handkerchief, holding a stuffed tinkerbird. Perhaps to emphasise his lifelong devotion to ornithology, he wears a yellow tie patterned with pheasants.

For thirty years, Colebrook-Robjent had paid his farm-hands and local boys to hunt down nests, remove their contents, and bring them back to his farm in their entirety, resulting in a collection of over 14,000 nestfuls. He kept immaculate records of their finds. A typical diary entry from the 1980s details that on 3 February a small boy named Fred collected a nest with a clutch of four eggs with a blue ground (background colour). Three days later, another boy, Moses, collected a clutch of three eggs with a white ground, and Levi a further three with a brownish-olive ground. The following day, one of his young labourers named Dunne picked up a clutch of three pale salmon-coloured eggs ... and so on. It was thirty years of immaculate ornithological detail, a zoologist's treasure trove.

Claire's first visit had not gone well. The major had been irritable, suspecting her of being there to spy on him and report his illegal egg collection. Attitudes to egg collecting had shifted, and by the mid-twentieth century what had been an acceptable hobby for Victorian naturalists had become a criminal offence. Major Colebrook-Robjent had been informed on once before, summoned to appear in the Choma Magistrates Court and – a humiliating moment for him – charged with theft. Eventually he was cleared and allowed to leave; he was fond of recounting how the judge had not only declared him innocent of all charges but also pronounced him a 'Professor of Ornithology' whose work was of great benefit to Zambia. Whatever Claire said to pacify him plainly worked. She and Mike were given permission to draw on the extraordinary and meticulously documented Colebrook-Robjent collection of over 350 different species of African birds' eggs.

It was astonishing.* To Claire's delight, Major Colebrook-Robjent had not only collected and documented prinia eggs, demonstrating how they changed colour and design over time; he had also correctly identified the slightly larger impostor cuckoo finch eggs every time they were found in a prinia nest. Claire and Mike were able to trace the progress of battles of colour and pattern that had been hard fought over decades. Each time the prinia had come up with a design variation in order to distinguish its eggs from the interloper's, so too had the cuckoo finch (see Plate 6). If a prinia laid eggs of pale salmon with brownish blotches, so did a cuckoo finch a little later. Creamy ivory eggs with purplish tracery? If the prinias laid them, then the cuckoo finches followed suit. If the prinias moved the goalposts and produced pale blue eggs with squiggle patterns and a UV kick to them, the cuckoo finches moved into squiggle-marked blue-to-UV eggs too. Most tellingly, the prinias had recently experimented with a new pale olive colourway, which the cuckoo finches had not yet managed to counterfeit. This was the proof that Claire and Mike were looking for. The variety and beauty of the prinias' eggs were the by-product of a deadly serious race for survival.

The great egg race was an arms race.

The Unconscious Counterfeiters

The sleuths' work had paid off. The Curious Case of the Counterfeit Eggs was another instance of natural selection. Cuckoo finches lay as many eggs in their hosts' nests as they

---

* The Colebrook-Robjent collection is now housed in the Natural History Museum at Tring.

can,* in the hope that some will match the prinias' signature designs. Eggs that are detected suffer the usual fate of substand-ard counterfeits: they are tipped onto the ground. But an egg that manages to fool the prinia will grow into a cuckoo finch, whose eggs will in turn incorporate the successful counterfeit design. As the prinias become increasingly expert designers, the cuckoo finches evolve into ever more ingenious counterfeiters. As the prinias get better at recognising and rejecting the cuckoo finches' eggs, the cuckoo finches get better at mimicking the prinias' new designs. Neither ever wins, but each side keeps the other in check. It is a race that exemplifies the Red Queen hypothesis.†

Nature does not discriminate; she helps the prinia improve its designs, but equally she assists the cuckoo finch in its counter-feiting. The invisible hand has produced an unconscious forger ceaselessly in lockstep with its unwitting and unfortunate victim. Nature has done more than produce enchantingly deceptive butterflies and other gentler forms of inauthenticity; she has also generated what, in a human context, we would call crime – egg counterfeits on a par with any art forger's, con tricks with sleights of hand as slick as any grifter's.

As I read Claire's papers, I began to fancy that, as well as his swagger and his penchant for yellow-waistcoated fancy dress-ing, the cuckoo finch shared the 'something for nothing' lifestyle of 'Yellow Kid' Weil. I saw parallels between the bully bird who

---

* The more parasite eggs laid in a nest, the harder it is for the host to distin-guish the fakes from their own.

† The Red Queen hypothesis proposes that species continually need to change in order to keep up with the competition. It is named after the Red Queen in Lewis Carroll's *Through the Looking Glass*, who points out to Alice that in her kingdom, 'It takes all the running you can do, to stay in the same place.'

dupes others into raising its young and the conman who dupes marks into giving him their money. Both are freeloaders. Cuckoo finch and conman both gain at the expense of others. But we should not confuse consequences with causes. In one case, the deception is automatic, unconscious, encoded; in the other, it is deliberate, conscious, calculated. The conman's mark is all too frequently complicit; the cuckoo finch's victim is unwitting. One difference stands out. We have no doubt that conmen are morally wrong; but birds are clearly morally irreproachable. Surely we can't blame a *bird*?

Cuckoo Noir

But blame them we do, and we always have. For 2,000 years, cuckoos have been a byword for plumed and feathered villainy. Pliny the Elder called them 'naturally craving and greedy' in his *Natural History*. Geoffrey Chaucer referred to them as 'furious gluttons', castigating them for their ruthless attitude towards the birds that raised them. The habits of cuckoos and their fellow brood parasites belong less in genteel detective fiction than between the pages of a pulp crime novel. Their world is one of deadly sibling rivalry, relentless fakery, delinquency, murder; their lives are a study in violence, blackmail, and sudden death.*

In *Cuckoo: Cheating by Nature* (2015), Nick Davies, professor of behavioural ecology at Cambridge University, relates his love affair with the bird that he has studied all his life. He details the chilling evolutionary tricks that cuckoos and other parasitic

---

* Coincidentally the tag line of pulp crime novel *Dig Me a Grave* (1952) by John Spain.

birds use to tighten their stranglehold on their hosts. In this world of Cuckoo Noir, the villains are swift – some cuckoos can lay their own egg and carry off (and swallow) the host's egg in a single swoop lasting less than ten seconds; disturbingly young – some cuckoo species have evolved juvenile delinquent chicks with concave chests that help them to scoop up their step-siblings and shovel them over the side of the nest; gifted and sinister mimics – some cuckoos can imitate the call of host birds, distracting them so that an impostor egg can be slipped into the nest. It doesn't stop there. Other cuckoos have evolved tail stripes reminiscent of their hosts' predators, flaunting the bars of a sparrowhawk or kestrel to forestall attack by the host bird while they slip a changeling egg or two into her nest.

All this bad behaviour came as something of a surprise to me. As a child, I first became aware of cuckoos as the much-anticipated harbingers of spring. Every year, the vernal season was heralded by letters to *The Times* from readers vying to have heard the first cuckoo of the year.* I had assumed this was a quaint custom about a uniquely British bird, but cuckoos are spread across two-fifths of the globe, an indication, perhaps, of the success and adaptability of their parasitic lifestyle. Charting the birds' annual return from their warm winter playgrounds to their chosen breeding grounds, Nick Davies envisages waves of cuckoos passing north, right across the temperate regions of the Old World.

> In many languages, it's the call that gives the bird its name, so the waves are of cuckoos announcing their own arrival. Across Europe, the first calling waves reach the Mediterranean in

---

* One correspondent had to write a second time to admit, embarrassedly, that what he had heard was in fact a workman *imitating* the call of the cuckoo.

March: 'cuco' in Spain and Portugal, 'cuculo' in Italy, 'koúkos' in Greece. They continue, up through central Europe: 'coucou' in France, 'kuckuck' in Germany, 'koekoek' in the Netherlands, 'kukulka' in Poland, 'kakukk' in Hungary. And they reach northern Europe from mid-April to May: 'cuckoo' in the UK, 'käki' in Finland. The waves pass north through Asia, too: 'guguk' in Turkey, 'gugoo' in Azerbaijan, 'kuku' in Kashmir, 'pug-pug' in Nepal, 'akku' in Bhutan.

Are there eager birdwatchers across the world, I wonder, blogging and bragging that they have heard the first cuckoo? Celebrating the arrival of spring, when what they should be doing is warning the reed warblers and the dunnocks and the meadow pipits that a plague of parental-care parasites is about to descend from the skies?

I'd promised myself that I would try not to use emotive language in this chapter. I can see that from the human point of view it's easy to get worked up about a bird that abandons its young, indulges in egg rustling, infanticide, and the rest (there I go again), but from a bird's point of view it is simply a good survival strategy to be a brood parasite, and a good survival strategy is what nature selects for. Around 1 per cent of the approximately 10,000 species of birds share some or all of the cuckoo's habits of shirking, home-wrecking, and imposture. Had you not seen how hard the unwilling foster parents fight back, you might wonder why more birds don't take up this attractive (in evolutionary terms) lifestyle. Instead, in this inter-species arms race, a delicate equilibrium – a nature-enabled system of checks and balances – holds sway.

'Cuckoo' has become adjectival shorthand for a freeloading, nest-parasitising lifestyle, with cuckoos and cuckoo finches by no means the only 'brood' or 'nest' parasites in the animal world. There are fish brood parasites (cuckoo catfish) and insect brood parasites (so-called cuckoo bumblebees and cuckoo wasps) who share the birds' freeloading lifestyle.* Some of their fellow parasites put the cuckoo's gangsterism in the shade. The cowbird of North America, which shares the cuckoo's laissez-faire attitude to parenting, has evolved a protection racket that an organised crime syndicate might envy. Memorably described by Edward Howe Forbush, author of *Birds of Massachusetts and Other New England States* (1925), as 'free lovers', with love lives that are 'neither polygamous nor polyandrous – just promiscuous', cowbirds lay an egg a day and distribute them between up to 200 different hosts.† Should a host bird dare to throw an interloper egg out of her nest, a gang of cowbirds will swoop down, tear her nest to pieces and peck open her eggs: the avian equivalent of sending the heavies round. Host birds (such a misleading term, I feel; it should really be 'victims') have now learned that it is better to give in to the *Goodfellas*-style threat of nest destruction and pay 'protection money' by raising the cowbird chicks as their own. So successful is this Mafia strategy that cowbirds do not need to disguise their eggs. Why bother with mimicry when scare tactics will do the job for you?

---

* The cuckoo catfish targets the thick-lipped chichlid fish, laying her eggs in the chichlid's mouth. Cuckoo wasps are strictly speaking kleptoparasites, meaning that they steal their hosts' stored food supplies rather than waiting to be fed by them.

† Forbush continued: 'They have no demesne and no domicile; they are entirely unattached. Their courting is brief and to the point. In this pleasant pastime the male usually takes the lead.'

The Free Rider Life

What all these avian existences share is an element of 'something for nothing', the ability to reap benefits without incurring costs. As Carl Zimmer, author of *Parasite Rex* (2000), puts it, parasites 'reroute the physiology of life to suit their own ends'. It's an extremely successful, and therefore extremely popular, lifestyle. John N Thompson, a professor of ecology and evolutionary biology, says that parasites exhibit 'the most common lifestyle on earth', which one way or another affects 'nearly all other living species'. Zimmer says simply that 'the majority of animals are parasites'. Once you look beyond the cuckoo finches and the cowbirds, not to mention those bees and wasps with the cuckoo lifestyle, and take account of the flexible, 'eat anything', opportunistic creatures – flies and mites, flatworms and nematode worms – small enough to pass unnoticed as they make their way into or onto their hosts, it turns out that upwards of 40 per cent of all living species are parasites. There may be 4,000 mammal species but there are 6,000 species of tapeworm *alone*.

When a zoologist calls an organism a 'parasite', they're not being pejorative, simply describing a lifestyle. But the rest of us feel rather differently. The original meaning of parasite, a person who eats at the table of another or who obtains hospitality or patronage by obsequiousness and flattery, finds an echo in the expression that economists use for a person who lives at the expense of another, or of society in general: a 'free rider'.* To be a free rider, to benefit from goods or services without paying anything towards them, is a way of life with clear benefits for

---

* Economists are not overly keen on anything 'free'. The economist's world is a transactional one where, famously, there is no such thing as a free lunch.

the individual, but it creates problems for the rest of society. Free riders make us uncomfortable. We instinctively feel that people should aspire to use their talents to the full, play their part, pull their weight; that there is something fundamentally inauthentic about those who hitch a ride on the coat-tails of others. *

It's because we're uncomfortable with human free riders that we have such an ambivalent attitude towards animal parasites. We know full well that the cuckoo doesn't choose its lifestyle. Yet we are just as likely as Pliny the Elder or Geoffrey Chaucer to pass judgement on it, to castigate what in a human would be revolting fecklessness and immorality. Taking as our starting point that individual aspiration is what makes us fully human, we proceed to condemn non-human creatures for lacking individual aspiration, for being content to batten on others. Matters only get worse as we delve into the deeper realms of parasitism: we are charmed by the beautiful butterflies' mimicry, even though they are freeloading on another insect's design, but we have very much less affection for other parasites – those that live *in* us, for example (tapeworms who take up residence in our guts), or *on* us (ticks that live on the skin and consume the blood of their hosts). As science writer and parasite enthusiast Ed Yong points out, some parasite lifestyles, including 'bloodsucker, disease-carrier, host-castrator and flesh-devourer', belong firmly in the horror genre.†

---

* There's another, perhaps even more fundamental factor that contributes to our dislike of the free-riding Homo sapiens. In the animal world, the parasite benefits at the expense of a host from a different species. In our human world, free riders are exploiting their own species.

† To which I would add head-burster. Check out the 'killer fungus', Ophiocordyceps unilateralis, which, as a *Scientific American* blog tells us, 'uses a particular species of ant to complete its life cycle. To live, it must

Not everyone finds such things distasteful. Parasite revisionists (motto: 'Equal Rights for Parasites') like to point out that many subsequently useful relationships began as freeloading ones, and that parasites are capable of reformation too. Parasitism, the revisionists' argument goes, is a lifestyle on a knife edge, always liable to shade into mutualism (and back again). We should see humans as ecosystems on legs, and recognise that at least half, maybe more, of the cells in the human body began in parasitic relationships which then slipped into something more reciprocal and beneficial.* More generally, efforts to destigmatise parasites that are beneficial to us are growing apace; advocates for the newly fashionable biome are behind much of the drive to rehabilitate many microbes.

But most of us remain prone to anthropomorphise, to project our own values ('beautiful' butterflies, 'antisocial' cuckoos, 'repellent' tapeworms) onto creatures that have evolved, not

zombify an ant. The fungus forces an ant of the species Camponotus leonardi to get a "death grip" on the underside of a leaf – a position prime for the fungus's transmission. The poor infected insect – once adorned with a harmless looking spore – then has its tissue slowly eaten and replaced. All that remains of the ant at this point is the exoskeleton, a husk. A deceased ant if there ever was one, save for the spiralling fruiting bodies of the fungus now protruding from the ant's head and body. These bodies burst forth from the ant, eventually releasing spores ready to begin the cycle anew.'

* For a while a figure was bandied about suggesting that we were ten parts former parasites and one part human-originated cells – a statistic definitely not for the queasy. 'Proportionally,' said one perfectly respectable biologist, 'from your left knee down to your big toe is your own cells and the rest of your body is other stuff, a lot of it parasitic.' More recently, in a calculation described as being done on both the front and back of an envelope, the figure was put at 50:50, making human cells and their parasitic sidekicks equal shareholders in your body.

chosen, their free-riding lifestyle. Anthropomorphism is an almost irresistible instinct: attributing human traits, habits, and emotions to non-humans is what we do automatically. I'm as guilty as anyone. To me the prinia's story was full of characters from an Agatha Christie novel, while the cuckoo was starring in a B-movie film noir. The cowbirds had just stepped out of a Martin Scorsese movie, the parasites out of one by Ridley Scott. To the newspaper journalists who picked up Claire Spottiswoode's research, the African cuckoo finches were feckless parents, welfare 'cheats', ASBO birds. We just can't help projecting our world onto theirs; our default is to see animals as cuter or more colourful, nobler or noisier, dangerous or more disgusting, human beings.*

We're liable to forget that in the animal kingdom, freeloading is a lifestyle, but not a lifestyle *choice*. We characterise cuckoo finches and cowbirds as villains rather than look for the reason why they behave as they do. Evolution is a mechanism, not a narrative. The twist in this particular whodunnit of art forgeries and chick murders is that *nobody* dunnit. It just happened. As storytelling animals ourselves, we are happiest when life is a kind of karmic jackpot: when crime is followed by punishment, sin by retribution, and when everybody gets what's coming to them. But that, as the celebrated geneticist Steve Jones has pointed out, is theology, not biology.

---

* In the early twentieth century there was a row about just this, known as the 'Nature Faker' controversy. President Theodore Roosevelt, who we'll meet properly in Chapter 6, weighed in against the then prevailing literary fashion of giving woodland and riverine critters cute human-like characteristics and storylines. Endearing otters giving swimming lessons to their offspring and woodpeckers creating casts out of mud and grass to mend their broken legs were just two of the more egregious examples. Culturally conservative toads who apparently enjoyed hymns but detested ragtime were another.

The Wider View

To be able to take the long view is a uniquely human gift. With it we can trace evolutionary relationships and make sense of the underlying mechanisms. Unlike the birds involved, we know that the prinia's battle began 20 million years ago, and that cuckoo finches, despite the bad press, are just descendants of a bird who once happened to leave an egg in a stranger's nest, and whose particularly large and rambunctious chicks survived to pass on their genes to others who did the same.

We are also the only creatures able to see things from another creature's perspective, to try to put ourselves in another creature's place. Claire Spottiswoode and Mike Stevens used their understanding of bird vision – took a bird's eye view, if you like – in order to make sense of the prinia-cuckoo finch egg competition. Without an understanding of bird vision, it would have been harder for our detectives to make sense of one of the most beautiful arms races in nature.

But there are limits. We can take a bird's eye view and see what they see, but we can't feel what they feel, or think what they think. If we are honest, we haven't a clue what it's like to actually be a bird, and no bird is likely to be able to tell us anytime soon. We can't get inside a bird's head any more than we can understand what it is like to be any animal, though when I was eight I read *Black Beauty* (tagline: 'Translated from the Original Equine') dearly hoping that we could. In his famous 1974 paper 'What Is It Like to Be a Bat?', philosopher Thomas Nagel pointed out that we can never know what being a bat feels like *to a bat*. All we can tell is what *we* might feel if we were shrunk to size and given a pair of stretched-skin wings and some rudimentary sonar. We can be bat-people, but never bats.

When you want to see things clearly, it pays to use the right language. Instead of projecting our world onto animals, we need to see our place in the natural world for what it is and for who we are. Although our world overlaps with theirs, we should not call the prinia 'plucky' or the cuckoo finch a 'cheat' outside the pages of a book or a TV documentary.* We are a small and quaint but troublesome tribe, subject to the same forces as all other animals, but with some interesting and exceptional skills. 'Cheating' implies two things unknown to any animal other than ourselves: a code of behaviour, and a decision taken deliberately to ignore it. It's a word that belongs in our world, not theirs. However much we enjoy it, we need to switch off our anthropomorphising habits if, having seen what links us to animals, we want to know what separates us from them.

---

* Some TV documentaries take my breath away. 'The female is fluffing up her feathers, hoping her charms will attract a mate.' Is she? Hoping? Really?

6

COMPETITORS

The Hunter's Dilemma

'One of the chief attractions of the life of the wilderness ... is its rugged and stalwart democracy. There every man stands for what he actually is.'
Theodore Roosevelt, *The Wilderness Hunter*

'One does not hunt in order to kill; on the contrary, one kills in order to have hunted ... If one were to present the sportsman with the death of the animal as a gift he would refuse it. What he is after is having to win it, to conquer the surly brute through his own effort and skill.'
José Ortega y Gasset, *Meditations on Hunting*

One cold morning in December 2014, on the last day of the muzzleloader deer season, Ryan Muirhead and a couple of his hunting buddies were driving around the snow covered roads of Kittson County, Minnesota in search of whitetail deer when, about 30 yards from their truck and a short distance from a barbed wire fence, they spotted what looked like a very large brown tussock poking out of the icy ground. As they approached, they saw it was a huge bull elk lying trapped on its back, its massive antlers embedded in the boggy mud under the snow. It was still breathing and panting horribly. 'He was on his back, chest heaving, steam pouring from his nose', Ryan recalls. 'He'd been kicking for quite a while and he was worn out.'

Examination of the tracks revealed that the elk had been one of a herd that had jumped over the barbed wire fence but, having made it over, somehow tripped and landed on its back as the rest of the herd went on. 'He'd stuck himself like a turtle upside down. No way was he moving', said Ryan who, as a deer hunter, did not have the all-important permit 'tag' that would allow him to shoot elk in the highly regulated Minnesota state territory. The group could see that the elk was an exceptionally large specimen, nine foot by ten at least.

Even with the beast's antlers mired deep into the muddy ground, the huge velvet-covered spikey branchings were almost certain to be big enough to be a 'trophy rack'– and I have to tell you, dear reader, that in the competitive world of hunting there is nothing quite like the sight of an enormous pair of antlers to get a hunter's pulse racing. If you google the words 'trophy rack', as I'm afraid I had to do, having only encountered the phrase used satirically before,* you find yourself in the strange and sometimes contradictory world of big game hunting. For today's hunters, the trophy is one of the – if not *the* – most important aspects of the sport. More so, for many, than the hunt itself.

A favourite way to flaunt trophy antlers is the 'field' or 'kill & tell' photograph, of which there are a great many on the internet. They consist of smiling, mostly overweight, mostly white men squatting beside a freshly killed beast. In a typical pose, the hunter sits astride the animal, grasping the antlers in order to

---

* Or perhaps I mean metaphorically? A trophy rack is what your trophy girlfriend has.

hold its head up to the camera, which generally means the hunter is framed and – if the kill is impressive enough and the hunter short enough – dwarfed by the elk's antlers.

Although Ryan Muirhead and his friends didn't know it at the time, the antlers of the bull trapped in the Kittson County mud would eventually measure among the largest ever scored since records of American big game began to be kept in 1895. All they knew at that point was that the bull was still alive, but was not going to be able to free its giant antlers from the mud without help. Torn between awe and pity for an animal so clearly in pain, and that most powerful of hunterly competitive instincts, the desire not to come back empty-handed, their minds were in turmoil. Ryan recalls them staring at the elk, and the great beast looking up at them, unable to move. 'We just sat there for a while trying to think what to do', Ryan said. 'We were in awe.'

One of the things that separates us from the rest of the animal kingdom is that we formulate principles, honour codes, and rules that we very much associate with authenticity. Hunting has its rules as much as any sport, and there is an authentic way and an inauthentic way for hunters to do things. For the last hundred and fifty years or so, the American way has been set out in the code of 'fair chase', the gold standard of what it means to be an authentic hunter in the elemental battle between man and elk (or moose or deer or bighorn). Real hunting, according to the code, is ethical, sportsmanlike, and lawful. Real hunters play fair by their quarry. Real hunters take only free-ranging wild game animals, and would never do so in a manner that gives the hunter an improper advantage. Most of all, for the chase to count as 'fair', the animal must have a sporting chance of getting away.* So in the competitive world of modern hunting, an elk helpless in deep snow but with an almost certainly record-breaking pair of antlers poses a dilemma: To cheat? Or not to cheat?

To be sure, the hunter's dilemma would not be a wolf's dilemma. Wolves, along with coyotes and cougars, are the elk's natural predators. Hunting is a chancy business, and wild dogs and wolves have been known to start feeding on their prey before it is dead, so it's fair to assume that faced with a stricken and entangled elk, it would be an unusual wolf that stopped to ponder this or any other ethical predicament.

The most passionate and vocal advocate of the doctrine of fair chase is the Boone and Crockett Club. Named for the famous hunters Daniel Boone and Davy Crockett, the club was founded in 1887 by Theodore 'Teddy' Roosevelt (a passionate hunter, later to be 26th President of the USA) and a group of fellow enthusiasts. In the course of a dinner, Roosevelt proposed that the guests form an organisation to work for the preservation of the large game of North America by promoting 'manly sport with the rifle'. The club's mission was both timely and necessary. The 1880s had been a time of unparalleled economic expansion in North America. As pioneer settlers moved westwards, wildernesses were overrun and land swallowed up faster than ever before. The founders of the Boone and Crockett Club, alarmed by the destruction of habitats and the devastation of wildlife by 'market hunters', including the near extinction of the American bison and the plight of the passenger pigeon, a beautiful but fatally slow and delicious bird whose population had plummeted from billions to near zero in less than fifty years,

---

* Though it is worth pointing out that hunting has a history of very unfair chase too.

made sustainable hunting and the safeguarding of native species a central tenet of the Club's ethos.*

From the start, the Boone and Crockett Club forged close links with nascent conservation movements. Curiously trademarked slogans such as 'Pioneers of Conservation™ since 1887' and 'Where Hunting Happens, Conservation Happens™' feature prominently on its website. The latter mantra seems somewhat circular. Are they conserving animals in order to kill them? Or killing them to conserve them in some way? In fairness, given the history of megafauna driven to extinction in North America – a list that is long, mournfully evocative, and very largely due to unregulated human hunting – any slogan that can help save a species gets my vote.†

To illustrate the authentic hunting spirit, the Boone and Crockett Club likes to tell the story of Theodore Roosevelt's encounter with a bear. One day in 1902, Roosevelt, by now President of the USA, was taking a break in Mississippi. Knowing his passion for field sports, his hosts had laid on a bear hunt for him. Anxious that the President should be the one to shoot the beast, but concerned for his safety, local hunters ran the bear to ground first. Having taken the precaution of thumping it on the head with a rifle butt and tying it to a tree, they called on Roosevelt to deliver the *coup de grâce*. Presented with

---

* The last surviving passenger pigeon – a species whose flocks had once been so large they have been described as having 'neither beginning nor end' – was a solitary female named Martha, who died in Cincinnati Zoo in 1914.

† The list of extinct megafauna includes mammoths and mastodons; Bison antiquus and the beautiful armadillo; the American mountain lion and the American mountain deer; giant tortoises and giant tapirs; Jefferson's ground sloths and camelops (native American camels); Western horses and stout-legged llamas; spectacled and giant short-faced bears; the smilodon, a sabre-toothed cat; the list goes on ... and on.

a half-stunned and tethered bear, Roosevelt adamantly refused to shoot. He idealised the hardy outdoorsman lifestyle and wanted nothing to do with a trophy that he had not earned through fair chase. When the story came out, *Washington Post* cartoonist Clifford Berryman made it the basis of a celebrated drawing entitled 'Drawing the Line in Mississippi'.* Within just a few days, Morris and Rose Michtom, owners of a Brooklyn penny store, had sewn some small fabric bears as toys for children and asked the President's permission to call them 'Teddy' bears in his honour. The episode cemented Roosevelt's standing in the public's mind as a man of principle, as well as burnishing his reputation as a protector of American wildlife.†

Eventually Ryan Muirhead and his buddies decided that something had to be done to help the animal. 'He was an old bull and he wasn't going to live forever, but you don't want to see him die like that if you can help him', said Ryan. They got help from a local rancher, who lent them a two-by-four slab of wood to use as a lever, but it took eight men to prise the elk's antlers from the muddy ground.

'We got him rolled over thinking he was going to dart, but he was so tired, he had no steam left … His legs were like Jello … He kind of staggered to the fence and fell down. We all backed off and let him be.' The elk's back leg was bloody where it had

---

* The caption was believed to allude both to Roosevelt's sportsmanship and his criticism of lynchings in the South.

† As ever, the full story is not quite as good as the myth. The President instructed his guide, a former slave named Holt Collier, to finish off the poor bear, with its bashed-in head, which Collier duly did – rather messily – with a knife. Though the episode inaugurated a Teddy bear bonanza, actual black bears fared rather less well. Their population has dwindled from 80,000 to around 750 in 2016; they were declared an endangered species in 1992.

Fig. 6.1. The Clifford Berryman cartoon of President
Roosevelt that inspired the birth of the Teddy bear.

been kicking at its antler in a vain attempt to raise its head from the mud, and its chest was heaving. It was worn out and unhappy to find itself in such close proximity to humans. After resting a few minutes, it stood and began walking. As it stumbled into the nearby woods and out of sight, it stopped and looked back and Ryan swears he saw a look of gratitude in the elk's eyes.

'I don't know if it was a "thank you" or what it was. Then he made his way into the woods, and it was pure quiet; you couldn't even hear him moving he was so quiet. We stood and watched him disappear.'

'All hunters should be nature lovers', declared Theodore Roosevelt. Fair chase harks back to a primal, pre-civilised world, where animals were free to roam and humans could form an elemental connection with them, just as Ryan felt he had communed with the elk. It's a romantic view, given that fairness, like cheating, is a concept unknown in nature. But fair chase does something more important: it lays out the conditions for equilibrium. As long as hunter and quarry remain evenly matched, it recreates the ideal of nature in balance.

Problems arise, though, when this equilibrium is disturbed by competition between hunters themselves. Once upon a time, a pair of antlers might have been pinned to a panelled wall or hung in a corner of a hunting lodge. Now, there is the whole world of social media across which to display your trophies. Once, you might have taken private pleasure from the size of your kill; now, you can compare it to every other hunter's. Ironically, one driver of competition may have been the Boone and Crockett Club's keeping – and, more importantly, *publishing* – accurate records of antler size and shape. Begun as part of a wildlife management programme, the catalogue has taken on a life of its own. A listing in the Club's Big Game Records is now the American elk hunter's single most coveted prize. It's no longer enough to have a set of antlers as a souvenir of a thrilling chase, no longer enough to have a fine trophy to display; these days your rack has to be demonstrably bigger than the next guy's if it is to count for anything at all.* Record bull antler measurements can now be compared as readily as Pokémon scores. An eighth of an inch can make all the difference.

---

* Trophy racks have become what economists call 'positional goods'.

Shopping and Hunting

There are many things – some fairer than others – that a hunter can do to increase his (and it *is* most often his) chances of success. Most seem to involve a lot of shopping, with sometimes comic results. Top of most shopping lists is camouflage gear. This makes you both less visible to your prey and more easily identifiable by your fellow hunters. Designs vary according to the terrain and climate of your quarry; you can choose from 'Mountain Mimicry', 'Mossy Oak Country', 'Woodland', 'Western Snow', and a host of others. It will not have escaped the astute reader that this is, in fabric form, the human equivalent of animals' cryptic colouration,* no different to the spots that help the jaguar disappear in the leafy jungle, or the stripes that allow the zebra to recede invisibly into the African grasslands.† You might see camo-wearing as a bit of a cheat, but few in the hunting world do. Equally uncontroversial are the gadgets – available from all good hunting stores, lodges, and online retailers – that mimic animals' distinctive calls. 'Bugler' pipes can reproduce the roars, whistles, and grunts of excitable bulls, the oestrus bleats of does, and the bawlings of fawns in order to lure the bull elks out into open country.‡ Two

---

* Colouration that makes animals difficult to distinguish against their background, making it harder for predators to find them.

† The latest theory about why the zebra has stripes is that African midges and tsetse flies don't like stripes. Travel tip: pack striped pyjamas.

‡ Hunters Specialities™ advertise their Heavy Horns Rattle Bag as 'a great tool for bringing in deer and elk during the pre-rut and rut. Hand-selected hardwood rods are specifically sized and shaped to reproduce the sounds of antlers locked in battle. Its durable bag lets you rattle one-handed, and the elastic silencer binds the rods.' For this you get a trademark? For some bits of wood in a bag and an elastic band?

133

that caught my eye were Knight & Hale's E-Z Grunter® Extreme Call, 'a versatile all-season call', and the evocatively named Who's Yrr Daddy Elk Call from Rocky Mountain Calls, which promises the 'hot nasally cow sounds that bulls want to hear' and is, they hasten to assure us, 'sure to bring the Big Daddy elk within range'.

You can also use scent-mimicry without being regarded as inauthentic in any way. Cow elk urine is the big seller here, handily available in stick, spray, or liquid formulations. If they are stalking elk during the mating season, hunters can douse themselves in this pungent pee, which has the dual advantage of camouflaging their human scent while simultaneously tempting the bull elk into view. Moccasin Joe Ambush Products™ offer Hot Elk Cow in Heat Lure (available in several versions depending on the species of elk), which they claim is guaranteed to make normally restrained and prudent bulls 'throw caution to the wind'.

If you are the kind of fastidious hunter who would rather not be dabbing urine all over your body, there is one other legitimate mimicry device you might like to consider. The Miss September Feeding Cow Elk Decoy from The Montana Decoy Co., printed on foldable stretched canvas, is a near life-sized photo of a cow elk taken from behind to emphasise her white fluffed bum. 'This relaxed look of a cow elk feeding lets other elk know everything's OK … a natural draw', as one seller puts it. The idea is that you pop it (her?) open at an opportune moment to attract the bull elk whose antlers you hanker after. Effective, perhaps; ridiculous, definitely. A word of warning, though, if you are considering spending $99.99 to buy it. Several purchasers have gone online to complain that the snap-open mechanism didn't snap open easily enough, and I can sympathise; wrestling with Miss September is not a dignified way to hunt.

Arguably the most 'natural' or 'authentic' way to hunt is to track animals on foot. Some purists even eschew guns, restricting themselves to bows and arrows.* But increasingly feverish attempts to ensure that a trophy is bagged every time have led to more controversial forms of hunting. The use of all-terrain vehicles, 'smart scopes' (rifle sights with built-in electronic rangefinders), drones, night-vision optics and thermal imaging that enable hunters to see game in the dark, is deemed unfair, and trophies bagged by such means are ineligible for entry in the Big Game Records. Cash-rich and time-poor hunters who pay to have game herded from the air by helicopters, to give them a better chance of actually hitting something, are particularly reviled. This, the Boone and Crockett Club points out, is nothing like fair chase. So much does the Club disapprove that any trophies gained from such highly mechanised hunts are disqualified from their records.

But nothing makes real hunters' blood boil quite as much as the recent development of so-called 'canned shoots'. For those for whom hunting is no longer about effort and skill, the challenge and excitement of man pitting himself against nature, the multimillion-dollar business of canned shoots provides a world of luxury hunting lodges and captive-reared 'wildlife', of escape-proof and fenced-in commercial shooting operations that guarantee the customer will leave with a trophy at the end of their stay. For between $5,000 and $20,000 (depending on rack size, luxuriousness of accommodation, etc.), 'game farms' with names like Big Velvet and Big Trophy Ranch offer punters the

---

* Despite its authentic 'feel', bow and arrow is not necessarily the most ethical way to hunt. The Minnesota dentist Walter J Palmer, whose 2015 shooting of Cedric the lion in Zimbabwe caused an international outcry, is a bow hunter who proudly states that he doesn't carry a gun to 'finish off' the animal. From the time Palmer shot him, Cedric took more than ten hours to die.

chance to kill a 'shooter bull' – an animal bred to produce abnormally large antlers, and very likely fed on proteins and hormones. Some are even said to be drugged, to make them lethargic and easier to shoot. Since the animals are penned, any pretence of fair chase evaporates; the hunt is reduced to a single pull of the trigger. Not only are the hunters shooting animals that can't escape, but, unlike wild animals, farmed elk have no fear of humans and will not run away. As the Boone and Crockett Club tersely observes, this is not hunting; it's wandering into a farm and shooting the livestock.

A clue to the changes that have crept up on hunting is given by the 'No Kill, No Pay' slogan that some game farms display on their websites. However much hunters hark back to a mystic or mythical past, where man and elk were evenly matched in battle, the truth is that hunting today is less about the chase and more about hunters vying to outspend other hunters in order to get a trophy they can brag about.* A canned shoot is not so much hunting as shopping, and an ecological contest has morphed into one that is very largely economic. What was Darwinian competition has moved firmly into the world of Adam Smith. Rivalry between hunter and hunter may give rise to legitimate economic activity, but their hunting is by any estimation fake.

This poses two separate but interlinked problems. The first is cheating. If one person cheats, others may feel driven to cheat as well. Ryan Muirhead's dilemma is every hunter's dilemma: they may want to hunt authentically, but they also want to compete with other hunters. And as competition escalates, fair chase

---

* Actually, I'm not sure it was ever that evenly matched. Most of North America's now-extinct megafauna were killed with nothing more hi-tech than stones and spears.

hunters see themselves being replaced, literally outgunned, by cheats. We know from other competitive fields, such as athletics, what happens when people have to cheat to compete. If one athlete dopes, others will feel the need to do so too. No one gains a competitive edge for long – and more often than not athletes suffer permanent or long-term damage to their health. A similar dynamic is playing out in hunting. All that escalation and expense, from camo to bells, smells, and whistles, and from ATVs and helicopters to the horrors of farmed elks; yet no one is better off in the sporting sense, and many are worse off financially – and, you might say, morally as well.

The second problem is damage to the sport itself. The revulsion felt towards canned shoots, particularly big game hunts that set up endangered African animals to be killed by 'bragging rights' tourists, has led to calls to ban hunting altogether. So the actions of these hunters are jeopardising the very existence of the sport they claim to love. We are used to the idea that unrestricted competition is healthy, that it will lead to the nirvana of good for one, good for all, but here it is letting down the very group it is meant to benefit.* What is good for individual hunters (more kills, bigger trophies) is not good for hunting as a whole. Canned shoots and other faux chases may benefit individual hunting businesses and their over-pampered and spoon-fed clients, but they are undoubtedly bad for the hunting fraternity overall. When the competition is simply to stay ahead of the competition – to bag not just a trophy but a *bigger* trophy – then the race is never-ending. As time goes on, it drives an ever-bigger wedge between the interests of the individual hunter and the sport as a whole. Runaway competition like this cannot

---

* Incidentally, unrestricted greed and competition are not what Adam Smith advocated.

be halted unless all concerned agree to stop the behaviour that leads to it. As a social scientist would put it, hunting is facing a classic 'collective action problem'.

It is something of an irony that many hunters fail to appreciate the problem before their eyes. Have they never asked themselves how their quarry came to have the antlers they find so desirable in the first place? Did Ryan and his buddies not stop to wonder how their elk had evolved the magnificent (and potentially fatal) great branches of bone that were trapping their owner in the mud? Had they done so, they might have noticed both a familiar pattern and a familiar problem.

Rising like a crest from the brow of the male elk, growing to around four feet wide and forty pounds in weight, antlers are a wonder of nature. The reason elks have developed these unfeasibly large bravura headpieces is the same reason cuckoo finches have become better egg counterfeiters, cheetahs and gazelles faster runners, and butterflies better mimics: they are characteristics that improve the animal's chances of reproductive success. During the 'strut and rut' mating season, bull elks use their antlers to battle for dominance over other males in the herd, and to establish a harem of cow elks. These contests are a noisome spectacle of posturing, trumpeting, 'bugling', and antler wrestling. Pacing back and forth, rival males size each other up; if neither backs down, a bloody and vicious heads-down, charging-and-goring battle ensues. The winner is invariably the elk with the bigger rack. Having won, that more antler-endowed elk reproduces and passes his 'bigger rack' genes on to his offspring, and so on and repeatedly across the generations, until the top recorded racks, so the Boone and Crockett Club tells us, have now reached a span of five feet or more. What must have started as bony protuberances, useful for the odd bit of headbutting, have evolved, via a testosterone-fuelled build-up, into an impressive weapons system.

But although bigger antlers benefit the individual bull elk (more cows, more offspring), they are a liability for the species as a whole. The elk grows a new pair every year,* and the nutritional demands that places on it are so great that biologists actually classify antlers as a handicap. They're also dangerous. Bull elks chased by wolves or coyotes try to flee into the forest, only to find themselves trapped by their antlers in trees or thickets, and at the mercy of their predators. And it is of course outsize antlers that make bull elks so attractive to hunters. What makes antlers majestic also renders them pointless. In the end, all the effort and resource dedicated to bone growth leaves the elks no better off: still fighting, still strutting and rutting, still trying to get ahead, but now burdened by vast and futile weapons stockpiled on their heads.† Their arms race does not involve cheating, unlike that of our trophy-hunters, but the pattern of runaway competition that only leads to outsized and unhelpful results is the same.

Although hunters seem unable to see the parallels between the natural and man-made worlds, Robert H Frank, professor of economics at Cornell University, certainly does. He sees ecological competitions that have unfortunate side-effects and economic contests that lead to unfortunate outcomes as equally

---

* Antlers are the fastest-growing bones in the animal kingdom.

† If you are seeing parallels with the spectacularly spendthrift Cold War nuclear arms race, you are right. What may have seemed beneficial to individual countries ('my weapons cache is bigger than yours') led to repeated huge and wasteful spending on nuclear weapons in a futile attempt to overtake the other side's temporary advantage and close the so-called 'missile gap'.

illustrative of what he calls 'Darwin's wedge'.* He coined the term to characterise the gap between individual and group interests that so often results from runaway competition, whether for bigger antlers on their heads (elks) or bigger antlers on their walls (hunters). Frank's insight is that economics and evolution are two sides of the same coin, two ways of looking at the same competitive behaviour. Both Darwin and Adam Smith, both evolutionary biology and economics, are concerned with the mechanics and effects of competition for scarce resources, and it makes sense to look for parallels between them. It's an insight that has profound implications for the study of inauthenticity, as our look at elks and their hunters has shown. When we think about the inauthenticity that competition gives rise to, we need to think about fundamental economic and evolutionary forces at the same time.

To be sure, Frank is far from being the only one to have realised that the pursuit of individual interests does not always lead to outcomes that benefit the group as a whole, and that collective action is required if and when we wish to prevent that happening.† His point is that, since unbridled individual competition damages the collective interest in the fields of economics and ecology alike, we should adopt the same attitude towards it whether the competition occurs in nature or in the man-made world. Frank urges people, organisations, and governments to set limits to futile and unfruitful competition. He would like to

---

* In his book *The Darwin Economy: Liberty, Competition, and the Common Good* (2011), which is where I first came across the elk example. It propelled me into more ruminant research, leading me from elks to elk hunting, than I ever expected to do in a book about authenticity, or indeed would have thought possible. Thank you, Robert.

† I like to think that any economists reading this are nodding and muttering, 'Uh-huh. Nash equilibria are not always Pareto efficient.'

see more discussion of ways to limit individual gains for the good of the species.

Antler Reduction

Limitation talks are precisely what the elks could do with too. The elk versus elk arms race has locked the species into an evolutionary struggle beyond its control. Bigger antlers may favour the individual elk wrestling for female attention, but what would undoubtedly favour the species as a whole would be antler limitation talks, followed by some practical antler decommissioning. If, as Robert Frank suggests, the elks could put their hooves down, press a button, and reduce all their antlers by half, they would all be considerably better off. Non-proliferation would eliminate waste at a stroke: the elks would be able to strut and rut just as much as before, but they could use the energy and resources that would have otherwise gone into inordinate antler growth for something more useful. Antler limitation would reduce the external dangers to the species too. Elks are not equipped to deal with a classic collective action problem, which is a shame. Cutting down on the height and width of their antlers would have saved a great many elks from wolves or coyotes in trees or thickets, and might even have saved the Kittson elk from its fate in the icy Minnesota mud.

Ryan Muirhead couldn't get the elk out of his mind, and returned to the place where he had left it. Since the bull was on Minnesota state land, he knew his best chance of claiming the antler rack was to be there when the animal died. Next day, Ryan returned to the site with his wife Josie. 'I just had to go back. I knew he wasn't going to make it far.' They found the bull 600 yards back in the woods. 'He was hunkered down in the willows, and we got within 40 yards before he picked his head up and looked at us. He didn't try to run. He was coughing, wheezing. He probably had pneumonia from being on his back that long in the cold. You could see where he'd dragged himself 25 yards through the snow to get back in the willows. At that point I knew he was done.' Over the next six hours Ryan watched the elk from a distance, returning now and then to the truck to warm up. 'It was sad to see a wild animal like that not be able to get up and run and do what he wanted to do. He'd pick up his head every now and then, but he could barely lift that rack. And finally, he just stopped picking up his head.'

The Kittson County elk perished because elks can't stop their antler race. Hunting may also perish, along with its associated conservation and animal welfare work, if hunters don't stop their trophy race. But the difference between us and the elks is that we can take a group or species-level view. We can recognise Darwin's wedge when we see it; we are able, if not always willing, to save ourselves from our own excesses. We've seen in previous chapters that competition – the competition for survival – is what leads to cheating and fakery in our world, and animal mimicry and free riders in the animal world. Competition may be a fact of life, but the difference between us and animals is that we can choose how to respond to it. We have degrees of freedom unavailable to any elk. Only we can regulate and negotiate. Only we can invent codes and laws, create principles like fair chase, set up hunting regulators, pass judgement on cheats and law-breakers. The paradox of the race for trophies is the paradox of competition more generally, that sometimes we need saving from ourselves, and that we are the only ones who can do it.

There are obvious areas – nuclear weapons, carbon emissions, sugary drinks, even the belief that more is always better – where if we all agreed to cut back we would all benefit. And of course, if we were moved to, we could cut down on all sorts of fakery from brand fakes to bogus pharmaceuticals. We can put our hooves down and say it's not OK to have things that benefit only the individual and not the group. Though of course we mostly don't. Even if we couldn't bring ourselves to exercise this superhuman level of restraint, we could vote in governments to do it for us, because governments could quite easily sort some of these things.

But since this chapter is meant to be about the mechanism of competition and its malfunctions, rather than morality and politics, I shall say no more on the subject of who should or shouldn't put their hooves down, and return instead to Ryan Muirhead, who is about to nail the trophy of his dreams.

Ryan Gets His Rack

For all the complex emotions that Ryan went through as he watched the majestic animal in its death throes, a trophy is a trophy, and Ryan and his wife had a cathedral-ceilinged living room which was rebukingly bare of any trophies. The bull elk's enormous rack would fill it impressively. They did not have to wait for long. Within days of the animal's death the verdict was handed down. The elk had died of natural causes, and the Minnesota Department of Natural Resources was granting Ryan a permit to possess its antlers.

'I was in awe just to see him again', Ryan said. 'It was just crazy.'

As soon as he was able, Ryan took the cape and head of the elk to the Sportsman's Taxidermy Studio in East Grand Forks to be mounted. Randy Dufault, official measurer for the Boone and Crockett Club, had green-scored the rack at 456 4/8 inches, though the antlers would have to dry for 60 days for the final score. By any measure, said Dufault, the rack was the largest he'd ever scored. If the score held up after it dried, he said, it would rank no. 5 in the world.

The Muirheads' giant trophy now has pride of place in their living room. Visitors marvel at antlers so massive – over a foot in circumference at the base – that even a full-grown man can't get his hands around them.

In my view antlers always look better on an elk, but who am I to argue with the Minnesota Department of Natural Resources? Ryan Muirhead got his hunting trophy because the elk hadn't been killed by hunting. But that means it wasn't a hunting trophy in any sense of the term. Ryan's rack is fundamentally inauthentic. Boone and Crockett Club recorded the antlers as part of its data collection – they are currently ranked the fourth biggest in the world – but it pointedly declined to mention Ryan's name in the listings. His trophy had nothing to do with fair chase; there wasn't even a chase. Let's be honest here: Ryan fluked into those antlers. He got the trophy through being in the right place at the right time, not through any kind of hunting skill. As a human being he looks to be a decent guy – I was moved by his feelings for the dying elk – but as an elk hunter, he looks to be something of a phoney, to put it politely. I was obscurely disappointed to find that he had posed with the dead elk for one of those kill photographs (see Plate 7). We all aspire to some sort of status symbol, and although I find the ambition for a pair of dead animal's headbones odd, I suppose it's no more odd than aspiring to a more expensive designer handbag or a supersized yacht.

But the real surprise to me was not Ryan's desire to acquire a trophy-that-wasn't, but the reaction of his hunting peers. I expected to find that the hunting community would be ambivalent about this all-too-easy and bogus win. Maybe a few lips would be pursed in disapproval at Ryan getting something for nothing. Some finger-wagging would have been nice. But not one of the comments I found online suggested that there was anything inauthentic about Ryan's taking home what could fairly be regarded as a found trophy. The dominant themes in the hunting chat rooms and internet comment page discussions of Ryan and his rack were enthusiasm and awe.

'Just wow', said a post from spectr17 on California-based Jesse's Hunting and Outdoors site ('your premier online resource for the hunting, fishing, gun and outdoor community … share information with folks in our friendly forums'), 'never see any buck or bull end up like that. I've seen pics of them hung up in trees, from fighting and hung up in fences but not upside down in mud.'

'In any event, a rare thing. Cool that he got to keep the rack', commented BelchFire in response.

'WOW! That is just amazing! Can't help but feel sorry for that bull! Nature can sure be cruel!' added HWkirby on the Alberta Outdoorsman site ('Alberta's only hunting, fishing & trapping magazine').

There was even a sprinkling of envy of Ryan's good luck. 'Gotta agree it is pretty sad that I didn't get to shoot it!' said darrin6109 who, if her photograph is to be believed, is a stunning buxom brunette with a future in glamour modelling.

And from the Bowhunting Network, who you might have thought would be sticklers for authentic hunting, there were congratulations for Ryan on his 'once in a lifetime find' and a message that they were 'proud to call you brethren'.

Which I guess just goes to show that it's not just nature that loves a free rider.

PART 3
ON THE AUTHENTICITY
OF THINGS

7

MULTIPLIERS

Death of a Counterfeiter

'The idea of money is older than the idea of counterfeit money, but older, perhaps, by no more than a few minutes. There is evidence of the use of both the genuine article and the counterfeit article in the earliest recorded civilizations, and it has been established that primitive tribes had both good money and bad money before there were any civilizations to record. It seems that immediately after certain people realized that they could easily make tokens to represent cumbersome property, such as collections of animal skins and stores of foodstuffs, certain other people awoke to the fact that they could just as easily make tokens to represent the tokens that represented the cumbersome property. The two ideas are so closely related that they are practically twins, and, like the products of the ideas, they are hard to tell apart. If it were not for counterfeit money, the story of money might be simply beautiful. As it is, the pattern formed by the fateful entwinement of money and counterfeit money is intricately grotesque.'

St Clair McKelway, 'Old Eight Eighty'

'To Counterfeit is Death.'

Warning on American colonial currency notes

149

On 22 March 1699, a boisterous crowd gathered at a small village to the west of London called Tyburn. The throng was in a holiday mood: hangings were entertainment as much as public punishment, and the executions that morning had included a popular highwayman who, with theatrical flair, had travelled to the gallows in his coach, stopping at taverns along the way, as well as five lesser scoundrels.

Now it was the turn of William Chaloner. Counterfeiter, traitor to the realm, and public enemy, a man whom the judge had derided as 'notorious'. The king himself had heard Chaloner's petition for pardon just four days before, and had refused to grant it. A gifted copier and counterfeiter, Chaloner had in the course of his career forged groats and shillings, silver pistoles and golden guineas. Even the most up-to-date forms of money – lottery tickets and the very first notes issued by the newly incorporated Bank of England – had posed no obstacle to his ingenuity. Arriving in London as a penniless Warwickshire weaver's son, Chaloner had begun as a maker of imitation tin watches – the fake Rolexes of their day – and as a peddler of sex toys, thereby picking up, as his contemporary biographer put it, 'a few loose Pence, and looser Associates'.* A man of great audacity and casual ruthlessness, he reputedly sent more co-conspirators to the gallows in order to save his own skin than all his predecessors. Skilled enough in the ways of London's underworld to direct accomplices and witnesses from his prison cell in Newgate, sufficiently eloquent to advise the

---

* The biographer was the anonymous author of *Guzman Redivivus: A Short View of the Life of Will. Chaloner, the Notorious Coyner, who was executed at Tyburn on Wednesday 22 d of March 1699: with a Brief Account of his Tryal, Behaviour, and last Speech*. Gallows literature, cheap pamphlets containing accounts of lurid murders and sensational hangings, were the red-top tabloids of the time.

House of Commons how to deal with counterfeiting while simultaneously plying his 'Clipping and Coyning Trade', Chaloner liked to boast that he had 'Wit and Money' enough to escape the law, that none but 'Poor Fellows and Fools' were hanged.

This was an optimistic and typically cocky boast. For almost three hundred years, since 1404, it had been a capital offence to 'multiply gold or silver' by adulterating it with cheaper metals, thereby diminishing the value of the store of precious metals – effectively the money supply – at the Royal Mint in the Tower of London. But since 1697, in the reign of William III and Mary II, counterfeiting – the copying of the king's coin – had been deemed to be high treason, the most serious crime in the calendar. Chaloner ran the risk of more than mere hanging. Male counterfeiters could be sentenced to be hanged and drawn (disembowelled and castrated while still half-alive), women to be burned alive.* The stakes had been raised.

Many of the crowd gathered at Tyburn on that cold spring day had paid to be as close as possible to the action. They were hoping for a good show, a criminal who displayed bravado before uttering some fine words of recantation as the noose was slipped over his head. They were not disappointed. Although Chaloner was still railing at the injustice of his fate as he was hauled on a sledge from Newgate to Tyburn, he was seen to pray fervently as he finally ascended the scaffold. The crowd cheered as he took the black hood and put it on his own head, the sign of a man prepared to meet his maker. The applause continued as the ladder was pulled away, Chaloner kicking and struggling as gravity took its course.

---

* Sheep stealing, every internet historian's favourite example of a barbaric capital punishment, only became liable to the death penalty in 1741.

Many wealthy criminals paid the executioner to pull on their legs and speed their death; but Chaloner, who had coined £60,000 in counterfeit currency in his time (perhaps equivalent to over £11 million today), had seemingly no money left to pay the hangman to carry out this last and smallest act of mercy.

Chaloner's death raises a number of questions about authenticity. Currency is made up of coins and banknotes that are multiples, copies, of other coins or banknotes. Why are some copies deemed authentic, and others inauthentic, counterfeit? Who gets to do the deeming, to authorise the distinction? We regularly shame and punish all kinds of copycats, but why should the counterfeiting of currency be punished so much more harshly than any other form of unauthorised copying? If currency is so important and valuable that copying it incurs the death penalty, how was it that an unlettered weaver's son was able to imitate it so easily? And is there any money that *can't* be copied?

William Chaloner's failure was not his desire to multiply or increase money, an urge shared by the highest in the land, as we will see, but his making an enemy of the newly appointed Warden of the Royal Mint. He failed to realise that this warden was cut from a very different cloth to his lazy and corrupt predecessors in the post. After the Glorious Revolution of 1689, Britain faced an economic crisis. In large part, the crisis was due to the fact that the coinage could not be trusted. Not only were many genuine coins worth less than their face value because they were 'clipped' – their silver content literally cut away – but up to one in ten coins was a forgery, made of base metal. The royal treasury determined that they needed the finest mind of their generation to help solve the problem.

Which is what they got when Isaac Newton left his position at Trinity College, Cambridge, to take up his first public office as Warden of the Mint in 1696.

It is intriguing to imagine Newton, the father of modern science – a man regarded both in his day and in ours as 'the greatest natural philosopher the world has ever seen', whose *Principia Mathematica* took the learned world by storm, the scientist we know for the famous story of the apple drop, the genius who created the mathematics of flux and change, whose optics explained the magic of the rainbow, and whose laws unravelled the mysteries governing motion and gravitation – suddenly tasked with investigating the dregs of London's criminal underworld.* He brought to the task a boundless capacity for minute and detailed observation and logical deduction. He also brought a very personal dislike of those, like Chaloner, who for dishonourable motives transformed base metals into simulacra of silver and gold.

The Great Recoinage

The rudimentary processes of the seventeenth-century Royal Mint made a counterfeiter's task a relatively easy one. A particular problem was that much of the currency was machine-struck, the silver discs die-stamped with a pattern to indicate the value of the coin. Like a seal pressed into a molten blob of wax, this produced a design that was fully rendered in the centre, but with free-form edges that could easily be trimmed away. The

---

* Newton's expense account reveals that he paid an aide to 'buy him a suit to qualify him for conversing with a gang of coiners of note in order to discover them, £5'.

resulting silver clippings could be mixed with a base metal such as pewter and moulded into more-or-less convincing fakes in what were little better than backroom foundries. It is estimated that by 1695 coin clipping had resulted in the silver coinage in circulation having only something between half and two-thirds of its proper weight. Older money was so worn and badly clipped that it was barely viable tender. Losing trust and confidence in the currency, people began to hoard genuine coins, boosting the circulation of counterfeits. Newton's solution was audacious. He resolved to collect all the silver coins in circulation and melt them down; the silver would be used to mint purer, better, and – he hoped – less copiable coins. A Great Recoinage as the solution to the Great Debasement. The new coins would have milled edges, which would not only prevent clipping but would also be – so the thinking went – harder to counterfeit.

Having recalled the old currency, though, the Mint failed to produce new silver coins quickly enough to replace it. For a year, as Newton re-tooled the Mint, the nation was starved of cash, plunged into what would now be called a liquidity crisis. The great recoinage had brought about a great coin shortage – and with it, an irresistible opportunity for counterfeiters. In backrooms and basements, Chaloner assembled the equipment and expertise needed for his operations. Although the new milled coins were supposed to be uncopiable, he and his confederates devised moulds capable of turning out convincing imitations. The distinctive new edging proved to be less protection than decoration. Though Newton's recoinage proceeded at an astonishing rate – at its peak, five hundred men and fifty horses were driving the Mint's giant rolling mill, producing in three years twice the amount of money that had been coined in the previous thirty – Chaloner's network of forgers and fences were already easing quantities of newly counterfeited coins into circulation.

Crimes of Copying

In the words of Thomas Levenson, professor of science writing at the Massachusetts Institute of Technology, Chaloner had become 'a kind of criminal alchemist, able to multiply without limit coins that looked so persuasively like true silver and gold'. To his anonymous contemporary biographer, it was as though Chaloner had discovered the alchemist's Holy Grail, the philosopher's stone, capable of turning base metals into precious gold: 'And now he seem'd to have found the (so-much-sought-after) Philosopher's Stone; or (like *Danae* from *Jove*) had Showers of Gold daily falling into his Lap. The Trade went on briskly, Chaloner's Guineas flew about as thick as some years ago did bad Silver and everything seem'd to favour his Undertakings.'

The first reason to counterfeit money is ... well, money. For those born without it but who have wit and talent, and not too many scruples, copying and counterfeiting represent opportunity. The more money you multiply, the more opportunities you create for yourself.

Not all crimes of copying are equal. Some flatter (a fashion '*hommage*'), some lead to social opprobrium (literary plagiarism), while others, as we have seen, lead to the gallows. What separates coiners, or money counterfeiters, from other fakers is the extent of the impact caused by their operations. Their business is to increase illicitly and most of all in quantity. Their theft is not of ideas, but of resources. An art forger steals from a handful of people at most – the original artist, their dealer,

155

perhaps the owners of genuine works. Infringers of copyright or patent rights damage the original creator or inventor and those who manufacture, distribute, and retail their products and designs. But 'moneymakers', as counterfeiters were known in eighteenth-century America, steal from a whole country. As false coinage seeps into the economy, it weakens the body politic. The philosopher John Locke, a contemporary and admirer of Newton's, wrote that money manipulations had 'contributed more to Sink us, than all the Force of our Enemies could do'. It's not the imitation that impoverishes, so much as the proliferation. The author of the cheap-sheet gallows biography that followed hard on Chaloner's execution made the same point. Chaloner was an exceptionally wicked rogue because he was stealing not just from individuals, but from society as a whole: '[T]he Person of whom I am to Treat has out gone all President [exceeded all precedent]: He scorn'd the petty Rogueries of Tricking *single Men*, but boldly aim'd at imposing upon *a whole Kingdom*.'

The question we should ask, as in all cases of copying and counterfeiting, is: Whose interests does the imitation advance and whose does it threaten? Money counterfeiting is 'roguery' with the potential to impoverish a 'whole kingdom', which is why states have so often employed it as a weapon of war. Britain was the first nation to try to weaken its enemies in this way, when it flooded its American colonies with false currency during the War of Independence. The former colonies learnt the lesson: the North did the same thing to the South during the American Civil War. During World War II, Germany's Operation Bernhard aimed to counterfeit sufficient quantities of banknotes to undermine the British economy; later in the war Germany set prisoners in Sachsenhausen concentration camp to forging British and American notes in order to finance German intelligence operations. In the present day, North Korea routinely counterfeits millions of US dollars, waging monetary warfare alongside its missile posturings.

All governments know that money is a formidable weapon, and that they need to keep control of the money supply as tightly in their own hands as possible. States limit the supply of money in circulation in three ways: by monopolising the right to mint or print it, restricting the use of the state stamp or warrant on coins and banknotes, and enforcing serious deterrents for money multiplying. They know that proliferation is the route to domination. Nobody was hanging counterfeiters just because they were forgers in the sense that Lothar Malskat was, copying an artwork or two, or rustling up a few fake frescoes. Nor were coiners being disembowelled for offences against originality, for trespassing on someone else's creative genius. Moneymakers weren't doing it for art's sake or to prove a point.* Instead of making a couple of copies, or even a handful, they were making hundreds and thousands, sometimes more. Counterfeiting currency is a form of multiplication that removes not just control of the money supply from the hands of the state, but power itself.† It's not surprising that the powers that be tend to be so very keen to keep the ultimate act of commercial copyright – the right to mint and print money, as well as the right to create 'new' money ('quantitative easing', in the prevailing jargon) – to themselves. They killed the

---

* There have been a few who did it for art's sake. In the 1970s and 1980s, a much-arrested artist called J S G Boggs made exquisite hand-inked copies of American banknotes both as works of art and as a way of questioning what made money valuable in the first place.

† It's no coincidence that the statute of 1404 that made it an offence to 'multiply' gold or silver used that term.

counterfeiters not for copying money but for multiplying it, and because they understood that to multiply money is to multiply power.

A Penniless Monarch

It was unfortunate that, just at the time of the collapse of confidence in the king's coinage and the economic crisis of the early 1690s, the monarch found himself in urgent need of cash to finance a series of vastly expensive wars. Armies need to be paid for. But with coin in such short supply, there was nothing with which to pay for them. There were reports of suppliers refusing to provision the king's troops, and one account of three colonels waiting on the king to beg for money to buy boots for their men to march in.

Like his namesake Chaloner, King William was constantly turning his mind to the question of how to increase his supply of money. Although he needed £1.2 million to continue the war against the French and their allies, a series of money-raising measures had failed to produce it. By 1694, his credit was so dire that he could not raise funds even by offering a steep 8 per cent interest. At that point, William agreed to a scheme proposed by a prosperous merchant named William Paterson. A group of wealthy men would fund a new joint stock company to lend the king the money he needed, with repayment secured against future government revenues. The entity would be incorporated under the name of the Bank of England.

This helped to increase the amount of money in circulation by a process of timeshifting (we give you the money now in exchange for interest now and repayment in the future). By bringing forward future government revenues, King

William was able to pay his soldiers and continue to fight the French.*

The incorporation of the Bank of England meant that the king's creditors became the nation's bankers, and eventually its long-term debt managers. The Bank soon acquired more protection, privileges, and monopolies, including the all-important right to issue paper currency. And the status of that paper was demonstrated by the fact that the same 1696–7 session of Parliament that passed the statute that deemed it high treason to counterfeit coins passed another that made forgery of the new Bank of England notes a felony publishable by death.

Just how long do you suppose it took the ingenious William Chaloner to find a printer prepared to counterfeit the special marbled paper on which the new banknotes were printed, and associates able to forge the handwritten sums on them? His first forgery was detected in August 1695, just two months after the Bank's notes were first circulated.† Of course, printing money is only a crime when the wrong people are doing it. As physical objects, there was scarcely any difference between the notes produced by the Bank and by Chaloner – except that Chaloner's were liable to get him hanged. When it comes to banknotes,

---

* Another way banks can increase the amount of money in circulation is via the money-multiplier mechanism (yes, it's really called that) which enables banks to lend money in excess of their reserves, not just once but several times over, on the basis that it is unlikely that everyone will ask for their deposits back at the same time.

† According to the *Oxford Dictionary of National Biography*, 'The forger who marbled the notes had denounced Chaloner, who immediately handed over his false notes to the bank. To protect himself further Chaloner exposed a major fraud against the bank, one presumably in which he was himself involved ... Chaloner received a £200 reward. Hoping to capitalize on his enhanced credibility he then sent the bank a proposal to prevent counterfeiting of bank bills.'

however beautifully made, what matters is not so much the author as the *authoriser*.

The Last of the Magicians

But perhaps most surprising of all in this story of the coming of age of money is that Isaac Newton, the Warden of the Mint who made it his mission to hunt down and extinguish those like Chaloner who dared to create worth from the worthless, was himself a secret multiplier.

It is an aspect of Newton's story that has until recently been sidelined that the great scientist was a devoted student of the occult and esoteric discipline of alchemy. Many prefer to think of Newton as a 'respectable' man of science rather than the man described by the great economist John Maynard Keynes who, having bought 329 lots of Newton's manuscripts, over a third of which were alchemical, declared that 'Newton was not the first of the Age of Reason, he was the last of the magicians'. Newton studied alchemy for more than thirty years, and he devoted over a million words to it in his writings. He made copies of published as well as mysteriously sourced and unpublished texts, and wrote notes that probed the vast literature of alchemy as never before. The focus of all his research and laboratory experimentation was the search for the philosopher's stone.

To judge by his writings, Newton was devoting more of his time in the early 1690s to alchemy than to all of his other activities put together. But it was work that he kept secret – rightly and necessarily so. It was only in 1688 that Parliament repealed the statute of 1404 that prescribed the death penalty for multipliers – among whose number could be included any alchemist who actually managed to produce gold from base metal. In any event, alchemy was regarded as the province of charlatans and tricksters.* But the motivation of Newton's quest for the philosopher's stone could not have been more different. His goal was more exalted than mere personal monetary gain. In the words of his biographer Richard S Westfall, 'While Newton was not indifferent to his material welfare, it was never money that kept him from his meals and drove him to distraction. Truth and Truth alone held that power over him.' For Newton, as for many genuine alchemists, multiplication was fundamentally connected with the idea of the divine, with God and his handiwork. They believed that while everything in the physical world had a mechanical cause, there also existed a non-mechanical spiritual principle that was the key to God's creation of the universe. The fundamental aim of these alchemists was to replicate God's act of creation as described in the Bible. To understand the transformation of matter was to understand God; to seek the philosopher's stone was to aspire to the secrets of Godhead. Newton wanted more than just to understand the laws of nature; hubristically, not to say heretically, he wanted to experience at first hand the divine act of creation.

In an attempt to determine the laws of flux in matter, just as he had determined the laws of change and motion in objects, Newton spent years secretly collecting and summarising all the available knowledge on alchemy in his massive *Index Chemicus Ordinatus*, 34,000 words long and containing almost 900 entries. His 'Chymical' notebooks overflow with the results of

---

* Such as 'Count' Marco Bragadino (real name Mamugna) who, having claimed to have discovered the secrets of transmutation, defrauded the Duke of Bavaria and was duly executed. As a warning to other pseudo-alchemists, he was brought to the scaffold dressed in a suit of gilt tinsel and hanged with a yellow rope attached, according to at least one account, to a gallows 'gilded' with shining brass.

his laboratory experiments, some of them in the sober syntax of the lab bench, others scribbled in the secret language of the alchemist. *Decknamen* – alchemical cover names used to hide the identity of substances and things, such as Green Lion, the Caduceus of Mercury, and the Sceptre of Jove – make frequent appearances. But there is no doubt what it was that Newton was seeking to create. In 1692 he wrote to his friend the philosopher John Locke to say that he intended to investigate 'whether I know enough to make a ☿ [mercury, that is to say a base metal] which will grow hot with ☉ [gold]'.

By 1693 Newton was using a new technique, one already explored by both Locke and Robert Boyle, whose publication of *The Sceptical Chymist* in 1661 enshrined him as the first modern chemist. It was a kind of fermentation that involved seeding a base mixture with a grain of gold in the hope of propagating more of the precious metal. Newton began to believe that he had finally achieved his goal. His notebooks from the spring and summer of 1693 detail his growing elation and his unusually extravagant claims for his experiments. Believing that 'fermentation' could generate a chain reaction of base metals repeatedly reinfused by the philosopher's stone, Newton devotedly and obsessively listed ingredients and methods, proportions and weights. Describing every detail of his yearned-for transmutation of base metals into gleaming gold, he ended the miraculous recipes with the alchemist's most longed-for QED: 'thus may you multiply to infinity'.

For a matter of weeks, Newton seems to have believed that he had created the philosopher's stone, and with it the gift of being able to proliferate without limit. In the words of the science writer Thomas Levenson, this was 'the moment when Newton, and Newton alone, peered into the mechanism of divine action this side of heaven'. Then his notebooks fall silent. It seems that his alchemical project ended in disillusionment and failure. Newton suffered a major nervous collapse. By the autumn of 1693 he was plumbing the very depths of what has been called his 'black year'. Although various explanations have been offered for his breakdown – it may have been precipitated by years of intense thought and study, or by the disintegration of the only close personal relationship of his life – the failure of his attempts to recreate the mysteries of creation surely played at least a part. In any event, in 1696, after more than thirty-five years, Newton left Cambridge for London and the Mint. As warden, he would pursue coiners and counterfeiters with considerably more intensity and scientific precision than they had been accustomed to.

Chaloner's Last Ride

The job of pursuing clippers and coiners was ordinarily under-taken by the warden's clerk.* Newton was at first unwilling to turn detective himself. But once he did step into the breach, he applied his talents to the task to great effect: more than a hundred criminals were imprisoned as a result of his efforts in London alone. William Chaloner might have escaped the noose if he had kept a low profile, but that was not his way. He had not been shy about sharing his opinions on how to deal with the great currency crisis. Indeed, he published several pamphlets on the subject – a bold move, given his profession. His *Proposals Humbly Offered, for Passing an Act to Prevent Clipping and*

---

* When Newton was first appointed warden, William Chaloner recommended him to appoint one Thomas Holloway – a long-time criminal associate and accomplice – as his clerk. Newton declined.

Counterfeiting of Money (1695) had caused him to be noted by some as an expert in matters of coinage (as in many respects he was). Early in 1696, Chaloner sent a petition to the Privy Council from his prison cell in Newgate alleging that the staff of the Mint were counterfeiting guineas on the premises, striking base metal, and selling official stamps and dies to coiners. In 1697 he gave evidence to a committee of the House of Commons on the prevention of counterfeiting. The committee recommended that Chaloner should be allowed to work in the Mint to make tools for the manufacture of guineas, their edges milled 'with a Hollow or Groove' that would render the coin 'certainly impossible' to counterfeit. Newton refused to comply with the recommendation, on the grounds that it would contravene his oath of office.

The breathtaking cheek of a notorious counterfeiter not only proposing remedies for counterfeiting, but also offering himself to make the tools with which supposedly uncopiable high-value coins would be minted, can only be admired. But Chaloner had made a dangerous enemy of Newton. Chaloner's allegations that the management of the Mint, including the warden himself, were negligent to the point of corruption, and his brazen attempt to get into the inner sanctum of the Tower of London, where the Mint was housed, would not be forgiven or forgotten. From then on, for Newton, a deep and intense man, a good hater, and himself a failed multiplier, it was no longer just business; it was personal.

Newton began to assemble his evidence. In September 1697, Chaloner was committed to Newgate on a charge of high treason. Having bribed the chief witness against him to flee the country, he was acquitted at trial. Newton had him arrested again in October 1698. This time, the warden had assembled more witnesses than Chaloner was able to bribe or suborn.

In the end, the uneducated weaver's son was no match for the finest mind of his generation. In March 1699 Chaloner, who had escaped the gallows five times before, faced two counts of high treason at the Old Bailey. Of his former bravado not a trace remained; his cockiness had given way to blind terror. The trial was swift and merciless. On being sentenced to death, 'He struggl'd and flounc'd about for Life, like a Whale struck with a Harping-Iron.' In desperation, he wrote to the man who had pursued and jailed him, begging Newton to speak up on his behalf:

> most mercifull Sir
> I am going to be murtherd although perhaps you may think not but tis true …
> O Dear Sir do this mercifull deed O my offending you has brought this upon me O for God's sake if not mine keep me from being murdered O dear Sir nobody can save me but you.
> O God my God I shall be murdered unless you save me O I hope God will move your heart with mercy and pitty to do this thing for me I am
> Your near murdered humble servant
> W Chaloner

The letter went unanswered. Chaloner's ride had come to an end.

The Finest Scientific Minds

In his book *Genome: The Autobiography of a Species in 23 Chapters* (1999), evolutionary biologist Matt Ridley observes that animals will choose risky replication over a safe and barren old age. Humans are not so different in this respect. The life of a counterfeiter is as precarious as that of the butterflies we met earlier. The allure of mimicry, the carefree use of false colours and borrowed patterns, is irresistible even in the face of casual and commonplace death. Despite the twenty-seven counterfeiters he executed, Newton's efforts proved in the end to be no more than a temporary deterrent. He couldn't stop the forgers forging. Nor, it seems, could anyone else. The records of the Old Bailey are full of hangings and burnings of those souls determined enough – or desperate enough – to counterfeit. Although the burning of women for treason was abolished in 1790, the authorities continued to hang counterfeiters of both sexes. The barbarity was memorably satirised by George Cruikshank, who produced his 1819 caricature of a Bank of England note after seeing women hanged for passing forged notes worth as little as £1.

The first paper money printed in America was produced by the Massachusetts Bay Colony in about 1690, a response to the home government's policy of keeping the American colonies short of coin. Several colonial banks also began issuing private bills of credit and banknotes. Soon there were so many different types and designs in circulation that the counterfeiters had a field day. Surmising correctly that someone in, for instance, Maryland would be unable to tell if a Connecticut or Pennsylvania note was authentic, they flooded the market with forged and falsified notes.

Once again, it took an exceptional mind to fight back: Benjamin Franklin, scientist, polymath, diplomat. Franklin began his career as a printer. His firm manufactured paper money for Pennsylvania, New Jersey, and Delaware, and in 1737 he devised 'nature printing', an ingenious solution to the all-too-easy faking of banknotes. Using leaf-casts and copper

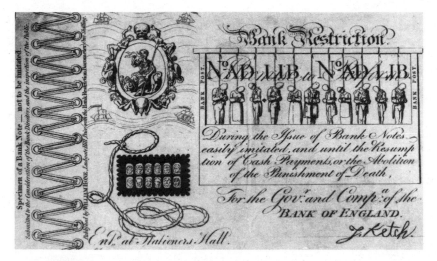

Fig. 7.1. Cruikshank's caricature of a banknote with shackles and scaffold and bearing the signature of 'Jack Ketch', the proverbial name for an executioner, in place of that of the Chief Cashier.

press plates to transfer the complex pattern and detail from foliage onto the back of banknotes, Franklin created the precursor to the raised and textured intaglio printing still in use today.*

But it never takes the counterfeiters and fraudsters very long to find ways around even the most advanced anti-forgery techniques. In 1862, the *New York Times* estimated that there were 6,000 varieties of altered, spurious, and imitation banknotes in circulation. By the paper's calculation, out of 1,300 banks (not taking into account 'wildcat, closing, closed and worthless' ones), only 100 had *not* had their notes counterfeited in some way. So bulky were the many illustrated

---

* Franklin's most imaginative anti-counterfeiting idea came to him in 1739, when he began printing bills for Pennsylvania on which he deliberately misspelled the name of the colony as 'Pensilvania'. A counterfeiter, Franklin figured, would correct the spelling on the assumption that the genuine bills were themselves fakes produced by a less literate criminal.

Fig. 7.2. A 1776 leaf-printed New Jersey six-pound note
bearing the inscription: 'To counterfeit is *Death*.'

manuals of counterfeit notes that prudent parties consulted in
the course of any commercial transaction, that their proportions
rivalled that of family Bibles. (As well as being bulky, time-
consuming, and inconvenient, these manuals could pose more
problems than they solved. John Thompson's *Autographical
Counterfeit Detector* of 1853 included 'authentic' facsimiles of
bank officers' signatures, an innovation far more likely to help
counterfeiters than businesses.) By the end of the American Civil
War, when fake banknotes were used by the North as an
economic weapon, fully a third of all currency in circulation in
the United States was counterfeit.

Any number of design and technical innovations have been used
to deter the forgers. One popular tactic was to increase the
complexity of banknote design, to make it difficult for engravers
to manufacture false plates. Another was to use special materials.
Many countries still use fabric, usually cotton or linen rag, to
make notes more durable (as you will know if you've ever seen a

banknote in your pocket after it's been through the wash); appropriately enough, the USA has sometimes used denim too. Modern detector pens use iodine ink that remains yellow or colourless on genuine fibre-based notes but turns the starch in fake paper-based notes black. This short-lived advantage has been eroded by ingenious counterfeiters, who have started bleaching genuine low-denomination notes to produce blank stock paper which produces the right result for the detector pens and is then reprinted as notes of higher denomination. Banks have retaliated in turn by adopting different sized paper for different denominations. And so the to-and-fro of the arms race goes on. The new digital printing techniques and high quality scanners that came on the market around the end of the twentieth century gave the advantage to the counterfeiters once more: with the disappearance of the need for sophisticated engraving or printing skills, anyone with an electronic printer or scanner could make money. The resulting fakes were often of only mediocre quality. But like the butterfly mimic that looks similar enough to its unpalatable model, a fake banknote only needs to be a good enough imitation to pass muster at a busy supermarket checkout.

I'm intrigued by the parallels between banknotes and nature's mimics. With inks that fluoresce under ultraviolet light, shimmering holograms embedded in its fabric, and sublime detailing almost too small for the eye to see, the twenty-first-century banknote is an object of beauty. It was not designed as a work of art any more than the prinia's speckled and spotted eggs were, but it is one all the same. The beauty of the banknote, like the beauty of the eggs, is a side-effect of the evolutionary arms race, a reminder that to multiply means to reproduce in more senses than one.

Multiplication is the wellspring of life. We are here at all because we can multiply ourselves, because one copy of our genetic blueprint produced another copy, and that copy produced yet another copy, and so on. Reproduction is what we do best.

A few years ago, in 2011, Timothy Geithner, United States Secretary of the Treasury, was extolling the new $100 bills, or 'Benjamins' (a nod to Franklin, whose portrait has appeared on the $100 bill since 1914). A high-tech triumph, they boasted an image of the Liberty Bell that changed from copper to green as the note was tilted, and special 3D technology used for a blue ribbon on the front that appeared to move from side to side as you moved your head. 'As with previous US Currency redesign,' Geithner was quoted as saying, 'this note incorporates the best technology to ensure we're staying ahead of the counterfeiters.' And I remember thinking, 'Staying ahead'? Is that the best you can do? 'Staying ahead' is not beating the counterfeiters, it's owning up to the fact that you're only going to be in the lead for a short time before they catch up with you.

In every generation, the finest scientific minds have been determined to discover what it will take to finally win the race against the counterfeiters. Our age is no different. Scott Aaronson, professor of computer science at the University of Texas at Austin and a leading light in computational complexity theory, has been researching the creation of a form of 'quantum money' using the electron-spin properties of sub-atomic particles. Unlike the Newtonian universe, governed by the classical laws of motion, where the behaviour of a body can be predicted, the quantum world is subject to Heisenberg's uncertainty principle, which states that we cannot know all things about a particle at the same time. It is impossible to copy a quantum particle's state exactly. If you could therefore somehow link money to a quantum particle, you could, in theory at least, make money that is impossible to copy. To be honest, the detail of the professor's PowerPoint presentation, with its references to such arcana as the Complexity-Theoretic No-Cloning Theorem, lost me early on; but his summing up is clear: 'This is science fiction, but it's science fiction that doesn't violate any of the known laws of physics.'*

In any event, as Aaronson points out elsewhere, in the Newtonian world no one has yet disproved the 'trivial' theorem of uncopiable cash, that 'any printing technology the good guys can build, bad guys can in principle build also'. In other words, whatever one man can invent, another man can copy. Whatever technology one side can muster, the other side will eventually muster – and master – too. In short, what one man can make, another can fake.

Money is essentially interchangeable, designed to be so, like all commodities. One barrel of oil is much like another. Gold is fungible, whether you measure it in ingots, coins, or troy ounces. But we like to think that there is a difference between the fungible and the expressive. Between the anonymous commodities we create for trade and the unique objects we create as art. The former are multiples, the latter are singular. Beauty, imagination, emotional power, belong in the realm of art, in our need to create works rooted in time and place. Artworks are artefacts with meaning, that are culturally specific, with a special stamp of authenticity and originality. Objects that are made unique by our interactions with them, by the artist and the era. Not by electron spin.

---

* This kind of quantum computing is currently only at the 'proof of concept' stage in very top research centres, so admittedly there will be a few practical problems to solve first. You need to build a quantum computer, then create quantum wallets, then find a way to prevent your quantum money from decohering …

There are many peculiarities and paradoxes in the annals of authenticity, but the one that takes us into the next chapter is this. Governments used to hang imitators, copyists, counterfeiters. Why do artists – and especially twentieth-century masters of the multiple – put them on the payroll?

8

ATTENTION SEEKERS

The Authentication Game

'Why don't you ask my assistant Gerry Malanga some questions? He did a lot of my paintings.'

Andy Warhol, interview with *Cavalier*
magazine, 1966

'Repetition is Reputation.'

Attributed to Andy Warhol

In the spring of 1618, Sir Dudley Carleton, the ambitious and upwardly mobile English ambassador to the Netherlands, receives a letter from the Flemish painter Peter Paul Rubens, with whom he is arranging an exchange of artworks. Rubens is willing to take a shipment of Carleton's antiquities – heads and figures in marble, acquired during the ambassador's stay in Venice – in exchange for some of his paintings. The question Rubens is writing to ask is, *which* paintings would His Excellency like to trade for his treasures?

Rubens has made a list of the pictures in his house in Antwerp, and offers Carleton 'the flower of my stock'. The list includes: 'A Prometheus bound on Mount Caucasus, with an eagle which pecks his liver', which he assures Carleton is 'Original, by my hand', adding that 'the eagle [is] done by Snyders' (an artist renowned for his skill in depicting wild animals); 'A St Sebastian, nude' and 'Daniel among many lions, taken from life', both by his hand; 'A Last Judgment', which Rubens tells him was 'begun by one of my pupils ... but this one, not being finished, would be entirely retouched by my own hand, and by this means would pass as original'. Or perhaps the ambassador might prefer 'A picture of an Achilles clothed as a woman', which Rubens describes as 'done by the best of my pupils, and the whole retouched by my hand; a most delightful picture, and full of many very beautiful young girls'.

Carleton writes back. He is not interested in any work by assistants or pupils; every brushstroke must be the master's. He selects only the autograph paintings, those done exclusively by Rubens himself. Rubens acquiesces cheerfully in this selection. At the same time, he exhorts his Excellency not to 'think that the others are mere copies, for they are so well retouched by my hand that they are hardly to be distinguished from originals'. What is more, 'they are rated at a much lower price'. The deal is satisfactorily concluded.*

A couple of years later, Carleton is again in correspondence with Rubens, this time on behalf of Henry Danvers, a courtier Carleton is anxious to curry favour with. Danvers has bought from Rubens a picture of a lion, tiger, and leopard hunt that he plans to give to King Charles I. But he's started to question whether his Rubens is, in fact, really a Rubens. He writes to Carleton to complain that the famous artist's touch seems to be missing from the painting: '[I]n every paynters opinion ...

---

* More than satisfactorily from Rubens's point of view, as he later enlists Carleton's help in obtaining copyright protection against reproductions of his work, and in 1620 the Dutch government forbids all engravers and etchers from copying Rubens's work for seven years.

[Rubens] hath sent hether a peece scarse touched by his own hand, and the postures so forced, as the Prince will not admitt the picture into his galerye.' When Carleton passes this on, Rubens is unabashed. He freely admits that very little of the work was done by him. As he points out, 'If I had done the entire work with my own hand, it would be well worth twice as much.' But if Danvers wants, he is happy to paint another, this time 'all to be done in my own hand'.

On one side, a famous and in-demand artist, for whom there are only so many hours in the day. Who can blame him for wanting to increase his output by using talented studio assistants? On the other, ambitious diplomats and courtiers for whom art is the currency of patronage and preferment, anxious to ensure that they are getting their hands on what is most genuine and hence most valuable. For them, a picture in the artist's hand, and solely in the artist's hand, is the real deal. For them, authenticity equals authorship.

The Doubtful Princess

The art world – that handy catch-all term for those who make, market, buy, and sell art in a shiny bazaar that includes high-end galleries and low-end artists' studios, institutions, and seats of learning – is endlessly examining authenticity. All too often, livelihoods depend on it. Any change in authenticity, an attribution (or worse a *de*attribution), will immediately be reflected in the price of a piece.

But sometimes you can't just drop a note to the artist to ask, 'Is this one of yours?' Take the case of Canadian-born collector Peter Silverman. In a New York dealer's one day in January 2007, he chanced upon an Old Master drawing by an unidentified artist (see Plate 8). Made in ink and coloured chalks on vellum, it depicted a young girl in Renaissance costume. As Silverman tells it, his heart started to beat 'a million times a minute ... I immediately thought this could be a Florentine artist. The idea of Leonardo came to me in a flash.'

If the artist is no longer around to authenticate a piece, the next best thing is an expert. The authentication of an Old Master is a matter of connoisseurship – expert judgement by eye – and provenance – scholarly historical research. Who painted it? When and where did they do so, and for whom? Did they make any copies? What were all the layers and stages in its making? Has it been restored? What has been its journey from owner to owner? Silverman found several experts who were willing to attribute his drawing to Leonardo da Vinci, the transcendent genius of the Italian Renaissance. Pre-eminent among them was Martin Kemp, professor of art history at Oxford University. Kemp agreed that Silverman's picture was by the great man. He even wrote a book detailing how he had come to that conclusion.

Kemp not only ascribed the picture to Leonardo, he also suggested that the girl was one Bianca Sforza, an illegitimate teenage daughter of the Duke of Milan, at whose court Leonardo worked in the 1480s and 1490s. Kemp named the drawing 'La Bella Principessa' – even though no one has ever suggested that Bianca was actually a princess. As well as Kemp's eye and art-historical expertise, a good deal of science was brought to bear on Silverman's picture. The vellum was carbon-dated to some time between 1440 and 1650. Pigments were analysed; high-resolution multispectral scans were done to reveal any earlier images in lower layers. A Canadian art examiner by the name of Peter Paul Biro studied the drawing and claimed to have found Leonardo's fingerprint on it. The idea of touching something that Leonardo himself might have touched was exhilarating.

Why are we so obsessed with 'artist's hand' authenticity? Is it because in our hearts we believe that a work of art is made in an almost divinely inspired moment of creation, that it loses its uniqueness, its 'aura', by being reproduced? In his most famous essay, the philosopher Walter Benjamin described the specialness of that inimitable instant: 'Even with the most perfect reproduction, one thing stands out: the here and now of the work of art – its unique existence in the place where it is at the moment.'

Buoyed by Kemp's book, excitable reports – many of them emanating from the owner of the picture – started to surface that the 'Bella Principessa' might be worth as much as $150 million. If it was really by Leonardo, it was not just by a genius, it also had the most valuable attribute that an Old Master can have: scarcity. Nothing excites buyers more than a limited or 'exclusive' supply. There exist fewer than a score of paintings attributed to Leonardo; authentic drawings by him can be counted in the low hundreds. Unfortunately for Silverman, though, a number of experts very publicly doubted that the drawing was by Leonardo. One museum director, who asked to remain anonymous, told Richard Dorment, chief art critic of the *Daily Telegraph*, that he believed the picture to be 'a screaming 20th century fake', conjured up from a 'compilation of obviously Leonardoesque elements that is not even close to Leonardo himself'.* In a pointed snub, the National Gallery in London

---

* In 2015, prolific forger and former jailbird Sean Greenhalgh claimed that he had drawn the girl in the portrait, basing her features on a 'snotty' girl called Sally he had worked with in the 1970s at a Co-op supermarket in Bolton. As was pointed out, if Greenhalgh had made the drawing, he must have done so at the age of less than 17.

declined to include Silverman's picture in a major exhibition of Leonardo's time in Milan.

The Authenticity Scale

There are ways an artwork can be authentic without being quite *as* authentic as the 'artist's hand' gold standard. Imagine for a moment you are in the artist's studio. The master has made a drawing or preparatory sketch, and then left it to his pupils to turn his design into a finished painting. In the standard terminology of the art world, this would be classified as a genuine 'Studio of …' – less valuable than a work done entirely by the master, but some of his skill, talent, and aura would still be there, reflected both in his students' paintwork and in any re-touching by his hand. Centuries later, legions of experts will pore over the paint handling, brushstrokes, and elements of composition in order to come to a view as to who did what, the price of the work depending on how much can be attributed to the master or whether, as one cynical collector has put it, 'the artist just breathed on it'.

The experts might conclude that the piece was of the period, but made by another, lesser, artist. In that case, it is conventionally labelled 'Circle of …' Or it might not be of the period at all. Ten years before Silverman's epiphany moment in New York, the then owner of the 'Bella Principessa' took it to be valued by Christie's auction house. She explained that her late husband had believed it to be by Ghirlandaio, one of the greatest painters of the Renaissance. After a cursory fifteen minutes' examination, a Christie's specialist in Old Master drawings declared it to be 'German School, early nineteenth century' – that is, by an unnamed German artist imitating Ghirlandaio or one of his contemporaries some four hundred years later. On the art world's authenticity scale this might be classified as 'Manner of …': 'a work executed in the style of the artist, but of a later date'. A nineteenth-century imitation of a Renaissance master is very unlikely to be as valuable as the original, no matter how similar they might appear on the surface. The disappointed owner accepted the verdict and put the drawing up for auction, where it sold for just over $22,000.

Twelve years later, when the art world was abuzz with 'newly discovered Leonardo masterpiece' fever, she sued Christie's for damages.*

Authentication is a process of valuation that itself creates value. Ultimately, though, the market is the judge. Whether the 'Bella Principessa' is worth $150 million or $22,000 will only be known when – if – she is actually put up for sale. Although Silverman claims he was offered $60 million for her in 2012, she has never appeared on the market, and the poor Principessa is believed to languish unseen in a Geneva Freeport warehouse.

Seeing Red

Another picture, this time a twentieth century one. Another buyer, and another very public dust-up. No need for experts here, both the style and the subject are unmistakable. The picture in Fig. 8.1 and in Plate 9 is one of a series of Andy Warhol self-portraits with a red background screen-printed in

---

* The court ruled that she had left it too late to make a claim that Christie's had misvalued the drawing, and dismissed her case. She was, however, entitled to get back the original frame, which Christie's had removed before selling the picture.

Fig. 8.1. Joe Simon-Whelan and the 'Warhol' that was
authentic until it wasn't.

1965, which was bought by a film producer called Joe Simon-Whelan in 1989. It was valued at a little, then a lot, and then … well, therein lies the problem, because when it came to authenticating the picture, the scale that had worked so well for Leonardo, Rubens, and co. simply didn't work for Warhol. The scale can't deal with a picture like this. It has no brushstrokes to prove that it was painted by Andy. Indeed it probably wasn't painted by Andy. It could just as well have been made by Andy's long-time assistant Gerard Malanga. As Andy once said, Malanga 'did a lot of my paintings'. But perhaps 'painted' is the wrong word since the picture required so few painterly skills that it could have been made by almost anybody, and frequently was. There's no 'original' from which copies could be made because there was never meant to be a single original; most of Warhol's work at the time consists of deliberately repetitive, machine-made series of multiples. There's no real connection to the 'artist's hand' either, because Andy famously said, 'I want to be a machine', and had rubber stamps made of his signature so that others could 'sign' his pictures for him. Not for nothing was his studio known as the Factory.

You might think that it doesn't make much sense to ask if a picture made in this way is 'genuine' or not. Isn't that the kind of traditional art-world thinking that Warhol challenged? Yet people have spent millions battling over whether this screen print is an authentic Warhol, and they must have been fighting over something. The question is not just how we tell how 'genuine' or how 'fake' this picture is, but whether it even makes sense to raise that issue at all. It's not a hypothetical question either. There was a time when it was a two million dollar question, which was what Joe Simon-Whelan thought he could sell the picture for. And then it became a seven million dollar question, which was the amount spent on legal fees by an outfit called the Andy Warhol Authentication Board in an effort to establish that the picture was *not* by Andy Warhol.

The story of Joe Simon-Whelan's Warhol – 'Warhol'? – says a great deal about the problems of authenticity in our modern world. What happens when all the things that used to make something 'authentic' no longer apply? It's not just a problem for well-heeled art collectors. Because 'authentic' is so often a proxy for value, the question seeps into our everyday lives, as we decide what to eat, what to wear, what to spend our money on. This is no art-world sideshow. The story of this picture's journey from worthless to precious and back again is the story of how value detached itself from authenticity and went its own way, of how the very meaning of authenticity changed, and of what came to take its place.

When Andy Met Gerry

It all began in 1963. A year after he had made his famous Marilyn diptych, completed within weeks of the star's death, Warhol was looking for an assistant. He had met Gerard Malanga, the man who was to become his most important associate, at a party given by some underground film makers, and then again a short time later at a poetry reading. 'Andy was experimenting with silkscreens at the time I met him,' recalled Gerard (who had experience of silkscreening men's neckwear), 'but when I started working with him the pace was accelerating. We started just churning them out in the summer of 1963 and carried on until the fall of '67.'

Silkscreening is essentially a sophisticated form of stencilling. The artist's design is printed onto transparent acetate film, which is used to create mesh screen stencils; paint is pushed through the screen onto the canvas or paper below. The paint sits on the surface, giving silkscreened images their tactile quality. Warhol, transitioning at the time from a career as a commercial artist (his drawings of shoes and handbags were popular with high-end fashion magazines and department stores), and keen to make his name in the art world, had hit upon an idea that was to make him very famous indeed. He would make his silkscreens from photographs rather than drawings. And not just any photographs, but powerfully iconic ones: movie stars, car crashes, electric chairs. Rendered in vivid colours, with little or no fine detail, repetitive reproductions of images captured by an automatic eye, they would become the defining Warhol look.

Andy would pick a photograph – a shot of Elizabeth Taylor, say – and send it off to the printers to be made into acetates and

Fig. 8.2. Andy (standing) and Gerard (sitting, in white T-shirt)
in Warhol's studio, September 1964.

screens. Gerard's job was to position each screen over the canvas
and push Liquitex acrylic colours (pink face, red lips, green
eyeshadow) through the screen; once the colours were in place,
Gerard would position the final screen to create the black
outline of the picture. If Gerry made a mistake with the posi-
tioning of the screens, Andy would say 'it's part of the Art' or
'it's Divine Accident, let's keep it in'.

Gerard and Andy worked fast. In the first year alone, they
produced eighty portraits of Liz Taylor, several versions of over-
lapping images of a gun-toting Elvis Presley in cowboy attire,
and a 'Death and Disaster' series that included *Orange Car
Crash Fourteen Times* (repeated images of a multiple-death car
crash) and *Suicide (Fallen Body)* (twelve repetitions of a photograph of Evelyn McHale, who had jumped to her death from
the Empire State Building).

In August 1967, fed up with the Factory scene and obsessed with an Italian society beauty called Benedetta, Gerard left New York for Rome. He had a one-way ticket, but Andy had told him that if he needed money to get back he would send it. After a month in Italy, he sent a postcard: 'PLEASE HAVE ANDY SEND ME MONEY. HE PROMISED. AM BROKE.'

Andy didn't answer.

Gerard has never talked openly about the episode, so it's not clear exactly when the idea of making his own 'Warhols' occurred to him. Short of money, he met an Italian princess who was keen to acquire a Warhol, and he set out to do alone what he had so often done with Andy. He picked out a photo of the revolutionary Che Guevara after his death in Bolivia, had a silk-screen made of it, and ran off two pictures on canvas, one for the princess and another to sell. He also made another fifty prints on paper. He wrote to Andy saying that he presumed this was OK with him and that if he didn't hear anything to the contrary, he would just go ahead with it. Andy didn't answer. Gerard wrote again, saying he was sure Andy wouldn't have any problem with him selling his silkscreen prints as 'Andy Warhols'.

The Malanga 'Warhols' exhibited at the Tartaruga Gallery in Rome in February 1968 sold out before the exhibition had even begun. But word had spread that the pictures were not all they seemed to be. Gallery owner Plinio de Martiis informed Gerard that forgery carried a 15- to 20-year sentence in Italy. Gerard wired Andy, begging him to endorse the pictures. 'I WILL BE IN AN ITALIAN MUNICIPAL PRISON WITHOUT BAIL … PLEASE HELP ME! PLEASE HELP ME!', signing it, 'PEACE, GERARD.'

Eventually Andy broke his silence. He agreed to authenticate the pictures – on condition that he received the proceeds of sale. 'CHE GUEVARAS ARE ORIGINALS', his telegram ran.

'HOWEVER MALANGA NOT AUTHORISED TO SELL. CONTACT ME BY LETTER FOR ADJUSTMENTS. ANDY WARHOL.'

This little-known episode, in as much as anything about Warhol can be 'little-known', is a significant moment in the history of art and authenticity. When the Malanga 'Warhols' became Andy Warhols by a process of retrospective authorisation, it marked a shift from artist's hand to artist's brand. A post-industrial transformation of the role of the creator from 'author' to 'author*iser*'. What an artist said about a work became as important as whether he had created it or not. Andy's mere word could turn a not-Warhol into a Warhol. As the astute critic Richard Dorment has pointed out, Andy 'had come to realize that a painting could be an original Andy Warhol whether or not he had ever touched it'.

In the modern world, as Andy was already aware, presentation counts for more than substance. Warhol also recognised that there was one step beyond the artist as authoriser: the artist as celebrity endorser. 'Maybe we can make some money off my name', he said to his business manager as early as 1965. On 10 February 1966, he placed an advert in the *Village Voice*: 'I'll endorse with my name any of the following: clothing, AC-DC, cigarettes, small tapes, sound equipment, ROCK 'N' ROLL RECORDS, anything, film and film equipment, Food, Helium, Whips, MONEY!! love and kisses ANDY WARHOL. EL 5-9941.'

A year after that, around the time of Gerard's Roman adventure, Andy launched Factory Additions, a business devoted to turning out prints on paper of his most popular images. For the first run, 2,500 prints in various colourways were made of Warhol's famous 1962 Marilyns by a commercial silkscreening company. The editor of one art magazine wondered whether 'machine-made assembly-line stuff – mass-produced art like Andy Warhol's Campbell soup tins', sold directly to the public, was going to put art galleries out of business.

The Video Party

Joe Simon-Whelan's red self-portrait had its origins in a photo that Andy had taken of himself in a booth in 1964. Warhol turned the photo into a series of silkscreened self-portraits. The following year, 1965, Andy announced that he was giving up painting in favour of film-making. Although he had made some experimental movies on 16 mm film,* he was keen to try out one of the then new, and very expensive, video cameras. The publisher of *Tape Recorder* magazine, Richard Ekstract, put together a deal. Andy would be loaned the video camera in exchange for his endorsement of it. Moreover, Ekstract would throw an underground party to celebrate the premiere of whatever movie Andy made. And if Andy lent Ekstract the acetates from which he'd made the 1964 self-portrait silkscreens, Ekstract would get a new series of ten printed to be exhibited at the party.

Andy gave Ekstract the acetates, and gave him instructions as to the shades of paint to be used in the silkscreens. Ekstract asked a friend called Herman Meyers, who worked in advertising, to arrange for the work to be done by the Norgus Silk Screen Company Inc. of New Jersey. When the pictures were made, Ekstract took the acetates back to the Factory.

---

* Mostly of whoever happened to come into the studio, and more than a few of Gerard having sex on the studio couch with a succession of female partners.

Fig. 8.3. Edie Sedgwick and Andy Warhol
pose with up-to-the-minute video equipment,
with a Red Series portrait in the background.

Andy and his Factory 'superstar' Edie Sedgwick were photographed underneath one of the self-portraits, draping themselves
around a bulky video camera that, to modern eyes at least,
resembles an outsize KitchenAid. Andy made his film, called
Outer and Inner Space,* and Ekstract threw a party for the
premiere. As always, publicity was a central part of the
exchange. 'He got half a column in the *New York Times*', said
Ekstract. 'To him that was a success.' As Andy was to say later
of this kind of attention, 'Don't read it; measure it in column

---

* Described in the *New York Times* as 'a masterpiece of video art made
before the term even existed'.

inches.' After the party, Andy gave the ten red self-portraits to Ekstract, who kept one for himself, gave two to the printers, and distributed the rest among people who'd helped with the project. The one that was destined to become Joe Simon-Whelan's went to Herman Meyers.

A few years later, in 1969, Andy gave another of the red self-portraits to his European dealer, Bruno Bischofberger. On the back of the canvas, he wrote 'To Burno [sic] B Andy Warhol 69'.

Andy Warhol died on 22 February 1987, leaving $220 million, an enormous quantity of artworks – around 10,000 paintings, drawings, and prints alone – and instructions for a foundation to benefit the visual arts. The foundation's trustees were to include two of Andy's oldest friends, Fred Hughes and Vincent Fremont. By May 1987, they had set up the Andy Warhol Foundation.

Shortly after Andy's death, the owner of the red self-portrait given to Herman Meyers in 1965 took it to Christie's auction house to be sold. Christie's submitted it to the Andy Warhol Foundation for authentication, and trustee Vincent Fremont stamped it with Andy's signature three times. With no doubt as to its authenticity, the picture sold for $28,000 (a sum that would get you a 'Bella Principessa' a decade or so later). Then in early 1988 Fred Hughes was asked to examine it by a potential purchaser. Hughes wrote on the leftmost edge of the picture: 'I certify this is an original painting by Andy Warhol completed by him in 1964 [sic].' Freeze-frame this moment. The picture is still very much an authentic Warhol, certified as such by two separate trustees of the Andy Warhol Foundation. And it is getting more valuable by the day. In August 1989, Joe Simon-Whelan, who had met Andy several times and admired him greatly, became its proud owner when he bought the picture for $195,000 'instead of buying a house'.

The Value of Art

When Warhol was shot by Valerie Solanas in 1968 and thought to be on the point of death, the fabled art curator Henry Geldzahler turned to his boyfriend and said, 'Do you know what that does to the values of the paintings?' – adding quickly, 'Don't ever tell anyone that I said that.' Geldzahler was absolutely right. Warhol prices did rise after his death, as art prices do once the market knows the artist won't be around to make any more. As prices rose, the Andy Warhol Foundation received an increasing number of requests for authentication; in 1995 the Foundation set up the Andy Warhol Authentication Board to deal with them. But the Authentication Board behaved oddly from the start. They wrote to the owners of Warhols inviting them to submit their works for authentication, but required a written undertaking that owners would not sue in the event of a negative verdict. Unusually, the Board refused to reveal their deliberations, on the grounds that such information might assist forgers. Most outrageously of all, if they decided a work was not a genuine Warhol, they would stamp 'DENIED' in red letters on the back before sending the picture back to its owner.

By 2001, Joe Simon-Whelan was aware that his picture might now be worth around $2 million. He decided to sell, and duly submitted it to the Authentication Board. What should have been a formality turned into a nightmare. On 2 February 2002 his picture was returned. To his horror it had been stamped 'DENIED' in red ink across the back. No reason was given. Joe's $2 million picture, twice authenticated by the Andy Warhol Foundation, had been rendered virtually worthless by the Authentication Board set up by the very same Foundation. Joe was beside himself. Advised to 'trace the history of the piece' and then resubmit it to the Board, Joe put his life on hold. He collected affidavits in support from an extraordinary array of witnesses: from Nicholas Serota, Director of the Tate Gallery in London; from Paul Morrissey, the manager of Warhol's Factory in 1965, who knew the details of the arrangement with Richard Ekstract; from the company that had made the red self-portraits; from Warhol's dealers at the time – and from Gerard Malanga, who knew more than anyone about Warhol's attitude to authenticity. Thus armed, Joe resubmitted the picture to the Authentication Board. In 2003 it was rejected for the second time. The Board stamped another red 'DENIED' on it, at a 45 degree angle to the first, making a crossed 'X' of double denial on the back of the picture.

At about the same time, the Authentication Board also rejected the red self-portrait that Andy had given to Bruno Bischofberger in 1969. In a statement that can only be regarded as surreal, they wrote: 'It is the opinion of the authentication board that the said work is NOT the work of Andy Warhol, but that the said work was signed, dedicated and dated by him.'

The Authentication Board were clearly struggling with definitions of art and authenticity. In the words of Georgina Adam of the *Art Newspaper*, 'The foundation want Andy Warhol to be a high artist with high ideals, they want him to be like Leonardo da Vinci. They don't want to think that he just signed a lot of stuff without even looking at it, but he did.' The Authentication Board were trying to restrict 'real' Warhols to ones where Andy was present as the work was being made, when Andy's point was precisely that he was trying not to be there. They wanted uniqueness, when Andy made multiples. They sought the artist's hand from the emperor of the brand. Unable to see that Warhol's artistic journey was one long retreat from the canvas, permeated by bouts of unreliable authorisation and jokes against the art establishment, they tied themselves up in knots.

Doubly denied, Joe retired stunned and upset. After a while, and emboldened by the many others who had received similar verdicts on their pictures, he picked himself up again and did something he really couldn't afford to do. On 13 July 2007 Joe filed a lawsuit against the Authentication Board. By the time the Authentication Board had spent $7 million before the case even came to trial, Joe gave up.

Art as an Asset Class

The fact that Andy's antics diluted the concept of authenticity in art hasn't troubled the operators in the art world bazaar. In the decades since Warhol's death, his prices have risen inexorably. In an era when returns on conventional investments have been generally low, investors have cast around for new things to put their money into. Whereas Andy's world had been one of artists, filmmakers, fashion magazines, celebrities, and rich collectors, now fund managers and even accountancy firms were taking an interest in the art market. One of Andy's 1963 Elvises sold for over $100 million; in 2010, Warhols accounted for almost a fifth of the whole contemporary art market. In the words of the *Financial Times*, Warhol had become a one-man art market index.

The buyers were a new breed of collectors, high net worth individuals who didn't seem to mind that Warhols were not exactly scarce, nor that they were not exactly authentic, nor that they were not always made entirely by Warhol himself. Many of the new buyers were less interested in the works themselves and more in what their purchases said about them. Warhols had become luxury or conspicuous consumption goods, status symbols, a quick way to show the world that you had arrived.

Warhol pictures are almost unique in how well they globalise and cross cultures because they are so easy to 'get'. As the art critic Robert Hughes explained in *The Shock of the New* (1980), our uniquely congested culture has changed how we consume art. An Old Master painting has layers of meaning that unfold as you look and re-look at the work. It belongs to a world of few distractions, a slow time of singular objects and the leisure with which to study them. Strip an image of complexity, says Hughes, and what you get is a sign, like a poster, or an icon with a single meaning. Signs that are universal, easily digested, and rapidly apprehended. Warhol's pictures are perfect for art's new habitat, which is, as Hughes put it, a forest of media. The new buyers are cash rich, but time poor. They have lots of dollars to spare, but very little mindspace. If you can establish something as a 'must have', you have bagged the scarcest resource of all – their attention.

At first, people thought they could solve the problem of choice with more information. The more you explained about a product or service (or a work of art or literature, or a political movement), the more value you would create in consumers' minds. But as Herbert A Simon, one of the founding fathers of decision-making theory, pointed out, information may be the problem rather than the solution. As Simon famously wrote: 'In an information-rich world, the wealth of information means a dearth of something else: a scarcity of whatever it is that information consumes. What information consumes is rather obvious: it consumes the attention of its recipients. Hence a wealth of information creates a poverty of attention and a need to allocate that attention efficiently among the overabundance of information sources that might consume it.'

Once, it was resources that were scarce. Now it is attention. Conventional economists have been slow to heed the changes of this 'comedy of plenty', claims Richard A Lanham, author of *The Economics of Attention: Style and Substance in the Age of Information* (2006), who calls the move from scarcity of resources to scarcity of attention 'the scarcity shift'. Our world has moved from one of 'stuff' (physical and material goods, commodities, 'things') to 'fluff' (attention, awareness). The scarcity shift moves the art world's centre of gravity from the objects that artists create to the attention that beholders bring to them. And, as Andy Warhol instinctively understood, attracting attention is a matter of style rather than substance.

Authenticity and Ubiquity

Since Andy's death, his Foundation has carried on his work of attracting attention. In particular, the Foundation has ensured that Warhol has become the most exhibited artist in the world. Not only did it set up the Andy Warhol Museum in 1994, endowing it with nearly 4,000 iconic Warhol works as well as archival material, it has also donated 52,786 works – including tens of thousands of photographs – to 322 institutions worldwide. In addition, the Museum lends works from its collection to museums and galleries around the world. According to its website, 'exhibitions organized or co-organized by the Warhol Museum have been seen by over 9 million people in 25 states and 36 countries' – a reach that any mass marketer would envy. If your museum doesn't have the resources, or doesn't want to go to the trouble of curating its own show, the Warhol Museum can let it have one of its twenty pre-packaged exhibition rentals. You can choose from, among others, *Happy Warholidays*

(Andy's 1950s Christmas-themed commercial drawings); *The Late Drawings of Andy Warhol, 1973–1987* (featuring iconic images such as James Dean, Campbell's Soup, Mickey Mouse, and John Wayne); *Love, Andy* (works exploring the theme of romantic love); *Dirty Art: Andy Warhol's Torsos and Sex Parts* (described as intended for mature audiences).

One thing that has helped to keep Warhol at the top of people's minds and top of the art sales charts is the very repetitiveness of his work. Not only are his images multiples, one of a series produced from the same acetate, but the images themselves are frequently repeats of other images: fifty Marilyns, fourteen car crashes, twelve suicides. As Andy is supposed to have said, 'Repetition is Reputation.'*

As the prices of Warhol's work continue to increase, they too become part of the attention campaign. High prices – often at auctions where the work has in effect been pre-sold by way of an irrevocable bid, ensuring that there will be no embarrassingly public failure on the night – generate news. They grab our attention. 'Another Warhol sells for record price' is a headline that makes Warhols even more desirable. Desirable because they're desirable, in the elusive, illusory, circular reasoning of our attention-grabbing, positional culture.

Warhol is everywhere, an art world titan. The saturation bombing of our collective consciousness has made him more than an artist: he is a commercial behemoth. The Foundation's licensing arm keeps him in full view at all times. Andy may have died in 1987, but he lives on in 'collabs' ... with Kidrobot for children's toys; with Levi's, Paul Frank, Uniqlo for clothes; with Philip Treacy for hats; with Rosenthal for china and glassware;

---

* In fact, it was probably Elizabeth Arden, founder of the American cosmetics giant, who said, 'Repetition makes reputation and reputation makes customers.'

with Royal Elastics and Adidas for footwear; with Seiko for watches; with Burton for snowboards – and, you'll be glad to hear, with Campbell Soup Company for soup. The 'assembly-line stuff' and the high-end stuff have melded into a single über-brand. Where is the artist's hand now, the unique aura of creative genius? Authenticity has been trumped by ubiquity.

In attention markets, quantity of attention counts for more than quality because there is a limited amount of it to go around. Sometimes the most famous artists are world-class artists; sometimes they are just world-class attention-seekers. Just as the best pupil in the class isn't necessarily the one who makes the most noise, or the one who puts her hand up the most. Or the best politician the one who garners the greatest amount of coverage. Airtime is not the only or even the best measure of merit, whether for painters or presidents.

Attention is a scarce resource. If we devote disproportionate attention to the deliberately, even provocatively, inauthentic art of Andy Warhol, then we necessarily have less attention to give to other kinds of art. What's more, because we tend to value what we pay attention to, rather than paying attention to what we value, we are in danger of attributing disproportionate value to the inauthentic as well. When attention becomes the metric of success, authenticity is the loser. If we are to be more than passive consumers, we have to do more than simply heed the attention-seekers; we have to seek out what is worthy of our attention. We have to learn to pay attention to the truly authentic, to what gets lost in the clamour of inauthenticity. Conflating famous-equals-good and unknown-equals-not-worth-knowing is an easy mistake to make.

In his book *The Attention Merchants: The Epic Scramble to Get Inside Our Heads* (2016), Tim Wu, professor of law at

Columbia University, says, 'As William James observed, we must reflect that, when we reach the end of our days, our life experience will equal what we have paid attention to, whether by choice or default. We are at risk, without quite fully realising it, of living lives that are less our own than we imagine.' We have to learn to value what we should, not what we are told to.

9

ABUNDANCE

The Battle for Tuxedoland, or
Why We Overrate Originality

*'I hope I have succeeded. For even if fashion is not
entirely art, we fashion designers must behave as artists.
That is to say by sacrificing everything, sometimes even
our lives, to devote ourselves only to our work.'*

Yves Saint Laurent accepting a Lifetime
Achievement Award in 1999

*'We'd done some pictures of just this pristine white barn
and it was a misty morning. And he said: "That's my ad."
It just said RALPH LAUREN COUNTRY. There were
no models, there was nothing … You wanted to step into
that picture, and you wanted to live in that world …'*

Buffy Birrittella in the 2019 documentary *Very Ralph*

In the winter of 1992, an assistant in the press office of French couturier Yves Saint Laurent was leafing through the magazine *Jours de France Madame*. Turning a page, they spotted a photograph of a model wearing what they took to be a recently issued dress by Saint Laurent, inspired by the cut, fabric, and feel of his famous *Le Smoking* dinner suit for women.

Pausing to take a closer look, the assistant saw – *quelle horreur!* – that the picture showed not Saint Laurent's twenty-five-thousand-dollar haute couture dress, but an all but indistinguishable thousand-dollar version, the 'Tuxedo' dress, by the American Ralph Lauren. As Saint Laurent's spokesman Monsieur Girard put it, 'At first we thought this was a misunderstanding or a misspelling of "Laurent" because the dress looked so similar to ours.' The suggestion of misspelling was calculated to chime with a Gallic prejudice that while the French were couturiers and designers, creative artists summoning the muse to their studios and ateliers, their brash New World counterparts were merely copycats and jumped-up *garmentos* – garment-trade peddlers. Ralph Lauren was born Ralph Lipschitz. It had long been suspected that his taking a name so similar to one of the world's most celebrated designers was no coincidence.

Saint Laurent's lawyers promptly sued. They claimed hefty damages for infringement of copyright – unauthorised replication of Saint Laurent's design – and asked the French courts to seize all versions of Ralph Lauren's tuxedo dress, to prohibit him from manufacturing any more, and to order him to publish grovelling mea culpas and apologies in ten newspapers.

The atmosphere was not improved when Pierre Bergé, CEO of Saint Laurent Haute Couture and formerly Saint Laurent's partner, threw a hissy fit on the front page of fashion bible *Women's Wear Daily*. 'It is one thing to "take inspiration" from another designer,' he said, 'but it is quite another to steal a *modèle* [design] point by point as Ralph Lauren has done.' Ralph Lauren promptly countersued for a million francs in damages for defamation, on the grounds that since he was 'known worldwide as a designer, he has no need to seek inspiration from Saint Laurent, nor does he'.

The case was about much more than a frock, and whether one designer had or hadn't copied another's design. It was a

battle of ideas and ideals, a tussle for territory and for posses-
sion of an increasingly valuable tradition. Not just a legal
dispute, but a cultural one, pitting the Old World against the
New. To whom did the elegantly sleek black-lapelled dress, and
the soft dark dinner suit that spawned it, really belong? Whose
origin story would win the day? Who, in short, was the rightful
heir to Tuxedoland?

'Le Smoking': An Old-World Story

Yves Saint Laurent was the last of the great Parisian couturiers.
The boy wonder of the House of Dior, he launched his first
collection under his own name at 24, and was dressing the
cream of French society and the international bohemian set by
the time he was 30.

In 1966, Saint Laurent created the first 'black tie' suit for
women, the most iconic garment of his career. By refashioning
the classic men's three-button dinner suit, with its characteristic
satin lapels and side-stripes, into the elegant female *Smoking*,
Saint Laurent revolutionised fashion. At first, the suit was
regarded by his couture clients as simply too daring. At a time
when few women were permitted to wear trousers to work, and
when it was inconceivable that an haute couture client would
wear anything other than a long dress to an evening event, only
one was sold from the collection. A few years later, however,
when Saint Laurent opened his first 'Rive Gauche' prêt-à-porter
boutique, ready-to-wear versions began to be snapped up by
younger women.*

---

* Which led Saint Laurent to comment that 'la rue court plus vite que les
salons' (the street runs faster than the salons).

As his partner Pierre Bergé said, where Chanel gave women freedom, Saint Laurent gave them power. By de-gendering and appropriating menswear, Saint Laurent's suits for women helped to emancipate them. 'The thing about a tuxedo is that it is virile and feminine at the same time,' said the film star Catherine Deneuve, a long-time Saint Laurent aficionado. *Le Smoking* became Saint Laurent's signature look, and he would return to it time and again, reimagining and reinterpreting it in a riot of fabrics – velvet, cashmere, lace, satin – and in styles as varied as capes, coats, boleros, dresses, skirts, and even shorts. *

In 1970, Saint Laurent created an haute couture dress based on the *Smoking* jacket. The slim black dress paid homage to the original with its double-breasted cut, matt black wool fabric, wide jacket-style lapels of contrasting glossy black satin, and double row of buttons. Some twenty years later, feeling the time was ripe for a revival, Saint Laurent reissued the dress with a couple of tweaks. Having launched the haute couture edition, he was preparing to release the ready-to-wear version in the spring of 1993 when he saw the lookalike dress from the American impostor. No wonder the man known as 'the prince of the dinner jacket' was incandescent with rage.

The Tuxedo: A 'New World' Story

When Ralph Lauren said that he had no need to go to Paris to seek inspiration from Saint Laurent, he was right. There was

---

* A 2005 exhibition at the Yves Saint Laurent and Pierre Bergé Foundation, *Smoking Forever* (which sounds better if you say it with a French accent), displayed 50 of the 230 'Smokings' that Saint Laurent created over the course of his 40-year career.

Fig. 9.1. Yves Saint Laurent's 1992 haute
couture *Smoking* dress.

plenty to be had much closer to home, and from a place rather
than a person. About an hour's drive from where Ralph was
born in the Bronx, at the southernmost tip of what is now
Orange County, New York, are the old hunting grounds of the
Ramapough Mountain Indians and the small town of Tuxedo.

In the Algonquian language 'Tuxedo' means 'Home of the Bear', or possibly 'clear flowing water' depending on whom you believe, but this creation story really begins in 1885 when tobacco magnate and polo player Pierre Lorillard IV built a colony of weekend summer 'cottages' there for himself and his wealthy friends. This was rapidly followed by a fine building by the edge of the lake, which housed the exclusive Tuxedo Park Club.

The autumn of 1886 was particularly warm. Ahead of the Autumn Ball at the Tuxedo Club, several young blades resolved to play a little sartorial prank on the club elders. Led by Pierre Lorillard's 22-year-old son Griswold – known to all as Grizzy – they lopped off the tails of their tailcoats before waltzing into the ballroom. A fashion legend was born.*

The tuxedo freed men from the constricting tailcoats of nineteenth-century formal dress, in which it was impossible to navigate any but the stateliest dances, and even sitting down had to be approached with caution. As America transitioned from the Gilded Age to the Jazz Age, as the flappers and jazz babes of the 1920s recklessly shortened their hems and bobbed their hair, conditions were ripe for the truncated tuxedo to flourish. A decade later, the silver screen ushered in a golden age for the dinner suit as Hollywood dressed its debonair leading men in tuxedos. World War II brought a temporary halt to the jacket's stellar progress, but as the countercultural 1960s and the revolutionary 1970s gave way to the conservative (in dress as in politics) 1980s, the all-American tuxedo, so evocative of earlier glamour, was due for revival. And one man, Ralph

---

* Although the prank didn't impress the author of the 'Town Topics' column of the local newspaper, who described them as 'idiots who should be in a straitjacket'.

Lauren, prophet and high priest of American aspiration, was at the forefront of its renaissance. So much so that he even gave its name to an evening fragrance for women: *Tuxedo*.

Ralph has built his empire on the idea that anyone can partake of the American Dream – or at least his version of it. His is a cinematic vision of life, unfailingly positive and optimistic, showcased in beautifully produced advertising spreads. Ralph Lauren Country is a place for people for whom 'summer' is a verb rather than a noun: impossibly chiselled racquet-toting blue-bloods dressed in crisp tennis whites sip champagne on manicured lawns. Gatsby-esque beings end the day tuxedo-clad, bow ties fetchingly unravelled, wearing velvet slippers inspired by 'the smoking slippers worn by lords in old English manors'.* In Ralph Lauren Country, you're not so much getting dressed as entering a narrative.

It's a narrative about America. It's hard to overstate Ralph's attachment to the all-American origins of his brand – not only the tennis whites and tuxedos, but the fringed cowboy jackets, the Stetsons, the Navajo silver jewellery. He wraps himself in the flag, sometimes literally. Here he is talking in vintage Ralph-speak about an 'iconic knitted navy sweater adorned with the American flag' that he made for a magazine shoot: 'When *Life* magazine asked me to be on their cover, photographed at our Double RL Ranch, I wanted to wear something that was just as American as my weathered jeans and jean jacket ... I decided to create a hand-knit sweater with the symbol of our country at its center.'

---

* This is not parody; the copywriting department really wrote it. Ralph, or at least the Style Guide on his website, also instructs you to repair for lunch in flannels, button-down Oxford shirt, and Italian brogues hand-stitched with a boar's hair quill.

The word 'original' derives from 'origin'. The origin of Ralph Lauren's designs is a *place*. For Yves Saint Laurent, on the other hand, it is a *person*: every Saint Laurent dress has its origin in the uniquely creative designer who first sketched it on his drawing pad. Whereas the Ralph Lauren brand story is that it comes from *somewhere*, Saint Laurent emphasises that designs come from *somebody*. Each version of originality reflects the designer's cultural heritage. And each claims protection for his version of originality from a different form of intellectual property right. Saint Laurent sought to defend *Le Smoking* by basing his legal action on the Old World protection of copyright (©). Ralph Lauren claims the New World protection of trademark (™).

As the name suggests, copyright is the legal right given to authors and artists to prevent unauthorised copying of the writing or designs in which they have expressed their original ideas. Trademark, on the other hand, started as a mark that denoted the source of goods, the place where they came from – the farmer's stamp on a bag of oats, the silversmith's mark on a cup. Customers come to associate the mark with the supplier, and then with the supplier's products; if the products are of good quality, then the mark itself becomes an assurance of quality.

Ralph Lauren has registered a number of trademarks. By far the most valuable are 'Polo', 'Polo Ralph Lauren', and the famous design of two mounted polo players that epitomises the upmarket and sporting American associations of the brand. (It's worth pointing out that polo is not remotely American, and that the Afghans who invented the game some 2,000 years ago would be frankly amazed to hear it described as such, and even more amazed to hear of it being used to sell piqué cotton T-shirts.) One of the benefits of basing your intellectual property rights on trademarks, as opposed to copyright, is that you can apply your trademark to goods that are completely unrelated to the ones that you first sold under the mark. Polo™ is so linked to Ralph Lauren's style that in 1978 he launched *Polo* scent for men.*

The case of Laurent versus Lauren was tried in the Paris Tribunal de Commerce in the spring of 1994. For an extraordinary moment, the courtroom became a catwalk as two models dressed in the rival dresses paraded before judge Madeleine Cottelle. Before retiring to consider her verdict she commented, 'The Saint Laurent dress is obviously more beautiful, but that can't influence my ruling.'

The Paradox of Originality

But what does it mean to copy? And does originality deserve the status we give it anyway? Across the Atlantic another judge, Richard A Posner, has written extensively on unacknowledged literary copying, or plagiarism as it is usually known. In his slim and entertaining *The Little Book of Plagiarism* (2007), Posner points out that we have a very different attitude to originality from our predecessors. In the past, creativity was understood to happen by degrees. It was a process of evolution, of 'tweak by tweak' improvements to what had been done before, rather than the whizz-bang, winner-takes-all novelty-mongering that we think of as originality today.

Posner illustrates what he means by the example of Shakespeare's description in *Antony and Cleopatra* of the queen

---

* Not, as you might expect, the smell of sweaty men and horses, but a 'woody chypre' with middle notes of pine-needles, leather, camomile, pepper, carnation, geranium, jasmine, and rose.

in her barge on the Nile. As is well known, Shakespeare lifted one of his most celebrated passages almost word for word from Sir Thomas North's 1579 translation of Plutarch's *Lives of the Noble Grecians and Romans*. Here is North's prose:

> [S]he disdained to set forward otherwise but to take her barge in the river of Cydnus, the poop whereof was gold, the sails of purple, and the oars of silver, which kept stroke in rowing after the sound of the music of flutes, hautboys, citterns, viols, and such other instruments as they played upon in the barge. And now for the person of herself: she was laid under a pavilion of cloth of gold of tissue, apparelled and attired like the goddess Venus commonly drawn in picture, and hard by her, on either hand of her, pretty fair boys apparelled as painters do set forth god Cupid, with little fans in their hands with the which they fanned wind upon her.

And here is Shakespeare's blank verse:

> The barge she sat in, like a burnished throne,
> Burned on the water; the poop was beaten gold;
> Purple the sails, and so perfumed that
> The winds were love-sick with them; the oars were silver,
> Which to the tunes of flutes kept stroke, and made
> The water which they beat to follow faster,
> As amorous of their strokes. For her own person,
> It beggared all description: she did lie
> In her pavilion, cloth-of-gold of tissue,
> O'erpicturing that Venus where we see
> The fancy outwork nature. On each side her
> Stood pretty dimpled boys, like smiling cupids,
> With divers-coloured fans, whose wind did seem

To glow the delicate cheeks which they did cool,
And what they undid did.

Shakespeare takes North's words and creates the purest poetry from them. North's Cleopatra is dressed as a goddess; Shakespeare's *is* one, glowing, mystical, contradictory, exotic, dangerous, alluring; even the wind and the water are in love with her. As Posner puts it: if this is plagiarism, we need more plagiarism.

In any event, it's not only Shakespeare who's being 'unoriginal' here. Thomas North's work wasn't 'original': it was a translation of the first-century Greek historian Plutarch. (In fact, North wasn't even translating Plutarch; he was translating James Amyot's French translation of Plutarch.) So although you could cast North in the Saint Laurent role, as the party 'injured' by Shakespeare's imitation,* he was at the same time the imitator. Which is Posner's point. If originality consists of a series of incremental developments – if intellectual progress is made by 'standing on the shoulders of giants', to use Isaac Newton's phrase – then the paradox of originality is that every creator will have a dual role as both copier and copied.

Why do we accord such status to originality? Writing about literary plagiarism, Richard Posner argues that, 'Readers are no more interested in originality than eaters are. They are interested in the quality of the reading experience that a work gives them. Originality becomes important only when the reading market is so dense that the readers become jaded and therefore require variety to keep them entertained.'

---

* Imagine if North had been able to sue Shakespeare for infringement, just as Saint Laurent sued Lauren – think of what we would have lost if he had won.

We've already seen that that denseness, that saturation, is a feature of our age of abundance. And just as we saw in the last chapter that the meaning of 'authenticity' has shifted as a result, so too the meaning of 'originality' has shifted. To say that something was 'original' formerly meant that a series of incremental creative improvements had resulted in something worthwhile that was different enough from what had gone before that it might be the starting point or origin for a new tradition. Now, 'original' has come to mean simply 'new', or at least new enough to be differentiated from the old in the ceaseless arms race of consumer markets. An overcrowded marketplace puts a premium on a very thin and specious concept of novelty; an original work is now no more than a work that is sufficiently different to another existing work not to be confused with it. But just because something is new, it doesn't follow that it is worthwhile. To quote Posner again, 'From an aesthetic standpoint the work might not have been worth making. It might be unimaginative hack work. But in a commercial society anything that fills an empty niche, however tiny, in market space has value and that value is diminished by plagiarism.'

Although you wouldn't know it from reading the fashion press, there are almost no original (as opposed to 'new') ideas in fashion. But commercial imperatives compel creatives to make febrile and egotistical claims of originality. Given our 'big bang' notion of originality, the more credit a designer claims for originality, the less credit they tend to give to those who went before, which is only a short step from claiming the earlier incremental improvements as their own, and an even shorter step away from seeing their competitors not as potentially creative improvers but as counterfeiters. It becomes worth their while to cry 'fake!' or 'copy!' at any product that looks similar.

It's no coincidence that Yves Saint Laurent brought his legal action against Ralph Lauren at a time when American designers, seen by many as barbarians at the gate, were about to break into the European high-end clothing market. Was the case of Saint Laurent versus his near namesake the howl of a genuinely wounded creative artist, or the last-ditch defence of a profitable corner of Tuxedoland?

Even Saint Laurent, who felt that fashion designers should behave as artists, understood that fashion is not like art. A work of art can be a urinal, a fabric-wrapped building, an unmade bed, a shark in formaldehyde, or a lobster telephone. Clothes are different. Clothes have a function. They have to *work*. As a minimum they need armholes, a neckline, a bodice, somewhere for your legs to go, and some way of not falling down. They have functions like warmth or protection, being figure-flattering, or signalling wealth or membership of some group. Clothes are very largely (though not exclusively) the product of circumstance, necessity, and use.

When Yves Saint Laurent sued Ralph Lauren for stealing his idea, Lauren retorted that he had no need to steal Saint Laurent's ideas; he had plenty of inspiration of his own, right here at home. No offence to designers and businessmen everywhere, and particularly no offence to the French whose romantic cult of the author and the creative individual is central to their iden-tity,* but do we really think the tuxedo dress would never have happened if Laurent or Lauren hadn't come up with it?

In science, where the lightbulb of invention frequently pops up over more than one head, we are used to the idea of more than one creator. We know that two people invented the

---

* Full disclosure: the author is half French.

telephone;* there are two rival conceivers of calculus;† five inventors of the steamboat; and at least nine candidates for the invention of the telescope, and they can't *all* get the credit, or the naming rights.‡ It is the case in fashion, too.

What if some designs are just too good or too of their time *not* to happen? Do they still need a grand designer? And if they don't, what might an alternative history of the tuxedo dress look like?

'Off With Their Tails!'

We've already seen how in the creation myth of the tuxedo, the father of the modern dinner jacket was the formal tailcoat. Once upon a time, men wore coats that were the same length all around. That was inconveniently cumbersome when riding, so the front part was cut away, leaving only the rear section, or 'tail', hanging down at the back. Once the tail was split into two, for greater ease when sitting on a horse or indeed sitting anywhere at all, the style proved such a success that it gradually became standard daywear and, in more formal and stiff fabrics, customary for evening wear too.

Around 160 years ago, tailcoats began to lose their tails and to evolve shorter, jacket-like lines of descent. The evening or

---

* Alexander Graham Bell and Elisha Gray applied to patent their speaking telegraphs on the same day.

† Newton and Leibniz.

‡ Stigler's law of eponymy states that no scientific discovery – including his – is named after its original discoverer. Stigler cheerfully acknowledges that he was not the first to discover 'his' law, pointing out that it should more properly be called Merton's Law after the sociologist who first formulated it.

'dress' tailcoat evolved into the dinner jacket and the fancy brocade or velvet smoking jacket; the morning tailcoat metamorphosed into the black jacket once worn (with striped trousers) by all professional men but now only by old-fashioned butlers. The longtails didn't die out completely. Morning coats are still worn by men whose activities are carried out standing up: not only bridegrooms, best men and ushers, but also courtiers and racegoers, as well as the staff at ritzy London department store Fortnum & Mason, who of course never sit down on the job. For as long as you are walking or standing upright, the long tails of an old-fashioned coat are not an encumbrance. But in the rest of life, where people prefer to spend most of the day sitting comfortably, form and function have marched hand in hand, and the tails have vanished from men's coats.

That this has happened completely unplanned, without design or oversight, shouldn't really surprise us. Having had about 150 years to get used to the once-shocking theory, most of us are able to accept that we are ourselves tail-less descendants of long-tailed ancestors. Humans are apes who share a common ancestor with monkeys; our ground-dwelling ape branch split from our tree-dwelling forebears over 25 million years ago. Although the timescales couldn't be more different, we lost our tails for the same reason the tailcoats lost theirs, which is that form and function are as inextricably linked in biology as they are in clothing. We too lost our tails as a result of the process at the heart of evolution: descent with modification. Our circumstances changed when we came down from the trees. Once we no longer swung from tree to tree, our need for tails vanished. Once our ancestors were walking upright on two legs, floorduster tails were simply an encumbrance.

The tail-less ape branch has spawned many sub-branches, including the various humanoids: Homo sapiens (us),

Neanderthals (partially us), as well as our simian ape-cousins: the orangutans, gorillas, chimpanzees, and gibbons. Species of long-tailed primates – or monkeys as we call them – are still very much around, though, like the long-tailed evening coats, they are hopelessly outnumbered and marginalised by the more successful tail-less types like ourselves. Some people even try to deny the fact that we are related to them. And perhaps that's the point: the winner rarely gives much thought, or credit, to all those who came before.

In the natural world, good designs frequently come about more than once, often from very different starting points. Perhaps none are more famous or startling than the parallel designs of the marsupial mammals that are almost uniquely found in Australia and South America and the placental mammals of the rest of the world. The likenesses between the mammal pairs shown side by side in Plate 10 are astonishing. The marsupial 'mouse' is indistinguishable from the placental variety. 'Our' wolf bears a strong resemblance to the marsupial Tasmanian wolf.* It is almost impossible to believe that the flying squirrel and the flying phalanger are not related.

In fact, the similarities, though striking, are superficial, mere matters of form and fur. Far more significant are the differences in internal plumbing.† Placental mammals give birth to relatively mature young who have been well nourished by the mother's placenta, whereas marsupial mothers give birth to rela-

---

* Reverse the 'Home' and 'Away' teams if you are reading this in Australia.

† Marsupial reproductive systems are like something out of *Star Trek*. Kangaroo genitalia facts: did you know that male kangaroos, like other marsupials, often have two-pronged penises, and that females have three vaginas?

Nature's impostors. Plate 1 (*above*) is a Monarch butterfly; Plate 2 (*right*) its almost indistinguishable mimic, the Viceroy.

Plate 3. Coloured sketches of butterflies made by Henry Walter Bates during his eleven-year expedition to the Amazon.

Plate 4. Fake snake. Not a poisonous viper, but a harmless caterpillar mimicking one. The larva of the Hemeroplanes triptolemus moth has evolved dramatic defences to ward off predators.

Plate 5. Shared warning signals. Bright colours and striking designs are used to indicate danger by Heliconius butterflies (*above*) and hazardous chemical and cautionary road signs (*below*).

Plate 6. Egg counterfeits. On the left are prinia eggs; on the right, cuckoo finch counterfeits. The variety and beauty of the constantly evolving designs of the prinia eggs are a by-product of the deadly serious race for survival.

Plate 7. Not so much a hunting trophy as a status symbol: Ryan Muirhead poses with the antlers of the elk that he stumbled across.

Plate 8. The doubtful Princess. A drawing attributed to Leonardo da Vinci by some experts, and denied by others. Whether she is worth $150 million or $22,000 depends on whose authentication you accept.

Plate 9. This is not a Warhol: the self-portrait that was twice authenticated by the Andy Warhol Foundation, and then twice denied by the Andy Warhol Authentication Board.

Placentals   Marsupials

Mouse

Marsupial mouse

Flying squirrel

Flying phalanger

Mole

Marsupial mole

Groundhog

Wombat

Giant anteater

Numbat (banded anteater)

Wolf (Canis lupus)

Tasmanian wolf

(Thylacine)

Plate 10. 'If a design is good enough to evolve once, the same design principle is good enough to evolve twice, from different starting points' (Richard Dawkins). Pairs of marsupial and placental mammals display astonishing similarities despite being from very different parts of the world.

Plates 11, 12 and 13. Virtual living. Robbie Cooper's intensely moving portraits of gamers and their avatars.

Virtual-world inhabitants can change gender (*top*), swap daywear for superhero costumes (*above*), and acquire extra powers (*below*).

In the twenty-first century, social identities will increasingly be shaped and expressed in the metaverse.

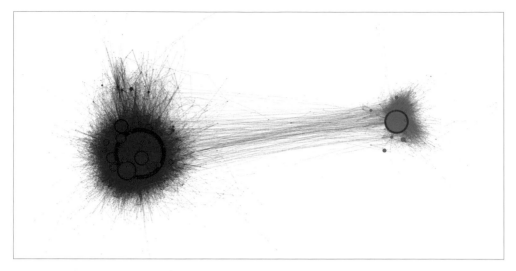

Plate 14. What a filter bubble looks like. A network map of Twitter conversations for and against the Syrian 'White Helmets' humanitarian volunteer rescue organisation. Notice how few sources and stories are shared – as indicated by the lines between the red and blue clusters – by comparison with the hundreds of lines that double back onto the same cluster.

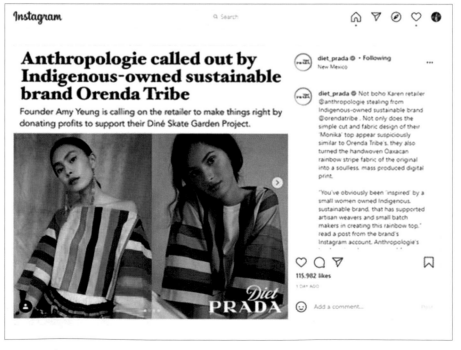

Plate 15. Fashion watchdog Diet Prada calls out a mass-market retailer for a suspiciously familiar-looking top.

tively unformed young who then continue to develop inside their mother's most distinctive design detail, the marsupial pocket or pouch.

The early European explorers and traders who first came across marsupials, initially in South America and then in Australia, were struck by their freakish similarities to animals they knew from home. Perplexity only increased when it became clear that there could be no family relationship between them. Although people looking at maps had long noticed that the protuberance of South America fitted into the curve of Africa as neatly as two jigsaw pieces, it was regarded as an amusing coincidence until 1861, when an Austrian geologist named Eduard Suess made a radical suggestion. Suess proposed the existence of an ancient supercontinent, Pangea, which around 200 million years ago had broken into continents that subsequently drifted apart from one another.* Around 100 million years after that, a southern continent, Gondwanaland, which included Australia and South America, detached itself from a northern continent incorporating present-day Europe. And between 80 and 40 million years ago, Australia floated off in its turn, creating a uniquely isolated continent. Australia has been separated from the rest of the world for so long that there is simply no possibility that any animal indigenous to Australia is related to, interbred with, or mimicking any animal indigenous to the rest of the world.

As with much else that we have seen in this book, it was Charles Darwin's theory of evolution that shed light on the mystery. What made the marsupial mammals look similar to their placental counterparts is, as we saw earlier, that form

---

* At the rate of around a centimetre per year, which is slower than your fingernails grow.

follows function. Animals are very largely shaped by what you might call their vocation or specialism. Because there is a niche in nature for a burrower, both groups contain a strong-pawed mole-like creature, a denizen of the underground streamlined for 'swimming' through earth and sand and equipped with powerful shovel-flipper feet. Precision dining is another specialist occupation, and both groups contain ant- and termite-eaters that use their long snouts to break up nests, and their sticky tongues to lap up the insects inside. There is a pouched marsupial mouse, a rowdy night dweller that looks almost identical to the more staid placental version.* Each group contains a squirrel-like glider that has developed wing-like flaps between its limbs; a 'cat' built for speed with spotted grassland camouflage; and a 'dog', in the form of the placental European wolf and the famous (and tragic) marsupial Tasmanian wolf, also known as the thylacine or 'pocket-dog'.

The marsupials' designs match the placentals', ecological niche for niche. But for the occasional tweak of pattern, colour, or fur, and that signature detail of the pocket, you could easily mistake the marsupial creatures for copies or designs 'inspired by' the placental versions. What these uncannily similar animal blueprints show is that function is the real originator of design, with evolution as its drawing board, and the savannahs, grass-lands, and treetops as its ateliers, design studios, and factories. In biology, a great many astonishingly and improbably similar good designs have emerged from a series of very different start-ing points without any need for a Grand Designer. Sometimes, all you need is a lot of little design changes that align with changes in function, and a lot of Little Designers.

---

* And, in the words of excitable newspapers, often 'sexes itself to death'.

Tuxedos and Trenches, Bikers and Gilets

The idea that we can understand fashion, like any other business, in evolutionary terms – as working through a dynamic of incremental selection and improvement and powered by function and the need to survive – seems so intuitively obvious that it's odd that it has taken so long to become part of mainstream economic thought. The evolutionary algorithm, with its Darwinian trinity of variation, selection, and reproduction, can explain an economy just as well as it does an ecology. As we saw with the elks in Chapter 6, it helps to look at businesses at the species level as well as the individual level. The ecology of the fashion business is vividly summarised by Eric Beinhocker, professor of public policy practice at Oxford University, in his book *The Origin of Wealth: The Radical Remaking of Economics and What It Means for Business and Society* (2006):

> Consider the shirt, blouse, or any other kind of top you are wearing – where did its design come from? Well, you might reply, it's obvious; a clothes designer designed it. But there is more to the story than just that. What really happened was more or less the following. A number of clothes designers took pre-existing ideas of what a shirt should look like and used their rationality and creativity to create all sorts of variations of 'shirts' and sketched them out ... looked at their various sketches and selected a subset of the designs that they thought consumers would like, and arranged their manufacture. The clothing company then showed its wares to various retailers, which likewise selected a subset of the designs they thought consumers would like ... You then walked into a store, browsed through a wide variety of shirts and selected the one you liked

and bought it ... The reason your shirt was evolved rather than designed is that nobody could predict exactly the kind of shirt you would want.

Here, then, is an alternative account of fashion design. We can compare it with the more romantic and evocative stories of Yves Saint Laurent's and Ralph Lauren's claims to the tuxedo and the dress it begat. This may be a more prosaic account, but it is also a more ecological one – in the sense that the process describes an ecology rather than privileging a single individual. It is one where, in design studios, workshops, and clothing stores across the world, unsung creators and unknown shoppers are bit-by-bit making the modest changes that will eventually shape what we wear. It is an account that allows for great designers like Yves Saint Laurent and Ralph Lauren, but crucially it does not depend on them.

We've seen that one problem with trying to identify a single point of origin for a garment is that it denies the possibility of two or more similar garments evolving – like the placental and marsupial mammals – from different starting points. In fact, a number of sleeveless coat-dresses have emerged from the fashion ecology. One of the best-known is the cotton 'trench dress'. Popularised by Burberry,* and resembling the tuxedo dress in styling and cut, the sandy yellowish-brown colouring of the fabric, the storm flaps and pockets, epaulettes, D-rings, and the residual 'gun flap' make clear its separate and rugged outdoor heritage. Although it may have started as a military coat rather than as formal evening wear, the trench dress, just like the

---

* One of the rival claimants to the original trench coat (the other is Aquascutum).

tuxedo dress, is a man's jacket that has evolved into a womens-wear staple.

Viewed together, the tuxedo dress and the trench dress are as alike as a placental mouse and its marsupial counterpart. Where biologists use terms like 'mutated', 'evolved', and 'adapted' to explain incremental changes, fashion talks of 'reworks', 'reissues', 'updates', 'features', 'detailing'. Although the trench dress has evolved separately and in parallel to the tuxedo dress, the similarity between them suggests that both fulfil a common function.

Whatever the function is, it is clearly a winner. The biker jacket has recently followed a similar evolutionary path. Keeping the zips, padding, and reverse collar details of the original, it has undergone a change of fabric from stiff leather to softer skins and even woven textiles, and has moved seamlessly into the female workwear category. It too has also spawned numerous offshoots: in some lengthening to a coat, in others also losing its sleeves to become a dress. It is now fully established as a perennial classic – fashion-speak for a successful species. Or take another mash-up that I hadn't clocked until recently: the sleeveless blazer (also known as the 'gilet') that has both shrunk into a shorter jacket form and elongated into a dress. The gilet looks set fair to emulate the evolutionary success of the tuxedo, trench, and biker. A headline in *The Times* caught my eye: 'How the gilet became essential'. 'In case you are one of the half-dozen people who doesn't have one already,' cooed the writer persuasively, 'here are five reasons why a gilet will prove the most-loved item in your wardrobe.'

Ubiquitous though they are, you might not notice that these hybrid items of clothing all serve the same function. Pierre Bergé came close to encapsulating it when he described Saint Laurent's designs as empowering women. I would call it the

Fig. 9.2. The tuxedo dress (left), trench dress (centre), and biker dress (right). Similar designs from very different origins.

function of smoothing a woman's progress through a man's world. Since men's clothes are invariably more comfortable and more practical than women's, 'feminised' menswear removes physical barriers to progression. And male attire reworked into womenswear has a signalling function too; it indicates that the wearer is a woman able to move in a world beyond the domestic arena, that she is equally at ease in the professional and public spheres.

Both Yves Saint Laurent and Ralph Lauren are, in their different ways, fashion geniuses. A truly great designer can absorb the culture, capture the mood of the moment, and create meaning out of fabric and thread, buttons and zips. Their creations can reflect seismic societal and cultural changes – and sometimes more prosaic ones too. It is only in the last fifty years that we have had both female emancipation and widespread central heating (told you it was prosaic), and it's a fair bet that a jacket-to-sleeveless-coatdress adaptation couldn't and wouldn't have taken off at any earlier point in history.

Overrating Originality

Three origin stories: the Old World, New World, and evolutionary versions, which trace a design back to a person, a place, and a process respectively. Each story has different implications for what it means to be 'original', as well as to be authentic. Whichever story we prefer, we need to bear in mind that 'originals' get all the good press, even though what is claimed to be 'original' may in fact be neither original nor especially useful. Rather than focus on 'originality' in fashion, we should be asking a more important question: whether something is worthwhile or worthless. Why should we regard something that is a small but worthwhile improvement of something that already exists as less 'original' than pointless novelty? The lesson of Shakespeare is that slow incremental inching towards improvement can sometimes be the most valuable creativity of all.

We need to remember that two similar originals can exist side by side. The lesson of the marsupials is that one does not have to be a copy of the other. Much less divides the 'original' from the 'copy' than people would have you believe.

All of which raises some important questions about our system of intellectual property. Should you be able to copyright what natural forces might have created anyway? Should you be able to register a trademark or patent just because you got your application in first?

The problem with giving credit for originality to something just because it's new is that novelty has acquired a picket fence of legal protection in the intellectual property system. A system that labels everything inside the fence as 'original', protecting it with © or ™, and labels anything outside that looks similar as a copy or counterfeit, means that the talented, the innovative, the entrepreneurial outside the fence are shut down – which makes us all the losers. Any successful designer will tend to give as little credit to their predecessors as they can decently get away with. The result is that claims of origin and originality sometimes shine too much light on too few individuals and neglect the long, slow evolutionary process of borrowings and of incremental improvement. Overrating and overprotecting 'originality' can benefit the few, but it disadvantages the many.

Intellectual property is not a law of nature: it's a concept that we've invented in the last 170 years or so. I'm not against giving legal protection to the fruits of human creativity (very few authors are), but we need to take a step back from time to time, to be clear who we want to reward, who we're trying to benefit, encourage, and protect. Is it creators? Just the one creator or also the many unsung predecessors on whose shoulders they stand? Businesses? Innovators? The public? If you think fashion and literature are insufficiently serious examples (I don't, by the way – I chose them because they are good illustrations of the wider principles we apply to intellectual property), then ask yourself: should a few individuals decide what counts as original, and therefore authentic, or should we have more of a say in it too? What's true for the creative industries like fashion is also true for many others. Some vital patents for drugs, plants, and genomes, to take just a few examples, risk being concentrated in too few hands. Recent research suggests that the patent system doesn't appear to increase scientific innovation at all, though it certainly benefits those who register the patents.

There have been eleven increases in copyright duration since 1962, without any corresponding increase in authors' lifespans.

There has been a significant increase in the patenting of plant varieties – even though the patent-seekers didn't create the plants in the first place. Patents have begun to be granted for 'business methods', most egregiously Amazon's patent on the 'one-click' ordering system. And country-turned-pop singer Taylor Swift applied to trademark such unique phrases as 'Party Like It's 1989', 'This Sick Beat', and 'Nice To Meet You. Where You Been?' You don't need a fine legal mind to realise that all may not be well with the way the intellectual property system distributes the lucrative rights to what it chooses to call originality. Sometimes you just need a sense of the ridiculous.

The Judgement in Paris

The judgement of the Paris Tribunal de Commerce was given on 18 May 1994, and made news across the world. The judge ruled that Saint Laurent's design was original and protected by copyright. Ralph Lauren was ordered to pay 2 million francs in damages for 'counterfeiting and disloyal competition', and further ordered to pay 200,000 francs to Rive Gauche, Yves Saint Laurent's ready-to-wear division. Lauren's tuxedo dresses were impounded and destroyed.*

But it proved to be the final flourish of the old regime. Today, more than 25 years later, the House of Saint Laurent is going strong, even though Yves died in 2008, and Paris is still the home of haute couture. But a Google search yields hundreds if not thousands of variations and versions of the tuxedo dress, all available at the click of a button. Saint Laurent may not have

---

* Ralph won his counter-action against Pierre Bergé for defamation, and was awarded 500,000 francs for the hurt and damage sustained.

known it, but he was trying to hold back an unstoppable surge. The barbarians are well inside the gate. Nobody in 1994 foresaw that the internet would double or treble the speed of the fashion cycle. In a world where a design can be copied the moment it appears on the catwalk, and be in the stores within a fortnight, the gap between the haute couture, ready-to-wear, and chain-store versions of a garment begins to collapse. Globalisation makes convergence and copying on a worldwide scale inevitable. There is no point in a designer bringing a court case about creative authorship and design copyright: even if the copyright infringer could be identified, the case would take longer to pursue than the few weeks the item would be in the stores.

Ralph Lauren is still going strong too. For his fall/winter 2019 women's collection, the 79-year-old Ralph transformed an empty warehouse on Wall Street into 'Ralph's Club', a 1930s-style speakeasy. The tuxedo, described by leading fashion commentator Anna Murphy as Ralph Lauren's 'aesthetic touchstone', was the centrepiece of his show, reworked in fabrics from velvet to fur, and in every colour of the rainbow from cherry red to canary yellow.

Lauren's 'Polo' logo is one of the most widely recognised on earth, and also one of the most counterfeited. He has fought other battles about origins and originality: his legal tussle with the United States Polo Association (founded 1890) over who had the better right to use a polo player as their logo spanned almost thirty years of continuous litigation.*

Griswold 'Grizzy' Lorillard, a passionate polo player like his father Pierre, travelled to England in 1886. His hosts were

---

* The United States Polo Association stubbornly insisted that they had 'a legitimate interest' in the image. They lost.

astonished to hear that Americans played polo too, having very much regarded it as a British game.

The story of how Grizzy lopped the tails off his tailcoat at the Tuxedo Country Club and thereby invented the tuxedo is all over the internet, and cited on Ralph Lauren's website too. But other creation myths are available. One suggests that Grizzy may have been more of a mimic than a creator, and that his inspiration came from a certain James Potter. Potter also visited England in 1886, accompanied by his attractive wife. The couple were invited to stay at the royal estate of Balmoral by the Prince of Wales, who was known to have an eye for other people's attractive wives. When dressing for dinner, the Prince favoured the less formal smoking jacket over formal dress tails; he encouraged his guest to do likewise, and even introduced Potter to his tailor, Messrs Poole & Sons of Bond Street. When Potter came back to America with his new tail-less evening wear,* he wore the shorter jacket to Delmonico's, the New York hotspot of the moment, where it was much admired, inspiring Grizzy and co. to try out the new style on that fateful autumn night. Tuxedos were already being worn *before* Grizzy had the idea for his prank, rather than as a result of it. Appropriately enough, by losing their tails, Grizzy and friends were not so much mocking as aping their elders, who had already adopted the European 'smoking' jacket – the very jacket that some eighty years later Yves Saint Laurent was so famously to adapt for women.

---

* But without his attractive wife, who had decided to pursue a career as an actress in Britain.

Stories that Stick

But there is something more important to note about the story of the tuxedo. The Grizzy version is more attractive to us than the Potter version, for all its royal connections and its whiff of adultery.* The Grizzy version is the story of an impetuous young man, impatient with tradition, taking matters into his own hands. Like Ralph Lauren's story, it is a dynamic all-American tale, and it has what marketing professionals call 'stickiness': people remember it and pass it on to others. It has become what both internet users and evolutionary biologists call a successful 'meme', a unit of cultural transmission that spreads at the expense of other, less successful ones. And memes have one great advantage. In a crowded marketplace, they find a very valuable piece of unchartered space in which to sit – the space inside your head. The next part of the book is about something that only humans, and no other animal, can do, which is to tell stories. As brands find it increasingly difficult to defend their market shares and economic niches against the competition, intangible stories can do what mere tangible objects cannot: they can grab a share of your mind.

---

* And, I'm sorry to say, what looks to be the true version is less attractive than both. There is no record of an American customer named James Potter in the ledgers of Messrs Poole & Sons. But Pierre Lorillard and other founding fathers of the Tuxedo Club *were* customers in the 1860s, around the time that the Prince of Wales ordered his first smoking jacket. Most likely it was they who introduced the dinner jacket to fashionable New York society, and thence to the Tuxedo Club.

PART 4
SELLING
AUTHENTICITY

10

INTANGIBLES

A Visit to the Fake-Hunters

'Advertisements are now so numerous that they are very negligently perused, and it is, therefore, become necessary to gain attention by magnificence of promises, and by eloquence sometimes sublime and sometimes pathetick. Promise, large promise, is the soul of an advertisement.'

Samuel Johnson, 'The Art of Advertising Exemplified'

'What Phil and Nike have done is turn me into a dream.'

Michael Jordan, 1993

I'm standing in front of an imposing *hotel particulier* in the swishy 16th arrondissement of Paris. Its classical lines, marble staircases, and delicately wrought iron balustrades belie the fierce sense of purpose inside. The Musée de la Contrefaçon is that most unusual of museums, one that specialises in counterfeits. I'm here to try to understand a problem that was familiar to Yves Saint Laurent and Ralph Lauren even in 1994, at the height of their spat over the elegant tuxedo dress: the problem of mass-market knock-offs and blatant counterfeits.*

---

* At the same time as its action against Ralph Lauren, Groupe Yves Saint Laurent was pursuing 300 cases against low-grade counterfeiters.

According to some estimates, the trade in fake products is worth $600 billion per year. An astonishing 7–10 per cent of all branded goods sold are counterfeit. It is estimated that 80 per cent of us have handled fake or falsified goods (mostly unwittingly, it should be said). Sales of luxury goods have tripled in recent decades, but fakes have grown even faster: one estimate suggests that counterfeits have increased by 10,000 per cent – an eyewatering two-hundred-fold – in just two consumer-demand-fuelled decades.*

It's not just the overall figures that boggle the mind. One French customs raid confiscates enough fake Louis Vuitton fabric to cover 54 tennis courts. A swoop on a Taobao seller nets 18,500 counterfeit bags, aprons, and footwear (enough to fill every shelf in a neighbourhood Tesco). A bust in Madrid impounds 85,000 counterfeits ready for the Black Friday and Christmas markets (equivalent to an out-of-town superstore entirely filled with fakes). In Istanbul, in 2020, almost 700,000 counterfeit haircare products are seized (picture four Glastonbury festivals with every member of the audience holding a bottle of fake shampoo).

Usually, when there are many more counterfeits than the real thing, you see a correction. Too many butterflies flaunting false warning colours, and predators start to take the risk. Too much clipped currency and you get a recoinage. But despite the growth of an authentication industry with an ever-expanding list of anti-counterfeiting tools – thermally activated tamper-proof seals, elaborate bar codes, security numbers, RFID (radio frequency identification) tags, colour shifting inks, holograms –

---

* Figures about fakes can only ever be 'best guess' estimates. No one really knows how many fakes are out there. You only know how many you catch, and you extrapolate from there.

all designed to create unique identifiers for products that are themselves far from unique, that doesn't seem to be happening.

I want to make sense of this discrepancy. At a time when so many say they are searching for authenticity, why are we buying so many fakes? Why can't the designers and the big brands stop, or at least slow down the counterfeiters? And how do you tell the difference between the real thing and the fake anyway?

Against the Barbarians

The Musée de la Contrefaçon is a typically French answer to that question. In a series of elegant interconnecting rooms, glass vitrines display products and their counterfeits side by side, helpfully labelled *vrai* and *faux*. In front of me is what looks very like the famous quilted '2.55' Chanel handbag, only this one, says the tour guide, is a Turkish-made knock-off. Where the original boasts regular and robust stitching, the fake is glued together. The signature 'quilting' is made of cardboard and cotton wool. At first sight, a Korean bag looks just like a Louis Vuitton; on closer examination, the famous trefoils have been replaced by a circle and a bar, the 'LV' logo by some superficially similar characters in Hangul, the Korean alphabet. Not a single element of the design matches the original, yet the overall effect is unmistakeably 'Vuitton'. The guide explains that this illustrates the difference between fakery by imitation and fakery by 'passing off'. In another cabinet is a 2,000-year-old Gaulish fake of a Roman amphora; what should be a Roman name on the stopper is replaced by random symbols. I get the feeling that the museum staff are quite proud that their oldest fake was made on French territory.

Rather unstylishly, I'm carrying my notebook, wallet, and keys in a supermarket plastic bag. Back at the hotel, I'd realised at the last minute that my shoulder bag was a fake Longchamp. Now I mentally compare it to the real thing that the guide shows me. On mine, the little gold *tchotchke* hanging off the zip is a plain gold ring, where it should have a leaping Longchamp horse and jockey. The inside does not have the delicious thick rubbery, almost sticky, quality of the genuine article. Compared to the real thing, the leather on my bag is oddly spongy and insubstantial, the stitching inadequate.*

I ask about the building. Is it true that it's a copy of an earlier seventeenth-century one in the Marais district? Does that mean – oh, the delicious irony – that the museum is itself housed in a counterfeit? The guide's eyes narrow slightly. I sense a *froideur*. 'It's a copy, not a counterfeit. Where there is no IP, no counterfeit is possible.'

To judge from the museum, the barricades of *haute luxe* seem to be holding – just about. But in the mid-market, counterfeiting has reached crisis point. Brand knock-offs that used to be sold in market stalls are now just a couple of clicks away on the internet. Many traders in counterfeits give markets – even online ones – a miss, instead selling peer-to-peer over social media. Worst affected are what are known in the unlovely jargon of marketers as 'masstige' products (a portmanteau word combining 'mass market' and prestige), goods that are premium but still affordable. No hard and fast line separates these from luxury goods, but instead of emphasising the former's craftsmanship and tradition, superior quality and exclusivity, masstige goods sell themselves on artisanal touches, wish-fulfilment, celebrity association, and fashion trend. As one commentator puts it, masstige focuses on 'aspirationality', 'the implicit distance between the world they represent in their

---

* Ten days after I got home, my counterfeit Longchamp fell to pieces.

230

communications and the product their consumers can actually afford to buy'.

I'm in Amsterdam to find out what is behind this explosion in mid-market fakes. Bjorn Grootswagers, regional director of the anti-counterfeiting organisation REACT, is visibly less relaxed than the folk at the museum in Paris. REACT have 30 years' experience fighting the counterfeit trade. They handle around 20,000 cases a year, working with customs and law enforcement agencies across 107 countries, and have back-office teams monitoring and taking down fraudulent websites 24/7.* Their 300 or so clients are a roll-call of the world's most powerful rights owners: not only the ever-present Louis Vuitton, but Adidas, Abercrombie & Fitch, Converse, Nike, Puma, Levi's, Tommy Hilfiger, FIFA, Ducati, Jack Daniel's, Jaguar, L'Oréal, Procter & Gamble, Unilever, Warner Brothers, Yamaha, PlayStation, Hello Kitty, Playboy.

To be honest, what with REACT's all capitals SMERSHy-sounding name and their international fight against the bad guys, I was expecting a big modern office thrumming with computers, and quite possibly James Bond-style secretaries carrying important messages from floor to floor in glass lifts. But as the taxi taking me from the station drives along the Amstelveenseweg boulevard, office towers turn into blocks of flats, and then into smaller and smaller terraced houses.

The driver asks me why I've come; he sounds unimpressed when I tell him. 'Why fighting fakes in Amsterdam? They don't make them here. I am from Turkey', he says proudly. 'And we make many!'

---

* In a very Dutch touch, they are at pains to point out that all goods seized are recycled responsibly.

We come to a halt outside a single two-storey, sharply gabled house with a little window set into the roof. In the front parlour which serves as a meeting room, I am plied with extremely good coffee by Bjorn and his colleague Mary-Ann Kouters. The shelves to my right overflow with the sort of knock-offs you might see on a stall in Oxford Street: polyboard squares holding fifty or so diamanté stud earrings in the shape of Chanel's double 'C', a floppy stuffed Paul Frank 'Julius' monkey, plastic purses with garish multicolour 'LV' logos. There are boxes of fake Ariel washing powder and a fake four-pack of Braun Oral B electric toothbrush heads – indistinguishable from one I'd opened that morning.

'When we started,' says Bjorn, 'if we stopped five thousand fakes a month we thought we were doing a good job. If we caught a hundred thousand a year, we would pat ourselves on the back.' He smiles. 'Then we changed what we did, and now we are stopping twenty-five million counterfeits a year.'

REACT used to inspect the markets and shops where fakes are sold. Now they monitor the points at which bulk consignments of counterfeits enter the EU, container ports like Rotterdam, Antwerp, and Bremen. One box shipping container can hold a thousand times more than a smuggler's suitcase. Pick the right port, the right ship, and the right box, and you can stop tens or even hundreds of thousands of fakes in a single swoop. But it's not easy. Around 120 million shipping containers whizz around the globe each year, 12 million of which pass through Rotterdam. Somewhere, in boxes within boxes, packed up, crated up, their contents hidden, are handbags and trainers, perfumes and toys, wallets and consumer electronics that look very like the official designer versions, but aren't. Bjorn and his colleagues have to pick out which of these identical containers might have counterfeits in it and ask customs officials to wheel

232

the giant box – 20,000 cubic feet of corrugated steel – off the ship to see if they are right.

For obvious reasons Bjorn can't tell me too many of the clues and techniques he uses to spot potential fakes, but he says he often finds himself flagging up what's *not* there, rather than what is:

> If it says just 'shoes' on the bill of lading that's suspicious, because if it's Nike shoes it would say Nike, and if it's Adidas it would say Adidas – so that's one red flag. Most of the counterfeit goods come from Asia, mostly China, we have a blacklist of factories of course, so if it's coming from one of those that's another red flag. We're often looking at shipping agents rather than factories, and they change their names all the time. They're called things like Unit 1234 and it's all in Chinese characters so it's not easy, but sometimes there are giveaways, say if the address is on a third floor – well, you can't ship from a third floor, can you? Or if they don't even bother with an address to make it look as though the goods are coming from a legitimate supplier and it's just 'Unit 1234, Guangzhou', then that's another red flag.

It's no coincidence that the country Bjorn mentions more than any other is China. Alongside its rise as a manufacturing super-power, China has become the world's largest counterfeiter, accounting for a whopping 60–80 per cent of all fakes produced.* There are fake ingredients (counterfeit cosmetics, for example, can contain toxic levels of lead, arsenic, and mercury), fake parts (counterfeit aircraft components caused some two dozen crashes in the USA between 2010 and 2016), fake brands (*Adidos*,

---

* Turkey is usually said to be the world's second or third largest source of counterfeits, so my taxi driver had a point.

PMUA, Naik), fake retailers (including dozens of bogus Apple stores across the country) – even, reportedly, a fake shopping mall in Nanjing crammed with fake outlets: *Bucksstars, Pizza Huh*, and a *McDnoalds* that features not two but three Golden Arches.

Dream Stealers

The twenty-first-century branded product is a rootless cosmopolitan. Made wherever manufacture is cheapest and sitting at the centre of a vast and complex biome of designers and manufacturers, suppliers and shippers, workshops and sweatshops, customs and border officials, it will likely be sold thousands of miles away from where it was either conceived or manufactured. Some products are made from up to a hundred parts supplied by a dozen or more contractors in different countries. Even the best-intentioned manufacturers (and not all of them are well-intentioned) may not know what is finding its way into their supply chain. As the world's manufacturers become concentrated into a few crowded industrial zones, techniques and technology are easily imitated or stolen. Craft skills can be replicated too. As Rain Noe, a writer on industrial design, says, 'If a human being contracted by Nike can accurately sew a pattern, a human being not contracted by Nike can too.'

But if China can make the same goods, to the same standards, and at a fraction of the price, isn't buying the cheaper unofficial version what any rational shopper should do? I put the question to Bjorn and Mary-Ann of REACT.*

---

* Almost never discussed openly by the brands themselves is the fact that many people must be complicit in buying fakes. The polite presumption is that if they do buy them, it must be in error, so I took a deep breath before I posed the question.

An intense look comes over Mary-Ann's face. 'Even if you made it exactly the same – which counterfeiters never do – you'd still be stealing from the brand manufacturer because the manufacturer has invested money in advertising, sponsorship deals, building the brand – goodwill is everything', she says, turning to look meaningfully at her colleague.

Bjorn nods. 'When you buy a brand, you're investing in the dream. You know Dr Dre who were bought by Apple? They make headphones that are good but not amazing. People buy them for cool. You are buying quality, but you are also buying being part of a group.'

He looks up at me and smiles. 'The designers aim to make a nice product with a nice dream. You buy it and your self-esteem will be good.'

When we buy a branded product, we buy it not just for its tangible qualities, but for the intangible ones too. We buy into the reputation of the brand and the reassurance that gives us. We buy into the image companies create around brands through glossy advertising and PR, catchy jingles and memorable slogans. We buy into the cool they conjure up by sponsoring the right parties, by getting the right actor or rapper to be the face of the brand, by getting the right people to be seen drinking it, or wearing it, or using it – all the contagious content and creative communiqués that are designed to make us, the consumers, feel good about it.

The intangible qualities of a product don't change the physical product, but they do change how you *feel* about it. Imagine two identical branded shirts side by side in the Musée de la Contrefaçon, each bearing the same logo of a dashing hunk on horseback swinging a polo mallet. One is *vrai*, the other *faux*. Which one would make you feel better about yourself when you wore it? The power of the intangible attributes of a brand is that they change not just how you feel about the product, but how you feel about yourself.

Many different words are used to describe the intangible qualities of a brand. Some talk about 'meaning'. Bjorn talks of 'the dream'. Mary-Ann uses 'goodwill', the term that accountants use to describe what makes a company worth more than its physical assets. Advertising men and women like to talk about 'image', that being the part they are responsible for creating. Marketing professionals prefer 'brand equity', a term that moves them closer to C-suite status. From the counterfeiter's point of view, it's easy: intangibles are simply the part of the product that they don't need to copy.

Intangibles are brainware: notions, feelings, perceptions, and conceptions designed by some of the world's most creative minds and destined, if the creatives have got it right, to take up residence in yours. Not for nothing is 'share of mind' one of marketing's most sought-after goals. Intangibles make their own journey from creator to consumer. While the physical product globetrots from designer to factory, warehouse to distributor, and thence into your hands, the voyage of its associated intangibles begins with the communications team at brand HQ, makes its way through the ether – via TV or social media, print or film – and thence into your head.

It suits companies that produce branded products to separate the tangible from the intangible, to locate manufacturing to wherever is cheapest and to spend more on beaming out the brand message. But what is becoming increasingly obvious is that the brands' business strategy suits the counterfeiters even better. What looks like strategic outsourcing from one perspective can look like a massive own goal from another.

If you look at it from the counterfeiters' point of view, it looks like a no-brainer. All they have to do is make a copy of the physical product at the lowest possible cost, and they can free-ride on the money that the real manufacturer has spent on advertising, sponsorship deals, and all the other costs of building the brand. Free-riding on all the effort it takes to develop and market a successful product (no one ever bothers to fake a failure) is a supremely low-risk way of making money.* It's betting on a winning horse after the race has been run. The more brands spend on promotion, and the less proportionally on the physical product, the bigger the window of opportunity they leave open for counterfeiters. Poor Bjorn, poor Mary-Ann, I think suddenly. The counterfeiters are stealing dreams, and all they can do is try to stop boxes getting through.

It's seldom you come across a battle where one side is actually making its opponents' work easier. What usually helps a species survive and thrive is making life *harder* for counterfeiters – as the little tawny prinia, squeezing out new colourways and dots and squiggles on her eggs to defeat the copycat cuckoo finches, would tell you.

A Natural History of Brands

Business is every bit as red in tooth and claw as nature, and for the same reason – survival. If companies devoted resources to attributing intangible qualities to their tangible goods, it must have been because it was a way to succeed. And as in nature, the process took place over time, so imperceptibly that they failed

---

* Although counterfeiting is illegal, the penalties are much lower than for drug trafficking and other forms of organised crime, which makes it a popular business for some very unpleasant people indeed.

to notice the rod they were ultimately making for their own backs.

Turn back the clock, if you will, and imagine an ancestral product. One that doesn't yet have the packaging and the promotions, the USPs (unique selling propositions), or any of the embellishments that would make it recognisably a brand of today. In other words, a commodity. How did that commodity become a brand? What is its Just So Story, its equivalent of 'How the Elk Got His Antlers'?

Like the ancestral elk – the one without his descendants' majestic antlers, just two little bumps on his head – our proto-brand displays none of its modern signature attributes. It is bereft of informational content, because its customers don't need any. In a hunter-gatherer world, you eat what you kill, consume only what you produce yourself. But once you start trading with others, they need information. Just the basics. Who grew this wheat? How much does it cost? Is there anything else mixed in with it? Once people start to live in settled communities, you need to agree on whose field is whose, and on which cattle belong to you and which to someone else. Now there's more information that needs to be communicated. You might identify your own cattle by *branding* them with a burning stick (*brandr* in Old Norse).* A brand in this sense becomes a mark of ownership, a mark of origin – a rudimentary trademark. And if your cattle are better fed or better looked after than others, the mark of origin

---

* Which is why every rookie brand consultant includes a picture of a cow in their client presentation. As professor of marketing Mark Ritson says in his seminal 'The Seven Unmistakable Signs of a Shit Brand Consultant' (2016): 'If they even say the magic words "Maslow's Hierarchy of Needs", throw something heavy at them and ask them to leave. Ditto, if they have a picture of a cow being branded in their slide deck or a quote about reputations taking decades to build, you know what you have to do.'

may come to denote quality too. As your farm gets bigger, you apply the same mark to the wheat and oats you sell as well. People begin to know that anything without your mark on it is likely to be inferior, and product differentiation is born.

As products start to travel further from home and into bigger markets, their producers need to give potential customers more information about them if they are to compete successfully. Because we are storytelling animals, this is often best done in the form of a backstory. Brussels lace, the über-luxury good of the sixteenth century, was superior because it was spun from linen thread more delicate and beautiful than coarse English flax. The story went that Brussels lacemakers sat in damp, darkened rooms, with only a shaft of light to illuminate their painstaking work, so that the still-moist thread did not dry out, and finer and more intricate patterns could be created than would ever have been possible with dry and brittle thread. The story is an important development. The most intangible element of the product mix so far, it serves to capture the imagination and keep the product at the forefront of the customer's mind. Now we have a mark of origin that is associated with quality, a good story – and a product that is beginning to look a lot more like a brand.

The move from product to brand gathers speed in the nineteenth century as new products begin to be transported by railway to unfamiliar markets. Consider the oat. Traditionally, oats were fed only to horses and invalids.* It occurred to an enterprising mill owner that marketing them as a breakfast food might be a lucrative idea. You're selling your oats to people a long way away, so you need packaging to transport them in.

---

* And Scotsmen. In his *Dictionary of the English Language* Samuel Johnson famously defined oats as 'a grain, which in England is generally given to horses, but in Scotland supports the people'.

And you can use that packaging as a billboard to explain to new consumers how and at what time of day they should be eating this product. If you can pick a memorable name, and an image for the box that conveys reliability and honesty, and even the strength of purpose that breakfasting on oats will give you, that would be even better. Which is what the Quaker Oats Company did in 1877 when they registered the first American trademark for a breakfast cereal.

Selling Authenticity

By the dawn of the twentieth century, we have what marketeers would recognise as modern brands. The classic four 'P's of the marketing mix – product, place (of sale), packaging, and promotion – are all in place. Over the next century or so, the globalisation of trade and communications would make three further 'P's – promise, personality, and purpose – even more important.

Promise first. In 1931, Proctor & Gamble used the results of a survey to advertise Camay Soap. The survey ('Imagine what a fascinating time I've had!' gushed the writer) asked fifty eligible bachelors what they looked for in a girl they would marry. Forty-eight of them agreed that they wanted 'a girl whose charm is natural'. Just in case anyone missed the point, the writer also consulted seventy-three dermatologists. All of them said that they would not hesitate to recommend Camay for the most delicate complexion. A tangible product (soap) had been freighted with an implied and intangible promise (marital prospects). For a small investment in Camay (10 cents for a bar) you could buy a very big dream indeed.

The second new 'P', personality, came of age in affluent postwar America. By the 1950s, quality had so improved across the

Fig. 10.1. A brand with promise. Have soap,
will marry.

board that products could no longer be differentiated on that basis alone. Now the brand manager's chief task was to give his product an identity that would set it apart from its rivals, and stand out on the increasingly crowded supermarket shelves. One way was to add 'personality'. Products were no longer just products; they became friends. Another way was to make them as eye-catching as possible.* Tide did both. The washing powder's orange and yellow 'bullet design' – still in use today

---

* One eye caught was that of Andy Warhol, who transplanted the bright emphatic packaging of Campbell's Soup and Brillo into art.

Fig. 10.2. Tide, the housewife's helper
and friend.

– made it instantly recognisable. Adverts showing houseproud housewives hugging a packet as if it were a long-lost friend – 'Tide's got what women want!' – made the all-important emotional connection.

The newest 'P' is purpose. Criticised by activists, brands have themselves become activists. We see them burnishing their societal credentials and inspiring others to do the same. Nike releases an advert, 'Dream Crazy', featuring Colin Kaepernick, the NFL quarterback who first knelt for the pre-game national anthem in protest at racial injustice. The slogan reads: 'Believe in something. Even if it means sacrificing everything. Just do it.' Dulux proclaims that it is not 'selling paint but tins of optimism', and donates half a million litres of paint to teams of employee-volunteers to give a face-lift to run-down urban neighbourhoods. We increasingly buy brands for the lifestyle they encapsulate and the values they represent. We want purchases that reflect well on us, products from companies that seem to share our view of the world. We are choosing brands the way we choose friends. We buy Harry's razors rather than Gillette's because Harry's give 1 per cent of revenue to men's mental health charities; we buy Timberlands because the company has pledged to reforest 50 million trees around the world.* Don't get me wrong – these are unimpeachably good causes. There is nothing wrong, and everything right, with supporting them. Nor is there anything wrong with expressing your feelings through what you buy. My aim is simply to point out that the trajectory over the last century or so has been to sell you more and more feelings.

As companies sell us products increasingly freighted with intangibles, they are selling us the building blocks of personal authenticity. The pursuit of authenticity, the twenty-first-century version of the Romantics' search for the inner person – what Charles Guignon, one of the most insightful philosophers of the subject, has described as 'the project of becoming the person you are' – has become intertwined with consumer culture. Brands that sell you promise, personality, and purpose are selling you a path to fulfilment and personal identity. You buy brands that resonate with the inner 'you', and ones that help you to express it. You buy aspirational brands to help you play the part of the person you want to become.

---

* Please don't think I'm just talking about Millennials or Gen Z. As Professor Bobby Duffy has pointed out in *Generations: Does When You're Born Shape Who You Are?* (2021), it is a myth that our current younger generations are more focused on acting sustainably or with social purpose than previous generations.

Some cynics say that these companies are simply exploiting our quest for personal authenticity, creating a new form of conspicuous consumption to take advantage of it.* I'm not that cynical, perhaps because I feel that with personal authenticity it is the end rather than the means that matters. And while I'm (mostly) fine with intangibles-as-authenticity as a marketing strategy, I can also savour the rich irony that selling authenticity has contributed to the incredible increase in fakery I came to Amsterdam to investigate.

The Arms Race (Again)

Selling intangibles is such a good strategy that no individual brand dares stop. Manufacturing cheaply, adding more and more value to the product via narrative and image, is a good recipe for survival. But if everybody is employing a similar strategy, the only way to compete is to go bigger on intangibles than the next guy. And therein lies the problem. More spend on intangibles and less on the physical product may be the perfect recipe for an individual brand, but it's a disaster for brands as a whole.

This should sound familiar. I hope your mind is now turning back to elks with ever more unfeasibly large antlers, and the problem of the competition to stay ahead of the competition. Image-building, brand-titivating, social media babble, creative advertising, celebrity endorsements: all the activities that lead the consumer to think warmly of your brand are the brand manager's weapons – and their equivalent of the elk's antlers.

---

* This is in fact exactly what Peter York says in his entertaining polemic *Authenticity is a Con* (2014).

The story of the last 50 years or more of marketing has been the story of a runaway arms race. Just as the elk with the biggest rack invariably wins the strut 'n' rut contest, so the brand with the biggest budget to spend on intangibles almost invariably wins in the marketplace too.* The prospects for a brand with diminished 'share of mind' are woeful indeed – akin to being the losing elk in an antler-wrestling contest.

But as we've already seen, selling intangibles is a gift to free-riding counterfeiters. The more companies spend on this kind of brand-building, the more they fuel the disproportionate rise in fakery that brand-building leads to. And that is potentially calamitous for brands as a species.

Faced with a similar situation, the elks were unable to put their hooves down. The possibility for collective action among brands, the possibility that they might decide together to put their foot on the brake and agree that everyone should simultaneously cut spending on intangibles – a move that would leave the competitive hierarchy untouched while allowing them all to spend more on their workers and their products – is almost zero. It would require the brands, firstly, to admit the problem openly among themselves; secondly, to trust all the other brands to do the right thing and not to cheat by secretly increasing rather than reducing spending on intangibles; and, thirdly, to expose the value or otherwise of the different parts of their brands to wider view. No wonder they would rather tackle the counterfeiters than the causes of counterfeiting.

---

* Which is how we've got to the stage of the $1,000 branded T-shirt. I've just come across a Balmain 'embellished sequined jersey T-shirt' at $1,350.

The Weightless Economy

What is a company's brand worth? It's easy to value the physical aspects of a product, harder to value its intangible aspects. How do you measure the sum of all the positive brand associations inside customers' heads? Sometime in the 1980s, a new discipline emerged, that of brand valuation consultant. A person who could reassure you that although you couldn't put a finger on the intangible elements of brand value, they could put a figure on it.

Contemporary brands are produced by companies very different from the smokestack industries of a century ago. Manufacturing is outsourced; marketing is ever more important. As the products they sell become increasingly freighted with intangibles, the value of these companies becomes increasingly intangible too. Where once their assets were largely physical – buildings, plant, stocks – now their balance sheets are jam-packed with intangibles, products of the intellect neither seen nor felt. Aspirational brand companies are less concerned with old-fashioned manufacturing skills, more interested in protecting their logos, slogans, and designs with trademarks, patents, and copyrights – property of the intellectual variety.

Unless you are a business analyst, it may come as a surprise to you to learn that the stock market is now made up of companies which are very largely made up of intangibles. Our national, corporate, and personal wealth has shifted from mostly concrete to mostly abstract. Brand economist Jan Lindemann found that, whereas in 1975 over 80 per cent of the market value of the US companies that made up the S&P 500 Index consisted of tangible as opposed to intangible assets, by 2005 the proportions were reversed: over 80 per cent of stock market value was intangible. Almost by stealth, the weightless economy had arrived.

The fabric and texture of life is changing. Our age of abundance means that we are surrounded by more stuff than ever before.* An empire of stuff increasingly bought by clicking 'Add to Cart' on a website, with no human or physical interaction, and delivered by anonymous couriers with no face-to-face interaction.

Turbocharged by the COVID-19 pandemic, our daily lives are less interpersonal and face to face, increasingly computer-generated and online. We are moving into an age where more and more daily life moves from the physical to the virtual. Working life used to be defined by the noisy whoosh of the office watercooler; now it is the hum of the home computer. The next generation may inhabit an even more disembodied world than ours.

Time will tell how we adjust, as we surely will, to this peculiarly weightless wonderland. In this economy, the crucial skill for business is no longer engineering or distribution, product development or the traditional marketing mix, but the skill of constructing a narrative. Describing the 'you' a product expresses, conjuring up a vision of what you might become, or painting a picture of a more purposeful life. Above all, the selling of intangibles privileges those with storytelling skills. What is needed are those who can link a product to a zeitgeist, or help it to stand out in a sea of sameness; those who can tell stories that engage with you on topics you care about, and stories that keep us together in a fragmented world. It is no

---

* Professor Frank Trentmann, author of *Empire of Things: How We Became a World of Consumers* (2016), estimates that the average modern German will have accumulated 3,000 items by the time they reach adulthood.

coincidence that twenty-first-century marketing emphasises storytelling and its close cousin, mythmaking.

This – and the tragedy of truth decay – are the subjects of the next chapter.

11

MYTHMAKERS

How Snapple Lost Its Juice

*'If they have to put the word "natural" on a box
to convince you, it probably isn't.'*
Eric Schlosser, *Fast Food Nation*

I may have mentioned that I love to tell stories.

I'm not alone. Marketers, brand managers, advertising execs, even – and especially – CEOs love to tell stories too. There are two types: the ones they tell us (product backstories, origin myths, and so on) and the ones they tell each other – which they usually call case studies. This chapter is one of the latter. But observe the marketers closely in coffee shops, their laptops aglow and faces anxious; at airports, noses buried in motivational bestsellers. Listen to them at conferences and unconferences,* Foo camps and Bar camps,† in MeetUps and PechaKuchas‡ – anywhere you can hear how they talk when

---

* A conference where the agenda is created on the day and collaboratively.

† Foo camps and Bar camps are also exponents of the 'there is no agenda until the attendees make one' movement.

‡ A kind of Japanese speed-dating PowerPoint presentation. 'Open, spontaneous, fun, informal, silo-breaking' is how they are described on the PechaKucha website. You are allowed 20 images for 20 seconds each, so 'over in 7 minutes' would be an equally good description.

they are among themselves. What they are really telling each other are cautionary tales. Popular ones include:

How Toyota Strayed From The Path Of Reliability And Ruined Its Reputation

~

Naughty Nike Who Paid Little Heed To Conditions In Some Of Its Factories And Whose Brand Equity Suffered Horribly As A Result

~

How Coke Disdained Its Loyal Customers By Launching New Coke And Was Made To Pay The Price

These stories tap into our – no, not our – a brand manager's, or an advertising executive's, darkest fears: product failures, launch fiascos, calamitous campaigns, and ruined reputations. The story structure is simple: Brand X, who from humble beginnings achieves great success, commits a Terrible Error, a Cardinal Sin which results in a Fall (a fall in sales – we're talking business here, remember, not theology) for which the brand manager or advertising executive may be fired. But not every cautionary tale needs to end in disaster: the nervous executive can be assured that if they heed the moral of the story (most usually realigning the brand and reconnecting with core values and/or consumers), Redemption and a return to Grace will follow for Brand X. The cautionary tale can become a fairy tale.

One of the most famous marketers' tales is the story of Snapple, a company that produced, and still produces, a range of juice and tea drinks known for their 'All Natural' and 'Made from the Best Stuff on Earth' slogans. You can download the story as a PowerPoint slideshow, or you can look for free at one of the numerous essays on the subject by marketing students (although many of them seem to have almost no grip on anything that happened before the twenty-first century). Or you can buy the Harvard Business School case study, which stops just at the moment of greatest crisis for Snapple, and asks MBA students to supply a solution that will lead to an appropriately happy and profitable ending. Or you can pay Mike Weinstein – aka 'The Rule-Breaking Beverage Guy' and erstwhile CEO of a company called Triarc, which once owned Snapple – to come and tell his story to your managers in person.*

In all versions, the tale can be summed up as:

How Snapple, Which Lost Its Way, Got Its Juice Back Again

The Rise

The story of Snapple begins with Arnie Greenberg, whose folks ran a sardine and pickle store in Ridgewood, Queens, NY. Arnie, Lennie Marsh, and Hyman Golden were friends from way back and, in 1972, the three New Yorkers founded a company called Unadulterated Food Products to sell juices to health-food stores. They chose the slogan '100 per cent natural'. Eight years later, the company introduced a line of products with the name 'Snapple'. The name came from one of its original products, an apple juice that had a 'snappy appley taste'.

The gang of friends had an unorthodox approach to product development and innovation. New flavours, including Passion Supreme, Vitamin Supreme, Apple Crisp, and Cranberry Royale,

---

* 'Snap Judgments', according to Weinstein's website, is 'a fast-paced 45-minute talk complete with historical slides, old TV commercials, and unique learnings from the rise, fall, and rescue of Snapple.'

were launched almost at random, with no sense of an underlying strategy to the product mix. As Douglas Holt, an expert on cultural branding, has pointed out, they continually rolled out odd and seemingly ill-conceived blends, only a few of which became hits. They relied on their most zealous customers for product and packaging ideas, rushing goofy and oddball requests into production without so much as a focus group. All it took to launch Ralph's Cantaloupe Cocktail – a drink that featured customer Ralph Orofino's face on the label – was the fact that Ralph liked melons. Everything was accidental and imperfect, wacky and erratic. Snapple was the loveable underdog, David to the industry Goliaths, turning the established way of doing things upside down. Radically and proudly different from the Coca-Colas and PepsiCos, it eschewed supermarkets and malls where the 'Big Soda' brands were to be found, distributing instead through smaller delicatessens, convenience stores, pizza joints, and gas stations across the New York area. Its packaging and promotion were unusual – 'offbeat, cluttered and almost gloriously inept', in Holt's words. One early spokesman, the less than charismatic Czech tennis player Ivan Lendl, was unable even to pronounce the brand's name, promoting it instead as 'Schnaaahpple'. The company's tiny office was inundated with fan mail. Over two thousand letters poured in each week, along with videos, songs, artwork, and poetry, all paeans to the glories of Snapple.

As the company grew, it kept the amateurishness that had attracted legions of devoted fans. The company's truck dispatcher, Wendy Kaufman, was promoted to become its spokesperson. Wendy had once written a fan letter to an actor that was never answered, and so she made it her mission to answer personally as much of the fan mail as she could. A five-foot-two Long Island native with a big personality and a 'Noo

Yawk' accent that could strip paint, Wendy featured in numerous TV ads, opening each 30-second segment with her trademark salutation, 'Hello from Snapple!'. She was the cornerstone of Snapple's claim to authenticity.* TV viewers could see that the chatty and chubby Wendy was the real thing, not a celebrity paid to endorse the product. She would read a query from a Snapple devotee, answer it,† and the ad would cut to the customer's home, where a TV crew was present to capture their reaction. Unscripted, with all the bloopers left in, the ads were a sensation, and 'Wendy the Snapple Lady' became a star in her own right. Her outsize personality attracted the attention of the public as well as television hosts, including Oprah and David Letterman, on whose show she read out Letterman's Top 10 Least Favourite Snapple Drinks. It was all wonderful and welcome publicity.

Snapple's ethos was authenticity first and last, 100 per cent natural marketing. When a woman wrote in to say that her dog Shane came running every time he heard a Snapple cap being opened, they invited her to have Shane filmed for an advertisement. When they tried it with the cameras rolling, the dog refused to move. True to their principles, they ran the ad anyway, complete with uninterested dog.

As part of the quirkiness typical of the brand, Snapple started to include 'real facts' inside the bottle caps. The first ever Snapple

---

* In an interesting elision that bolsters the myth, the story is always told with Wendy as an unlikely Cinderella, plucked from the anonymity of the dispatch room to become Snapple's advertising princess. As a matter of fact, she was a friend of Arnie Greenberg's family, and had been at university with the agency head who conceived Snapple's mould-breaking vérité advertising.

† When mail grew to almost 500 letters a day, Snapple hired another woman named Wendy Kaufman so she could answer mail, too, and no one would be the wiser.

Fig. 11.1. A Snapple 'Real Fact'.

'Real Fact': 'A goldfish's attention span is three seconds.' (Real fact: it isn't.)

For the young, feeling sidelined by the Reaganite '80s, Snapple assumed an almost mythic status as the countercultural antidote to the fizzy pops and sodas of mainstream America.* Authenticity, in its modern sense, is about marching to the beat of your inner drum, about not heeding society's call. Snapple allowed consumers to feel that they too could flee the morass of conformity by their choice of drink. As a scene from *Chicago Hope*, a networked TV drama broadcast in 1998, put it:

---

* Interestingly, whether you call fizzy drinks 'pop' or 'soda', or even use 'coke' as a generic, depends on where you come from. Academics have mapped regional variations in the USA and a crowd-sourced map, http://www.popvs-soda.com, shows broadly the same results: 'pop' marks you out as a Midwesterner; 'soda' as from the North-East or South-West; and using 'coke' to mean any fizzy drink at all is strongest in the Southern states, the heartland of Coca-Cola Corp. The beverage industry calls them 'carbonated beverages' or 'CSD' (carbonated soft drinks).

You remember the '80s, Philip?
Of course.
God hated the '80s.
He didn't like anything?
He liked Snapple.
God liked Snapple?
Not all the flavors.

Snapple was loved – and what was not to love? It was Kurt Cobain's *and* Jerry Seinfeld's favourite drink.

Business boomed. By the end of the '80s Snapple had introduced a range of iced teas,* including lemon, raspberry, peach, cherry, lime, and mint flavours, as well as 'Kiwi Teawi', and was selling over $50 million worth of 'The Best Stuff on Earth' every year. But companies need to make profits too. In 1986, barely breaking even despite $5 million in sales, Lenny, Hymie, and Arnie decided to cut costs. They slashed the juice content from 100 per cent juice to 10 per cent. With the big boys from Pepsi and Coke moving onto their turf, the founders, now in their fifties, were ready to sell up and cash in. Which they did in early 1992, selling 70 per cent of the company to a Boston investment firm for $145 million – as Greenberg said, 'More money than I ever thought existed.'

---

* They were 'the first iced teas that didn't taste like battery acid', said Arnie Greenberg when asked to explain their success.

The Fall

Meanwhile Quaker Inc. were waiting in the wings. The oats-to-beans-to-pet-food conglomerate had been eyeing up Snapple for a while, seeing it as an edgy 'fashion' brand that could bring in the customers their mainstream brands could not reach. Quaker's acquisition of Gatorade, a fizzy isotonic drink the colour of a footballer's wife's tan, had been a huge success some years earlier, and Quaker believed that by buying Snapple and yoking it to Gatorade they would become a major force in the beverage market. On the face of it, it was an unlikely plan. Gatorade was the antithesis to Snapple, a carbonated sports drink that fitted into the lifestyles of people who played sport or worked out at the gym: essentially families and jocks. It was drunk by people who bought their drinks in superstores rather than delis, who lived lives very different to the urban Snapple drinker.

In 1994, Quaker bought Snapple for $1.7 billion, a steep sum for a company with fewer than a hundred employees, no factories, and a handful of contracts with bottlers and distributors. Quaker decreed that from now on, there were to be no more corner shops and delis for Snapple; it was to be malls and supermarket shelves. Worried about the risks of urban 'quirk' to their mass-market brands, they fired Wendy Kaufman, as well as shock jocks Rush Limbaugh and Howard Stern, who had long been hired to endorse the product. Out went random, untested product ideas and hit-and-miss new flavours like Ralph's cantaloupes; in came Quaker's streamlined, rationalised product-development process.

It was a complete disaster. Sales nose-dived. Having been sacked, Howard Stern retaliated by urging his radio listeners to boycott 'Crapple'. Snapple began to lose its iconic stature. The management rationale that Quaker could optimise Snapple's value by 'applying its expertise in mind-share branding' failed to take account of the fact that consumers can, on occasion, make up their own minds. As sales figures continued to plummet, Quaker were finally forced to throw in the towel. In 1997, they sold the brand to a private equity firm called Triarc for $300 million – $1.4 billion less than they had paid for it. In the corporate carnage that followed the Snapple fiasco, the chairman and president of Quaker both resigned, with their marketing and advertising departments suffering extensive collateral damage.

And the lesson of this story is (are you listening carefully, brand managers?):

How Quaker Failed To Grasp The Principles Of Cultural Branding And So Lost $1.4 Billion Of Shareholders' Money

A cautionary tale indeed.

The Redemption

At this point Mike Weinstein, CEO of Triarc, enters our story. A genial fellow who likes to be described as 'The Rule-Breaking Beverage Guy', Mike knew that a brand in decline seldom comes back. 'We're in a fashion business here, and when your imagery isn't fashionable, often that's the end. But we've talked to a lot of consumers and we did a lot of qualitative research, and we've decided that in this case the brand still has inherent strength. People feel good about it. It will respond to the right marketing stuff.'

The first thing Mike did was to re-hire Wendy Kaufman, announcing that 'Wendy is the essence of the brand'. He ran a parade down Fifth Avenue celebrating her return and launched a new flavour, Wendy's Tropical Inspiration. As one analyst put it: 'Essentially, the company is moving to realign the brand with the vision that made it a success in the first place.'

Like Lenny, Hymie, and Arnie, Mike was happy to experiment. The Triarc guys were free of corporate pressure – it was genuinely OK not to succeed. On display in Triarc's lobby were garbage cans filled with products that had failed. Triarc could make Snapple authentic again because it shared the ethos of the original founders.

But 'founder authenticity' is not the only kind of authenticity a product needs. Another analyst identified the 'pivotal characteristics' of the brand. Snapple is 'fun', 'personal', 'vividly sensual'. Pivotal characteristic #1 was 'authentic'. The analyst's note reads presciently:

Authentic – The brand pivots on trust. It makes implicit health claims. Its name conveys healthiness.

Snap → active → healthy
apple → healthy

The fruitiness claim works on the same level as the vegetable content of V8 juice. Fruit is healthy, Snapple is fruity, so Snapple is healthy. If it is seen as faux fruit juice (e.g. Sunny Delight, Kool-Aid, etc.), then its claims (All natural ingredients; Made from the best stuff on earth) become just so much hype and Snapple drinkers are chumps.

Weinstein used the brand to make consumers feel good about themselves and used the image of free-thinking and quirky Snapple drinkers to make the market feel good about the brand – a neat self-reinforcing circle. He played on the fact that Snapple's niche was to be quirky and wacky, but in a safe kind of way. As Ken Gilbert, Triarc's senior vice-president of marketing, pointed out: 'Snapple users are really very average, normal people but the brand helps them to think of themselves as offbeat.'

In any event, the tale of 'How Snapple Got Its Juice Back Again' has the requisite happy ending of a prodigal brand returning to its core values. Perhaps we should let Mike Weinstein sum up the upbeat and inspirational finale: Triarc 'faced an immense challenge trying to rescue Snapple. Embracing the original vision of the three Snapple founders … [we] used innovation, speed, and creativity to engineer a miraculous turnaround. Within six months Snapple [had] returned to growth and profitability.'

It was a happy ending for Weinstein too. Not only was he named 'Beverage Industry Executive of the Year' and inducted into the 'Beverage World Hall of Fame', but Triarc sold Snapple within just three years for $1 billion, more than tripling its investment and – we have to hope – making Weinstein a very rich rule-breaking beverage guy indeed. It is at this heartwarming point that the brand managers' tale ends. The cautionary tale has become a fairy tale, and Snapple drops out of the marketing playbooks.

Real life is often messy and unsatisfactorily open-ended. The joy of fairy tales is the clarity and finality, as well as the 'ta-dah!' quality of the ending. The frog turns back into the prince and the camera closes in on the delighted face of the princess who up until then had been bravely puckering up to an unpromising-looking amphibian. Or, in the case of 'How Snapple Got Its

Juice Back Again', closes in on the delighted faces of shareholders and management as they gaze at newspaper headlines about the massive takeover pot of gold.

We can't fast forward fairy tales to see how things panned out ('Princess to divorce "slimy" husband. "I couldn't stand the burps"') but we can fast forward the Snapple story. Two decades after Triarc's triumphant turnaround, now owned by a megacorp called Keurig Dr Pepper, Snapple is up there with Big Soda behemoths Coca-Cola and PepsiCo.

At a casual glance the brand looks the same as ever. It's kept the quirky flavours coming: to celebrate 4 July 2014, Snapple issued a patriotic limited-edition drink called Lady LiberTEA. The label showed luscious fruit alongside the Statue of Liberty or, as Snapple put it: 'Behold. Lady LiberTEA, a tribute to our Nation's Heritage. She's a blend of our delicious black tea with RED raspberry, WHITE peach and BLUEberry flavors.' Snapple Apple still has its same Real Facts on the caps and still proudly trumpets 'All Natural' on the label. But a closer look reveals that it's not *quite* the Snapple of popular imagination any more.

One sign is a shift in the language. Like a whisper of rain on the wind, discordant only to the counterculturally attuned ear, the idiom changes. In 2010, the company's annual report proclaimed: 'At Dr Pepper Snapple Group, we are *flavored to win*' (my italics), before talking about its expected 'plans to grow shareholder value … building our brands, growing per caps and rapid continuous improvement'.* Now I'm not naïve.

---

* 'Per caps' is per capita consumption, so 'growing per caps' means persuading consumers to consume more of the same product. Currently Mexicans lead the world in per capita consumption of soft drinks, consuming over 1,000 soft drinks each on average per year. Go on, divide by 365 – that's almost 3 soft drinks a day, *every day*, more than double the rate in the USA, where they consume 'just' 400 per year. In Mexico, diabetes is the leading cause of death.

Phrases like 'shareholder value' and 'per caps' are obviously aimed at investors and markets and not at consumers, but it struck me as peculiar to use the word 'flavored' rather than Snapple's better-known USPs of being 'All Natural' and 'Made from the Best Stuff on Earth'.

Snapple has also parted company with Lenny, Hymie, and Arnie's New York East Village roots, moving its headquarters first to the Dr Pepper heartlands of Plano, Texas, and more recently to the town of Frisco, Texas, where Keurig Dr Pepper's new HQ overlooks the Dallas Cowboys practice facility. As part of the Keurig Dr Pepper group, Snapple now keeps company with supermarket brands like Squirt (so named because the drink claims to 'squirt' into your mouth like a freshly squeezed grapefruit) and a great many carbonated beverages including 7 Up, Sunkist, and Crush. Like a raddled old trouper rolling out the same tired performance, the familiar brand buttons keep being pressed and the old refrains trotted out. But something has been lost. From the press release for Lime Green Tea: 'Growth will be driven in part by promotions such as a green tea tie-in with St Patrick's Day, a rebate offering a free six-pack and new drinks such as a "ChariTea" connected to a celebrity's cause of choice … Negotiations are under way with several celebrities.' *Negotiations*? Snapple used to grow its own celebrities from real people. What is it doing buying them in? Snapple promotions used to be the cheerful mayhem of 'Miss Crustacean', cherrystone spitting contests, the dog that wouldn't run when the cameras were rolling; not a part of the commercial juggernaut that is America's St Patrick's Day celebrations. 'It's like when the Tin Woodman lost its heart', says Wendy Kaufman (Wendy the Snapple Lady). 'There is nothing in there any more.'

Of course, there's nothing really wrong about being a supermarket product, dressing up a brand in the finery of yesteryear,

Fig. 11.2. Snapple Apple front-of-bottle label.

keeping the quirk for the adverts and speaking a more special-ised and sober language to investors, provided that the product also, as the saying goes, does what it says on the tin. And this is where the real shock came. The words 'natural' and 'naturally' appeared three times on every bottle of Snapple Apple; so did the word 'apple', along with a picture of a whole apple and a sliced apple, on an apple-green background.

But in 2011 a sharp-eyed observer noticed that, if you turned the bottle around to look at the description on the back, you would get a surprise. A Real Fact: Snapple Apple contained no Apple at all. Snapple Apple contained only 'filtered water, sugar, pear juice, concentrate, citric acid, natural flavors and vegetable and fruit extracts (for color)'.

It seemed that Snapple, that poster child for authenticity, was selling an apple juice drink that contained no actual apple juice.

It did contain pear juice (because, apparently, pear tastes more 'appley' than apple) – but only 10 per cent pear juice. 'Ah-ha!' I hear you say. As the label said the drink contains 'natural flavors', those must be from apples, surely? I don't know, and I have no way of finding out, but my hunch is that if Snapple Apple had had actual apple extract among its 'natural flavors' it would have said so, as that would be an obvious marketing win. So I think we can assume that the 'natural flavors' in Snapple Apple originated elsewhere. Can you have an 'all natural' apple drink without any apple in it? And if you can, is it still – in any way that matters – authentic?

A Natural Aversion

What counts as a 'natural flavor' is defined by the Code of Federal Regulations of the US Food & Drug Administration (FDA). The detail is perhaps a little dryly technical for the non food-scientists among us,* but basically 'natural flavor' is a tasty or aromatic extract from anything that was once alive. So animals, plants, and vegetables are fine, but mineral extracts are not. Subject to that, a beverage or food manufacturer can put the resonant though non-specific term 'natural flavors' on the label without ever having to say where those flavours come from.

---

* The term *natural flavor* or *natural flavoring* means 'the essential oil, oleoresin, essence or extractive, protein hydrolysate, distillate, or any product of roasting, heating or enzymolysis, which contains the flavoring constituents derived from a spice, fruit or fruit juice, vegetable or vegetable juice, edible yeast, herb, bark, bud, root, leaf or similar plant material, meat, seafood, poultry, eggs, dairy products, or fermentation products thereof, whose significant function in food is flavoring rather than nutritional.'

So, although most people would expect a juice with apples on the label and the word 'natural' sprinkled all about to contain apples, the 'natural flavors' clause is the legal fudge that means that a food or beverage company can splash 'natural' on a product that may contain none of the fruit/herbs/spices/vegetables on the label. In the case of Snapple Apple those 'natural flavor' ingredients could have been derived from: apples (probably not), pears (maybe), some other fruit … or vegetable … or spice … or poultry … or seafood. All perfectly legally. Or those 'natural flavor' ingredients might even have been extracted from the anal glands of a beaver.* You won't know which flavour source Snapple is using in the product because it's not telling, and emails seeking illumination were fobbed off with corporate obfuscation and gobbledegook.

It takes more muscles to doubt than it does to believe. What the shopper sees at first sight in a convenience store or supermarket – an apple-bedecked label, buttressed by an elaborately told tale of authentic origins, a myth that has had time to embed itself in our collective consciousness – is what they are most likely to believe. To make the mark salivate with greed, the conman uses that staple of his toolkit, mish rolls: wads of cash with genuine banknotes on the outside and stuffed with worthless newspaper inside. If mish rolls were soft drinks, they'd be Snapple Apple: mouth-watering apples on the outside and stuffed with cheap flavourings inside. High on calories but low on juice; high on margin for the manufacturer but low on value for the recipient. Now we know what Snapple meant when it

---

* I'm not making this up. Extract of beaver tush (castoreum – the exudate from the castor sacs of the mature North American beaver) is used to flavour vanilla, strawberry, and raspberry products. Jamie Oliver gave the game away on the *Late Show with David Letterman*.

told markets and investors (but not consumers) that it was 'flavored to win': what corporate Snapple wanted them to take note of was its technical expertise in creating and sourcing the mysterious combinations of molecules that it adds to drinks to give 'apple' flavour to what was otherwise 90 per cent water and 10 per cent pear (not apple, sorry to harp on, but …) juice. Listen out, they are saying: our real USP is in laboratory-extracted flavours and the real tale is:

How Snapple Lost Its Juice, But Won The Fair Maiden Of Flavour, And Thus Found Its Way To Exceeding Profitability

How Sweet It Is

At some point between 2011 and 2013, so within a couple of years of the disconnect between label and contents being pointed out, the company reformulated Snapple Apple. It now contains apple as well as pear juice, along with the still-unspecified 'natural flavors'.

Ingredients are listed in order of quantity: water is number one, sugar number two. When Snapple won the contract to supply all of New York's schools and public spaces, it added vitamins and minerals to the drinks the kids would be buying from its vending machines. As was pointed out, however, they still contained more sugar than a 12-ounce container of Coca-Cola.* Dr Michael F Jacobson, co-founder and for a long time

---

* Snapple: 41 g of sugar; Coke: 39 g. You don't need me to tell you that sugary drinks are significantly linked to obesity. As a rule of thumb, every 1 per cent rise in consumption of sugary drinks leads to approximately five additional overweight adults in every hundred, putting more people at risk of premature death (including death from COVID-19).

executive director of the Center for Science in the Public Interest, called Snapple's products 'little better than vitamin-fortified sugar water'.

What is a worried consumer to do? They might go to the authorities to complain. But they will get no joy, for the weasel use of the words 'natural flavor' on 'juice drinks' and indeed sorbet bars* – and many other examples too tedious to mention since Snapple is by no means alone – is, as we've seen, perfectly legal.

They might try asking the FDA, 'Well, what do you actually *mean* by natural?' But they'd be stumped there too. On three occasions in the last thirty years, the FDA have been asked to define what 'natural' means, and every time they have said in effect, 'Nope. Sorry. No can do', and set their jaw firmly against resolving the ambiguity. No matter that they have managed to define such abstract and imprecise terms as 'light', 'fresh', 'healthy', 'low fat', and 'a good source of ...'; when it comes to 'natural', the FDA have nothing to say, claiming 'we're not sure how high of an issue it is for consumers'. Snapple clearly thinks 'natural' is a priority for consumers, or it wouldn't plaster it all over its product labels. Consumers think so too: natural food and drink is one of the fastest growing segments of the market. The refusal of the regulators to do what is after all their job is causing frustration all round, and leaves the industry free to give as little information as it possibly can.

Having written this book, I have a great deal of sympathy with anyone trying to nail down definitions of authenticity, and

---

* Snapple also sells 'naturally flavored' sorbet bars with mango, pineapple, kiwi, and strawberry on the label, but precisely zero fruit in the product. Curiously, Lady LiberTEA contained no peach, no apple, and no blueberry either.

whatever the FDA say, they will be criticised. But they ought to say *something*. They have the expertise and the mandate, the freedom and the responsibility to define 'natural'. As far as I'm concerned, they can use as many paragraphs and sub-clauses with as many infelicities of prose and legalese as they like, but they do need to have a go at saying what is natural and what is not. Until they do, until they get themselves out of this particular self-imposed fix, consumers are going to feel as if they are being treated – in the words of the analyst all those years ago – as chumps.

Does any of this matter? I'd say, yes, we should be concerned. Telling a tale that doesn't match the underlying reality matters, and it matters more when big business, rather than an individual, is the one telling it. In part because a corporation is larger and more powerful than an individual, but also because our expectations of trust are, in consequence, so much higher. Snapple is not uniquely or even especially culpable; this story is just an illustration of the power and the responsibilities of mythmaking.

We all love a good story. Mythmakers should be aware that stories, like products, have 'best before' dates too. At the start, the Snapple founders tapped into the yearning for a mythological all-natural Eden. A decade later, it was the desire to escape conformity and to express yourself, even momentarily, that propelled the brand's success. But a myth can pass into the collective consciousness and remain there long after it has parted company with reality or is serving any real purpose. There are few, if any, links between the original Snapple and Snapple as it is today. The gap between fantasy and actuality is enormous. A gap that would not matter so much were Snapple today not trading so heavily on the image, memory, and culture of the original.

Should we care? Aren't brands like the honest magicians who say 'I'm going to deceive you' and then do? When brands give us their magic, their enchantments in a bottle, don't we know we're meant to suspend disbelief as though it were a trip to the cinema? *Of course* these trainers won't turn you into an Olympic athlete, they smile. Everybody *knows* that a 'juice drink' isn't juice, they add, pitying your naivety. Only a child would believe that the lady was *actually* cut in half. What's wrong with a little bit of inauthenticity if it gets you through your day?

Perhaps there would be no need to care if it were just a matter of one brand. But it isn't. Although estimates vary, the number of brand messages we receive *each day* is somewhere between 1,500 and 3,000. There simply isn't time to decode and unpick all the brand stories as I've done for Snapple Apple. In a world of ever-multiplying claims and too little time, authentication matters. You may say it's just a soft drink, it's a treat, don't get so *serious* about it all. It's not a big deal – do calm down, dear! But each time we let inauthenticity slip past us we lose a little, and if it happens enough we lose a lot.

12

EXTERNALITIES

China's Gift to the World

*'A handful of qinghao [artemisia] immersed with two
litres of water, wring out the juice and drink it all.'*

Ge Hong, *Emergency Formulas to
Keep Up One's Sleeve*

*'"Victims?" he asked. "Don't be melodramatic, Rollo.
Look down there," he went on, pointing through the
window at the people moving like black flies at the base
of the Wheel. "Would you really feel any pity if one of
those dots stopped moving – for ever? If I said you can
have twenty thousand pounds for every dot that stops,
would you really, old man, tell me to keep my money –
without hesitation? Or would you calculate how many
dots you could afford to spare?"'*

Graham Greene, *The Third Man*

I magine there is a new and virulent disease. Highly infectious,
it's killing the weak and vulnerable quickly, the others more
slowly. The good news is that a cure has been discovered in
China. The bad news is that counterfeiters have moved in and
are selling fake versions of the cure. From the outside you can't
tell the fake pharmaceuticals from the real. Same boxes, same

blister packs, same capsules. But inside, the cure is diluted with so much mineral dust that you might as well chew on chalk for all the good it will do you. Some of the falsified pharmaceuticals do contain just a few grains of the real medicine. It's not enough to cure anyone; but it is enough to allow a new mutant strain of the disease to develop. A strain for which there is no cure.

'This is a very, very serious criminal act', says Professor Nicholas White, one of the world's most respected malaria experts, of this callous counterfeiting. 'You're killing people. It's pre-meditated, cold-blooded murder. And yet we don't think of it like that.'

We have all experienced the fear and misery of coronavirus, but unless you live in those parts of the world where it is still endemic – sub-Saharan Africa, the warm and swampy tropical and subtropical regions of Latin America and Asia – you are unlikely to have come face to face with malaria. And malaria is truly horrible. It invades the liver first, and then the red blood cells. Initial symptoms are flu-like: sweats and chills, headaches, fever, vomiting. Without prompt treatment, the parasites spread to the kidneys, lungs, and brain. Life-threatening complications follow: organ failure, oxygen deprivation, and, ultimately, death. Every year, over 200 million people contract malaria, and around half a million die from it. Over 90 per cent of them live in Africa, and most victims are children under the age of five.

The disease has been described as 'the unsurpassed scourge of humankind'. The malarial parasite has taken so many lives: by some counts, more than half of all the people ever born have died of it. Yet the kind of urgent and concerted international action we saw at the height of the coronavirus crisis is lacking. One reason is that malaria outbreaks are regional rather than global, so they are classified as epidemics rather than pandemics. As the World Health Organisation puts it, a pandemic sounds 'an alarm bell, loud and clear'. It triggers global collective action. But for malaria, the bell has not sounded loudly or clearly enough.

Organisations fighting the disease, from the WHO to the Gates Foundation, believe that with one final push we will be able to consign malaria to medical history. The disease is well on the way to being eliminated; the malaria map has shrunk spectacularly. There is a treatment that could get rid of it once and for all: artemisinin combination therapy, which combines artemisinin, the fastest-acting antimalarial yet devised, with slower-acting drugs that wipe out any straggler parasites. But it has to do so before new mutant and drug-resistant strains take hold.

Those fighting to eradicate the disease are in a race against time. They face a number of enemies. Not only the mosquitoes, and the malaria-carrying parasites they host, but also human parasites of a more familiar kind: counterfeiters.

As we saw in Chapter 5, parasitism is a form of freeloading. One where the parasites get the benefit, and their hosts – victims – pay the cost. It's an unbalanced, asymmetric transaction. We tend to view the transaction between the parasite and its victim as confined to the two of them, but as with any transaction, there can be spillover effects – 'externalities', as economists call them – for third parties. Such externalities can be positive (that is, they benefit the third party), as in the case of vaccination against infectious disease: each person that receives a vaccine not only protects themself, but also helps to protect the rest of us. Or they can be negative. We tend to think of fakery as a self-contained affair, one that concerns only the deceiver and the deceived, just as we tend to regard authenticity as a private matter. But the intertwined stories of these two very different parasites illustrate how wide-ranging such spillover effects can be. Their activities cause harm not just to their immediate victims but to all mankind.

A Tale of Two Parasites

The deadliest of all the malaria-bearing parasites, Plasmodium falciparum, is a single-celled organism. Plasmodium (as I shall call it) has adopted the freeloading lifestyle with a vengeance, living off not one but two hosts. It mates and gestates inside the female Anopheles mosquito and is then transferred to humans through her bloodsucking bite. Plasmodium-borne malaria has no effect on mosquitoes, but wreaks havoc on humans. The parasite does not need to spread malaria in order to survive – to Plasmodium, sick humans are just a side effect – though like any self-respecting parasite it takes care not to kill its host until its own replication is assured.

Even more lethal than Plasmodium are the human parasites, those who supply counterfeit medicines to malaria sufferers, knowing that in the absence of proper drugs they are likely to die. Poor and powerless, many of them among the most vulnerable and desperate people in the world, malaria victims are ripe for exploitation by the unscrupulous.

It is estimated that 30 per cent of anti-malarials sold in sub-Saharan Africa, and up to 50 per cent in South East Asia, are fake or substandard. If such fake or substandard drugs contained no active ingredients at all, then giving them to patients would be of no use to the patients, but would not harm others. But that is not the case. Very often, counterfeit drugs contain a tiny amount of the active ingredients of the genuine drugs that they imitate. And that is the source of the negative externalities that could impact us all.

Inside the body of a dying child, as the counterfeit anti-malarials encounter the parasites, a microscopic arms race begins to play out. The less-than-lethal dose of active ingredient that the fake drug contains is too little to kill off all the Plasmodium in the child's bloodstream; the more robust parasites will survive. The next time a mosquito bites the child, these hardy survivors will be transmitted back into the mosquito population, and from there to new human hosts. As the cycle repeats, hundreds and thousands of times, new and increasingly drug-resistant strains of Plasmodium begin to emerge. In South East Asia, where counterfeit anti-malarials have circulated for years, drug-resistant strains have been identified in several countries.* Experts know that unless they can wipe out the mosquitoes that carry these new strains, they will likely spread to neighbouring countries – and then we could be only a plane journey away from worldwide transmission. Counterfeit medicines will lead not just to drug-resistant misery for millions now but, if we lose the ability to fight the disease, misery for future generations as well. These spillover effects sweep out across geography as well as time.

Counterfeit anti-malarials are just part of a much wider problem. WHO research suggests that every year up to a million people across the world, including 250,000 children, die as the result of falsified and substandard medicines. From the 'life-saving cancer drug' that is anything but – as happened in

---

* There is a further issue: people using anti-malarials in an ineffective and unsupervised way, taking a couple of tablets and stopping once the fever abates – but before all the Plasmodium in their bloodstream have been killed. Which is why you must take any medicine, such as antibiotics, for the prescribed period even if you begin to feel better sooner. Otherwise, you are helping to make the antibiotics less effective in the future for yourself and everyone else.

2012, when cancer patients in California received vials of 'Avastin' that contained no active ingredients – to the counterfeit antibiotics that are estimated to have caused more than 8,000 people to whom they were given to prevent post-surgery infection to die over a five-year period in one Himalayan hospital. A hundred children died in Haiti in 1996 because their cough medicine contained lethal diethylene glycol (the principal ingredient of antifreeze) instead of soothing glycerine. Ten years later, exactly the same thing happened in Panama; hundreds died. Counterfeit medicines are uniquely evil: they pretend to cure, but frequently kill. At best they are useless; at worst deadly.

The majority of the world's 'Bad Pharma' comes from China.* One problem is that China monitors pharmaceutical producers but not the intermediate chemical companies that manufacture many of the ingredients, making it easy for impure ingredients to find their way into the medicines. But the real issue is that corruption and deceit infect every stage of the supply chain. Package designs are easy to counterfeit; pills can be bulked out with cheaper ingredients and sold to customers who, without laboratory or testing equipment, are powerless to tell whether what they are being given is a dud, or even deadly. It is not only the medication that is faked. From show factories where foreign businessmen are shown immaculate industrial units with wiring that goes nowhere, to drug trials of which up to 80 per cent are rigged or falsified, and from product safety certificates (experienced China hands estimate around one in three are fake) to anti-counterfeiting investigators who counterfeit products themselves in order to claim bounties for 'seizing' them, the subterfuge is systemic and all-pervading.

---

* Although India is a major player too.

There can be little doubt that the Chinese state is aware of the extent of the counterfeiting of its 'gift to the world' that is happening on its territory. Many of the companies selling fake pharma are state-run or state-empowered; the academic institutions falsifying drug tests are government-run. If we lose the race to eradicate malaria, much of the blame will lie at China's door.

A Doleful Irony

It is a melancholy irony that the miracle cure for malaria – and our current best line of defence against the disease – was discovered by the very nation whose counterfeits now threaten its eradication.

The story of the discovery of artemisinin is an extraordinary tribute to China's ability to mobilise and organise when it has reason to do so. Malaria is not an easy problem to solve. Both the Plasmodium parasite and its vector, the mosquito, have a regrettable tendency to develop resistance to anti-malarials and insecticides respectively, and any breakthrough tends to be short-lived.

The earliest treatment for malaria, discovered by explorers in the mid-seventeenth century, was quinine, extracted from the bark of the South American cinchona tree. By the twentieth century, quinine had given way to synthetic chloroquine. But Plasmodium acquired resistance to chloroquine, which put paid to the ambitious global eradication programme of the mid-1950s, and by the mid-1960s the world was on its third or fourth wave of anti-malarial drugs. 'SP' (sulfadoxine/pyrimethamine) looked promising, but resistance to it spread rapidly too. When a particularly severe outbreak of the disease coincided with the war in Vietnam, the battle against malaria acquired a new urgency. The North Vietnamese Army and the Viet Cong were losing more troops to malaria than were dying in battle. Somewhere between 50 and 90 per cent of their soldiers were so sick from the disease as to be useless. They pleaded with their principal supporter, China, to find a cure. In 1967, the Chinese set up a secret project to find a new drug to cure malaria, code-named Project 523 for the day (23 May) on which it was launched.

Five hundred scientists were directed to work on Project 523 (many of them for only a year before being purged in the Cultural Revolution). At first they investigated modern synthetic compounds. When several thousand existing drugs had been screened for anti-malarial properties to no avail, they turned to an exploration of the traditional and folkloric remedies that fall under the catch-all name Traditional Chinese Medicine.

Traditional Chinese Medicine was very largely the creation of the chairman of the Chinese Communist Party (also Great Leader, Great Supreme Commander, Great Teacher, and Great Helmsman), Mao Zedong. Some years earlier, faced with a shortage of doctors trained in Western-style evidence-based medicine, Mao had yoked together a thousand years or more of folk medicine, fairy tales, quackery, and some – but very few – real herbal remedies under the banner of Traditional Chinese Medicine, decreed it to be on a par with Western medicine, and directed that the promotion of Chinese medicine should be made a priority. 'Chinese medicine and pharmacology are a great treasure-house', he said. 'We should explore them and raise them to a higher level.'

Mao's integration and promotion of Traditional Chinese Medicine as standing alongside and equal to Western scientific medicine was, like his later 'Barefoot Doctor' campaign, above all a cheap way of providing care to the masses. His aim was to save money; he knew perfectly well that if offered a more effective, pricier alternative, the Chinese would not choose to turn to acupuncture, cupping, moxibustion, yin-yang theories, or herbal and dietary remedies. Mao knew that most of them didn't work; as he confided to his own physician, he never touched the stuff himself. But Traditional Chinese Medicine led to China's greatest medical discovery.

A young scientist named Tu Youyou was appointed to lead the Project 523 investigation of traditional ingredients. She and her team examined over 2,000 herbs, but without success. Then they alighted on one called *quinghoa*, also known as artemisia or sweet wormwood. According to the story, the breakthrough came when they uncovered a recipe in a physician's handbook, *Zhou hou bei ji fang* ('Emergency formulas to keep up one's sleeve'), written in 340 CE by Ge Hong. It suggested that to calm a fever believed to be malarial you should take 'a handful of qinghao [artemisia] immersed with two litres of water, wring out the juice and drink it all'. Crucially, the remedy recommended that the *qinghao* be extracted in cold water rather than being boiled as would typically be the case.

This was the great leap forward they needed. When extracted at low temperatures in an organic solvent, the plant derivative *qinhaosu* (artemisinin) proved extremely potent against that most virulent of malarial parasites, Plasmodium falciparum. For the best part of a decade Mao's China, obsessively secretive, kept this important discovery to itself. In the early 1980s, as Chinese scientific journals began to be translated into English, the world started to pay attention. By the late 1990s, Swiss pharmaceutical giants had registered patents for various combinations of artemisinin with other drugs, and were marketing them globally as a cure for malaria. The ancient Chinese remedy had become the medical marvel that would save millions. A wartime emergency had spawned a peacetime miracle. Tu Youyou, awarded the Nobel Prize for medicine in 2015, described artemisinin as 'a gift from Chinese Traditional Medicine to the world'.

What China gives with one hand it takes away with the other. The nation that discovered the cure for malaria is now allowing – even encouraging – it to be counterfeited. When it comes to malaria, 'the unsurpassed scourge of humankind', China is both the solution and the problem.

I can see no excuse for China's complicity in fakery. A nation that can land a mission on the moon, that can lock up a city and throw a cordon sanitaire around 60 million people, can surely track down the diluters and counterfeiters in its midst. China has shown that if it puts its mind to it, there's no limit to what it can achieve. It aims to become the most economically powerful nation in the world: it can make the choice whether to cure or to kill.

But it is not only China that is morally culpable. So are the wealthy Western nations that buy their own medical supplies from China. They – *we* – know that China is responsible for most of the world's Bad Pharma, that it is responsible for very many of those unnecessary million deaths a year, those 250,000 children who wouldn't be dying if it weren't for falsified and substandard drugs. So they increase their quality checks on Chinese-made medicines entering their borders. What they – *we* – don't do is censure China, or seek to hold it to account, or refuse to buy Chinese medicines and ingredients, because they know that if they did, their supplies of drugs would run out in a matter of months. They look the other way. It is not their citizens who are needlessly dying of malaria.

Nations, like individuals, reveal themselves in times of crisis: epidemics and pandemics demonstrate whether we are equal to the moment. Disease also lays bare our fundamental interdependence. It reveals that fakery and inauthenticity are, in the end, not a private matter. There are some negative externalities that affect us all. Authenticity is indivisible.

PART 5
A VIEW FROM NOW

13

THE IMPOSTOR I KNEW

A True Story

'Philosophy is perfectly right in saying that life must be
understood backwards. But then one forgets the other
clause – that it must be lived forwards.'
Søren Kierkegaard, *Journal*

There's a picture on my wall of the man who is the reason I began to write this book. The fantasist and fabulist I thought I'd never see again. He's in the far corner of my wedding photograph. Confetti rains down on a group clustered on the steps, but he is on the edge, somehow detached. The others are laughing and tossing petals in the air. A small bridesmaid is looking up in wonderment at the adult gaiety. His is the only blank face.

He was not an obvious faker. He was, and doubtless still is, a small friendly man, who I'll call Alastair.

Oh, hold on a minute …

The author of a book about authenticity needs to be upfront with readers – this is no place for an unreliable narrator. So let me assure you this is a true story. Events written in the first person happened to me, and the ones written as told to me by a third person were indeed told to me by that person. The purpose of this book is not to expose individuals, just to expose the

283

occasional truth, so I have changed only the following: my fantasist's name, the names of both his fiancées, and the name of the posh house he bought.

Now back to the story.

Over the two or three years we worked together, I learned the following things about Alastair, some directly, others indirectly or when he seemed to let them slip:

That he was from an aristocratic background.

That he had a serious and long-term illness.

That he had known tragedy: his father, a professor at Stanford University, had been killed in a drive-by shooting.

That he was working for the Security Services.

All by turns romantic and dramatic. None of it true. Interestingly, I now know this is a pretty good checklist of the most frequent and popular fantasist lies, though I didn't spot any of them at the time.

He came back into my life in a rather unexpected way, raising questions about authenticity both personal and factual. The problem with other people's personal authenticity is that it is, well, personal. Just because someone made up a few fibs about their life twenty years or so ago doesn't mean they're not an upright citizen now, does it? But since you can't see inside their heads, it's hard to know if and when someone has finally become their true self. There may be a point when, having tried on many skins, they finally find the one that fits them best, when they stop the clock and say 'this is my authentic self' – but should we believe them? Just how much effort are you supposed to make to check on what people say is true anyway? And what if they're not just 'people' but your friend and boss? Or is the answer to all these questions the one I took from the story of Stanley Weyman: that you can never know the whole story until the final reel?

Alastair was the nice guy I met on my first day at the office. Impressions: gingerish brown hair, short, friendly, wearing chinos with a red stripy shirt – the dress-down uniform of the 1980s. It was several weeks before I worked out that he was actually my boss. In a company stuffed with creative egos, he was the safe pair of hands, and more than that: he was a real whiz with computers and financials and could bash any number of spreadsheets when the need arose.

As was fashionable during the 1980s, the company was a boutique venture capital and consultancy business. During that brash and shoulder-padded decade, even as we worked improbable hours, we felt a yearning for an imagined past where there was no need to scrabble for money. The zeitgeist had been intensified by a landmark TV series of Evelyn Waugh's *Brideshead Revisited*, a gorgeously shot and beautifully acted tale of doomed aristocrats, 'all silk shirts and liqueurs and cigars and naughtiness', a televisual nostalgia for times past that marinated viewers in delicious snobbery. At its core was the cult of the country house, a concept that has had such a strong hold on the imagination that it is imprinted even on people who have never been to England or seen a country house. Alastair had read history at Cambridge and talked often and knowledgeably about title and descent. He had a large Kneller portrait in his tiny, starry-vaulted dining room, and from a careless remark of his I understood it was of an ancestor. As time passed, I met his friends: the Polish aristocrat in exile, the soon-to-be famous historian, the clever journalist, and the dashing MI6 spy who later went rogue and sold his story to the newspapers. At Alastair's wedding they were all there. Some time later, I was shocked to hear that his father had been shot dead in California. On his return from the funeral, Alastair showed us the order of service, with readings by his grand relatives. Misfortune piled onto mishap. He was often ill with kidney disease and constantly disappearing off to hospital. His marriage was in trouble.

Then came accusations of financial misconduct, and he was forced out of the company we both worked for. I resigned in protest – a decision that suited me fine at the time, as I was just about to begin an exciting new career in television, but which, I'm ashamed to say, I dressed up as a gesture of high-minded loyalty to my valued colleague and friend.

I didn't spot any of the lies at the time – not, I like to think, because I was wide-eyed and naïve, though I certainly was both of those things, but because I grew up in a very different world. One where there were no issues of trust. Not because everybody was trustworthy, but because in my little corner of North London everybody knew everybody. In the chicken-soup belt that stretches from Edgware (traditional, Orthodox, genteelly semi-detached), loops through Hampstead and Highgate (intellectual, liberal, scruffy), traverses the immigrant heartlands of Stoke Newington and the East End (newly hip and gentrified), and comes to rest in Essex (taxi drivers and the cash economy), everything from emotions to assets is laid out for all to see, like a faintly unappealing car boot sale. We were not on permanent histamine alert for liars or fraudsters as I feel we are today.

It was a noisy, extravert, and musical world.* At home, there

---

* It was a given in my family that anyone would be able to glance at notes on a stave, take up or sit down to whatever instrument it was, and pick out the tune. And not just play, but play together. Like the conversations where everyone talked at once, and increasingly loudly, but where, out of the cacophony, some kind of crescendo of meaning was reached. And there was a language not spoken, but slipped into to emphasise a point, the grace notes of meaning. '*Emes*,' they would say, 'It's true.' Yiddish could be playful as well as profound, a treble-note trill to counteract the bass clef. Like '*spiel*' ('play'), as in 'Old man Zahler's coming round for a *spiel*'. And the part I understood was that the bald man with the heavy German accent, and a smile that lit up his blood-

were three violins, a viola, and a piano always to hand, and, in the attic, the clarinet that my father Archie taught himself to play on the boat out to India during the war, and a mandolin prettily inlaid with mother-of-pearl.

My truth-detectors (and I imagined them to be like the waving antennae of a snail) never developed beyond the presumption that people and things are what they appear to be. My education took me no further forward. I studied the difference between reality and perception in Philosophy, but not in life, the difference between the natural and the synthetic in Chemistry without thinking to look for it in the wider world. An MBA taught me to read a set of business accounts, but nothing about the nature or fragility of promises, so it was as a serious, besuited, and totally unprepared business-school nerd that I first met my fantasist.

Not long after his divorce, Alastair met my beautiful friend Claire. They started going steady (as she told it) or had a brief moment of passion on a Caribbean holiday (as he did). They were in a relationship, she said; it was over after Antigua, according to him. After a while these discrepancies became awkward for me. I couldn't invite them to dinner, as she accepted for both of them, but then he would call to say that he was abroad, and not 'with' her anyway. But when I was round at his place, I spotted a pair of oversize tortoiseshell glasses beside the

hound face so unexpectedly, would arrive with his violin and my father would uncork the piano, and the music would begin. The part I didn't understand was why he didn't have a family. When you're a child everyone has a family, and my parents' explanation of 'he was in the camps' made no sense to me at all. I did once see the numbers on Zahler's arm, but they meant nothing to me either until many years later, when I remembered them and wondered how he could even bear to hear any words at all from a language so close to German.

bed that were unmistakably hers. He met my friend Serena (classic English rose, firm of jaw and fair of hair), and soon they too were an item. Serena, beaming, told me they were going to get married and live together in town. I spoke to Claire and she said they planned to get married and live together in the country. Two fiancées seemed like one too many to me.

I tried to confront him but got nowhere. I dropped by one day and found him with his spook friend, and he told me that he too was doing security work and I was not to discuss his whereabouts with anybody. I couldn't work out whether that was true or not. And I didn't know what to say to either of my friends, who had done nothing to deserve this betrayal. Do I tell Claire about Serena? Serena about Claire? Am I a bad friend if I don't? Or a worse friend to Alastair if I do?

I didn't need to worry too long, though, because his lies were about to come out. It was 1999 and Alastair, otherwise so savvy, had failed to consider one important thing. He may have had two fiancées, but there is only one Millennium. There is only one end-of-an-epoch New Year's Eve, which you must obviously spend with your fiancée. Easy with just the one, tricky if you have two, both waiting to greet the new dawn with you.

I spent New Year's Eve in bed with a raging temperature, listening to the sound of the fireworks marking the millennial shift, and wondering which fiancée Alastair was with, and what he'd told the other one. The firecrackers exploded and the catherine-wheels wailed, shrieked, and hissed, but the screeching sound in my ears was of a rollercoaster coming off its rails.

When you've been betrayed, a number of things change. You go through stages not dissimilar to the phases of mourning: grief, denial, anger at the loved one for leaving you, fear, and then, with any luck, acceptance and moving on. Your attitudes and behaviour also alter in a number of more or less predictable ways:

You decide not to trust people for the moment.

You decide not to trust people ever again.

You can't believe you were taken in.

You can't believe other people fell for it too.

Really annoyingly, other people start to tell you they knew all along the person was a fraud; they just never got around to telling you.

You resolve to be more vigilant in the future.

Eventually, I found out what had happened that night. Serena had arranged a New Year's dinner in her cottage, for her fiancé to meet her closest friends, but Alastair never showed up, leaving an empty seat to greet the visitors. Word came of a crisis, a breakdown, an illness, and then … he disappeared.

If there are real heroes in this book, they are people like Serena. Here's what Serena did after Alastair vanished. Full of raging energy, she took four months' leave from work to track down Alastair's real story. She talked to everyone she could find who knew Alastair and learnt what was, and wasn't, true about him. She did this from my spare bedroom, as she had sold her flat to move in with him when she thought that she was his one-and-only fiancée and that they were going to live together. Every day she came back with a new revelation, a new lie unpicked. When she searched Alastair's empty flat and retrieved a copy of the printed order of service from his father's funeral we were flabbergasted, because by this point we weren't sure that his father had died at all, at least not as described. We lapsed back into silence in awe at the lengths Alastair must have gone to in order to maintain his fantasy edifice.

Here's what I did. I read every book about truth and lies that I could lay my hands on: fact and fiction, yarns and super-serious philosophical tracts. I became obsessed by tricksters and impostors, historic and present day: what made them tick and the psychology of their victims. I analysed the anatomy of a con from every angle. I wondered whether we had been, in some way, complicit: Claire and Serena in thrall to some Mills & Boon romantic fantasy, me all too ready to take people at their own estimation. Most of all I wondered what the point of the lies was. He couldn't have married both Serena and Claire; he would have had to sort it out at some point. And were his breakdown and illness play-acting, done to get himself out of the mess he'd got himself into? His way of dealing with at least one too many fiancées?

After a while, life was too much fun to worry about Alastair and what he might, or might not, be doing. I was working in television – itself a fertile field for fantasists, though they mostly confine their storytelling to the screen. My beat was 'factual' television, which was just beginning the slow transmogrification into entertainment that would peak with today's constructed and scripted 'reality shows'. In my bluestocking way, I thought long and hard about the problems television poses for representations of reality: the imbalance of balance; the 'view from nowhere' that conflates neutrality with fairness; the faux objectivity of the edited interview; the pretend candidness of 'ObsDocs' (observational documentaries) and 'fly on the wall' filming. Back then, we were the few talking to the many, and we thought that as broadcasters we had a special responsibility to create truthful pictures of the world. We had no inkling of the problems the internet would bring.

I didn't hear anything more of Alastair, and I assumed that he was getting his life back in order. The waters closed over his small local impostures. Life moved on for the others too. Serena married a young Russell Crowe lookalike; Claire, an intrepid businessman who flew light aircraft. Happy endings for all, I thought – though I was wrong about that too.

Eleven Years Later

My son comes home from school very excited.

His violin teacher had been struck by the bow he was using and had asked to look at it more closely.

'She told me to take great care of it, as it might be very valuable. She said it might be a Voirin and it could be worth up to £20,000.'

His brow furrows. 'But we shouldn't sell it – it was Grandpa Archie's.' He seems genuinely worried. He is sentimentally attached to the grandfather he was named after but never met.

'Where did you get it?'

'From the attic.'

The motley collection of my father's instruments in the attic comprised three violins, a viola, and a cello, all in dusty cases, mostly missing handles and fastenings, and oozing strands of horsehair from bows inadvertently trapped as they were inexpertly shut. I was interested in the teacher's reaction to the bow, and I remembered one of the violins was quite old, so I took them to be valued. Tom, the restorer and valuer, ushered me into a small sitting room with oxblood walls covered in pictures and instruments and proceeded to disappear with each violin in turn into the workshop next door. He wore a long dusty-blue apron with a white T-shirt underneath, long shorts, and sandals on his bare feet. His hair was a mass of crisp grey curls and his half-glasses trailed cord about his ears and down his neck. Every few minutes he would scurry out of his workshop like a demented mole, hold up one of the instruments and utter some cryptic words.

'This one's 1960s Chinese. Not worth anything.'

Scurrying in again. Then out.

'This one's German. Someone's smashed the head and put a new top on it.'

'This one could be interesting. It's English. Based on the Long Strad.'

Tom warned me that the Voirin bow might be a fake, but I explained that, given my interest in authenticity, I would enjoy a fake almost more than the real thing. Almost.

As he examined the bow, he started muttering again: 'Pins are in the right place. It's *pernambuco*. Somebody's put this facing on the top, but I'd like to have seen what's underneath. Shape of the top is not quite right.' He looked at the maker's name. 'It says F Voirin, Paris.'

Hope blossomed.

And then the clincher: 'Voirin bows are usually stamped F N Voirin.'

He handed it back to me and said, 'More crosses than ticks.' And I thought to myself: of all the many and varied ways I have found to frame the subtleties of authenticity, that's probably the best and pithiest summary I've heard. *More crosses than ticks*. He's saying: 'It's probably a fake, but we haven't shut the door on it completely.' The Yiddish proverb *a halber emes iz a gantser lign* – a half-truth is a whole lie – had always seemed overly harsh to me. It was good to hear that the world of objects was more nuanced, more forgiving than that.

Might that be true for people? Can we apply some kind of 'more crosses than ticks' principle to them too? I was pondering these questions as I drove home with my collection of instruments. As I turned into a leafy West London square, to my astonishment I saw a familiar silhouette. At first I thought I must be hallucinating. But the curly reddish-brown hair was unmistakeable, as was the stance. I'd just taken a 'Voirin' bow to be checked out as a fake, I was adding another story to my anthology of authenticity, and there he was: my über-fantasist. It felt like some kind of sign, though of what I couldn't be sure. I drove the car up onto the pavement, parked at a rakish angle, and got out.

'Alastair!'

He turned. 'Alice Sherwood!' And we hugged.

It had been more than ten years, but it felt like no time at all. He said, 'You look exactly the same.' Then, glancing at my car, he said, 'That's *exactly* how my wife parks', and he gestured towards a vast Chelsea tractor parked nearer the middle than the side of the road. 'I've just been picking up the scooter my children left at school. Come and meet the moppets.'

The moppets were adorable in their little bucket seats. His wife, it transpired, was blonde, beautiful, and fresh, like an advert for family insurance or toothpaste, and it all felt very sunny and picture-perfect: the younger wife and all the trappings. Here was a successful, happy man. He may have tripped and fallen, but he had stood up and tried again.

'Let's have a coffee. Catch up? You're still in the same place', he said, as if he knew.

At home, Archie was playing the violin to a tempestuous piano accompaniment. He didn't seem at all fazed that the bow wasn't going to bring us riches. In fact, he was almost relieved that there was now no dilemma to solve. I too thought that a fake Voirin bow was frankly a relief: you can just use it to make music without making a museum piece out of it.

Sometimes, I reflected, it can be good to have more crosses than ticks.

I had made a checklist to give to any friends who were wondering whether someone they knew wasn't quite what they seemed to be. It said: listen to the stories they tell about themselves, and red flag any of the following:

If they tell you that they happen to be related to the aristocracy or royalty, or to a celebrity.

If they have a secret but important job. Like being in the intelligence services, or the SAS or the Paras.

If they have a secret but romantic sadness (such as the death of a loved one), or a slow-acting but sympathy-inducing illness.

And there was one more that I didn't know yet:

If they have *form*. Because if they lie about one thing, they will likely lie about others.

One summer day in 2013, I'm leafing idly through the paper when a photograph leaps out at me. Under a banner headline is a story about a company suing their former director for allegedly helping himself to millions of pounds of their money. They want to freeze his assets, ahead of claiming the money back. There is an unflattering and grainy photo of the director, which is plainly of Alastair. In the inky smudge of the newspaper, my friend and former boss looks indistinguishable from any other low-rent, high-stakes crook. The company is alleging that he stole their money to buy himself a lavish country estate called Sturridge Manor, as well as to prop up his own ailing businesses. There is a photo of the Manor which looks, well, *manorial*, but in a not very interesting way: Georgian frontage, honey-hued stone, eerily symmetrical, and with rooms stripped bare of any character. An estate agent might talk it up, but it's no Brideshead.

The headline doesn't come as a complete surprise: a gentleman bloodhound employed by the company has already been in touch with Alastair's old crowd in order to gain insights into the man and his modus operandi. It gets me thinking. Why had I not paid attention to the allegations of financial misconduct when we were working together? Should I have wondered if a love rat might be a financial rat as well? Maybe because Alastair was my friend. Maybe it was because I believed in redemption and that we shouldn't be defined by our youthful errors. Or am I just making excuses for laziness and a kind of laissez-faire complicity?

The old crowd get to talking among themselves. I tell our most upper-crust mutual friend that the order of service had turned out to be a fake, and how Alastair's connections to assorted aristocrats didn't stack up, and he says, 'I knew Alastair couldn't have been related to all those people, otherwise one would have *known* him, if you know what I mean.' At least one person turns out to have known all along that Alastair's father couldn't have been killed in a drive-by shooting somewhere near Stanford, for the simple reason that his father never was a professor at Stanford. 'I was curious', Alastair's old journalist friend says to me. As this was before the internet, he had rung up Stanford and found that they'd never heard of anyone by that name. An old friend from Alastair's days at McKinsey writes to me saying that it was inevitable that his compulsive lying would get worse and worse until stopped, adding sadly, 'I tried to talk to him about it a few years ago, but was met with denial and indignation. Haven't seen or spoken to him for years … I feel sorry for all the people he must have hurt along the way.'

Last Train to Fantasyland

Eight months later, the court proceedings end in a summary judgement against Alastair. More details emerge. When I read the judgement, I recognise many of the familiar details of a con. Alastair had gained the trust of a wealthy Russian clan and persuaded them that they needed a London family office to manage their investments and fund their lifestyle. A company of which he was already a director would be the perfect vehicle. He put forward two investment projects; he roped the family in by telling them that he had other famously wealthy families keen to co-invest. The family transferred millions of pounds to the company, and Alastair simply passed the money on to the solicitors who were buying Sturridge Manor for him and to his own struggling businesses. Over the following months, he produced a variety of 'convincers', including forged letters from two different banks showing that the family's money, as well as funds received from the fictitious co-investors, was in the company's accounts awaiting investment. When an audit which would have revealed the true state of affairs was due, Alastair tried to delay the inevitable; he created a fictitious accountant, from a real firm, complete with a fake email address, and proceeded to forge a correspondence with him. The non-existent accountant was 'elusive and subject to last minute changes of plan and sudden illnesses', a ruse that did not keep discovery at bay for very much longer.* To me, the most shocking aspect of what the judge called a 'disgrace-

---

* Connoisseurs of the genre will note that while Alastair's con contained the key elements of 'roping the mark' and 'giving the convincer', it crucially lacked the 'blow-off'. How Alastair was going to distance himself from those whose money he had helped himself to – short of leaving the country and changing his identity – I have no idea.

ful pattern of fraud and forgery' is that Alastair forged his mother's signature on a mortgage that turned her home into security for a £250,000 loan he had taken out without her knowing.

It turned out that Alastair had been made bankrupt not long before the hearing, and he represented himself in court. The judge seems to have given him every opportunity to set out his case. But as I read the judgement, I share the judge's bewilderment that a man so obviously 'of high intelligence and impressive experience' should put forward such a rambling and implausible story. Alastair relied on an 81-page witness statement that contained not a single corroborating document. He claimed that many documents that would have supported his defence had been in a Dropbox account, from which they had been mysteriously deleted. The judge's conclusion was unequivocal. Alastair's defence was fanciful and hopeless; he had no prospect of showing that he had been entitled to use the company's money for his own purposes.

I can only speculate what made Alastair do something as clumsy as this sudden pitch for riches. If I had to guess, I would say that it was a mix of desperation (he'd run out of money) and the gambler's last roll of the dice – the final chance for the glory he felt had eluded him; a grasping at the life less ordinary that he craved: Lord of the Manor, and a big house with portraits. He was past fifty, and a middle-aged man in a hurry. His friends and colleagues had had genuine career success: the historian now played on the world stage; others were leading journalists and literary agents or ran vast multimillion pound businesses. Unlike Stanley Weyman, who found his 'skin' as a journalist and stopped pretending, Alastair didn't manage it in time. The strangest thing of all was that this great rollercoaster ride had lasted a matter of months. Alastair was the owner of Sturridge Manor for less than a year.

I developed my own theory about Alastair, with his classic impostor profile of a fractured and missing childhood. It's easy to feel nostalgia for something you never experienced, and easy too to fill a gap in memory with something more appealing. Maybe Sturridge Manor was his Brideshead. Stories that catch us at key times of our lives are very potent. Perhaps the Manor Madness (as I thought of it), with its ridiculous camomile-lawn pageant of Englishness, was the false memory of a boy who, missing his absent father, poured a Brideshead fantasy into his empty history.

Putting Your Best Self Out There

In an idle moment, as I am writing this chapter, I google Alastair, expecting to find the usual links to the newspaper articles. But this time something new has appeared right at the top of the search results: a website created a couple of months after the final court hearing. I don't know what I was expecting, but not this. Not a website replete with sunlit uplands, old school photos, and pictures of him frolicking with a red setter.

Is he for real this time, I wonder? I'm a sucker for redemption stories (though you might think I should have learned by now), and Alastair's sheer optimism shines through in the uplifting quotes he's garnered. You know the sort of thing: 'Sometimes when you're in a dark place you think you've been buried but you've actually been planted.'

There's no mention of aristocratic forebears in the family section, nor of drive-by shootings. And it's hard not to warm to a man who writes that his greatest achievement is his three amazing children, with posts of children's drawings and loving notes to Daddy. I'm ashamed to say I find these a little cloying, and an unworthy thought flickers through my head that a man who can fake letters from banks and emails from accountants can surely rustle up a couple of kids' drawings. Then I remember that I met two of his children the day I ran into him, so they do at least exist.

There's an awful lot of stuff about cricket, with the odd Saxon church thrown in for good measure; film reviews; a travel page; a music section with his various top tens – including one category of songs for saying farewell: 'Just for those moments when you have to say adieu.' He quotes the most celebrated quip of the patron saint of getting away with it: 'My policy on cake is pro having it and pro eating it.' I look to see if he deals with the serious stuff, and the answer is simple: he doesn't. He details his childhood, adolescence and university days, and skips the next 30 years, including the years I knew him, and the years he was affianced to two of my friends simultaneously. The years that led to the court judgement and the loss of his house rate barely a sentence (he doesn't want to 'bore' us). My eye is caught by a quotation from Anthony Trollope's novel *The Small House at Allington*: 'My belief is that in life people will take you very much at your own reckoning.'

Perhaps that is what this website is about. It's Alastair putting his best self out there. We are all broadcasters now; the old one-to-many ratio has gone. Anyone with access to a computer can give the world an edited version of their life. A website under your real name, a presence on social media, an Instagram account (which it turns out Alastair also has) are all invitations to a private view of the authentic you.

While I'm unpicking Alastair's story, I spend an hour or so looking at the online parish records of the manor house and estate he so briefly owned. I know the historian (and snob) in him would have delighted in the details of tithes and titles, demesnes and moieties of the manor, and the seventeenth-century local dust-up between parliamentary and royalist forces would have been right up his street. But at some point his Brideshead fantasies turned into full-blown fraud. When I google 'manor lordships' one of the search returns is a remark-ably realistic medieval video game, Manor Lords, and I begin to wonder whether, if Alastair had been born just a few decades later, his castles in the air might not have been digital ones instead. What if the aristocratic make-believe, spy-game fanta-sia, drive-by shootings, and all his other rainbow reveries could have been lived not as a fantasy life but as fantasy *games*?

14

REAL LIVES

Virtual Worlds

'Virtual worlds are unreal. We mean by this that they are artificial, fictitious, imaginary, intangible, and invented ... Yet virtual worlds are real as well. All things artificial or invented do not fall entirely outside the ambit of reality.'

Greg Lastowka and Dan Hunter,
'The Laws of the Virtual Worlds'

'They're going to live online, so we need to teach them how to live online.'

Lance Priebe, Founder, Club Penguin

For over fifteen years Virtual Reality, VR, was the coming thing that never quite came.

Every year, the hypemen of virtual lifestyles told us that *this* would be the breakthrough year. This would be the year we swam with sharks on the Great Barrier Reef, took a hyper-realistic trip to Mars, stood atop Everest as the wind whistled past our ears, or BASE-jumped off a skyscraper. This would be the year of fully immersive and interactive experiences. Not actually, of course, but virtually.

And every year it wasn't.

Sure, some tech early adopters were happy to try the cumbersome headsets, wield a 3-D mouse and slip on the wired gloves, have motion sensors track their movements as they lumbered through an approximately rendered 3-D world (actually their sitting room), and pronounce it Unbelievably Awesome and The Future.

For the rest of us, however, headset-VR never quite took off.

Then suddenly, in 2020, it did. Not just with the usual suspects – black-T-shirted gamers, well-funded gadget-lovers, pallid adolescents, lone wolves who were 'something in IT' – but with what you might, for want of a better phrase, call ordinary people. During the COVID-19 pandemic, unable to explore the world outside and desperate to escape their four walls, people sought refuge from reality in virtuality. With up to 90 per cent of the world under travel restrictions, VR travel apps saw a big boost in downloads. In the UK, sales of VR goggles skyrocketed by 350 per cent. Everyday folk went to the expense of forking out anything from £6 for 360-degree 3-D cardboard goggles to around £600 for a top-end headset device, and the faff of strapping on what looks like a blacked-out scuba mask and moving the furniture, all in search of a good – or at least a *different* – time. They climbed and caved; they honed their light-sabre skills; they went on immersive and interplanetary expeditions.* People were turning to digital worlds, however burdensome, unwieldy, and expensive, for things they could no longer get in the real one.

'You can be standing on a beach in the Caribbean, with your feet in the sea watching the waves, or be jumping out of an

---

* Some even discovered their inner graffiti artist, virtually spray-painting walls and roof tops, alleyways and train cars. As the makers of Kingspray Graffiti (available in solo or multi-player versions) helpfully point out, hanging out with friends, bombing walls, and smashing bottles is more fun without the jail time.

aeroplane,' one woman was quoted as saying. 'It's a great way to escape from the reality that is pandemics and crazy world leaders.'

But Virtual Reality offers considerably more than a great way to escape from pandemics, social pressures, and geographical restrictions: it offers a chance to learn, to experiment with new experiences we might never otherwise encounter. We can try on new skins, test out different personas. The pursuit of personal authenticity calls for a voyage of self-discovery, for self-creation and self-expression, but daily life all too often hinders or precludes it. Might the bits and bytes that make up these invented spaces give us the chance to be the authors of our own lives? Might a global network of dumb machines and screeds of invisible code have the power to change what it means to be human?

Tech gets a bad rap when it comes to authenticity, but virtual worlds provide deeply immersive experiences that involve not just slipping on a mask, but the chance to try another life entirely. We're less than a couple of decades into this new and exciting world, but the possibilities are opening up. Might we be able to live lives less ordinary, to try on new digital identities, each time getting a little bit closer to finding out who we really are? And wouldn't it be wonderful to do that in a safe place where no one was deceived, because it was a place where trying on new identities was actually the point?

So convincing has the headset version of VR become that disbelief is almost suspended for you. Jeremy Bailenson is the co-founder of the Virtual Human Interaction Lab at Stanford University, where he researches the effects of spending time in an alternative reality. The multi-sensory room of his lab contains some of the most state-of-the-art VR in the world, combining headset renderings of different worlds with an impressive array of room-shaking, positional sound, and haptic devices (ones that send tactile sensations back to the user). As you move, what you see in the headset changes in real time just as it would in the real world. Your gestures are transported directly into the VR. Objects get bigger as you approach them, sounds get louder as you approach the source, shadows lengthen and shorten. Your body's movements and the onscreen visual reactions to it are perfectly synchronised, yielding an uncanny sense of reality.*

Bailenson likes to tell the story of having Mark Zuckerberg in his lab and getting him to walk the plank. The 'plank', or 'pit', simulation is 'one of the most effective ways to evoke the powerful sensation of presence that good VR produces'. Picture the scene: with a high-resolution headset strapped to his head, the Facebook founder can now only see a digital simulacrum of the comfily carpeted lab. In the control room Bailenson instructs his assistant to 'do the pit', and the programme begins. Suddenly Zuckerberg feels a shudder beneath his feet, and with a whine and a crash the virtual floor falls away, leaving him apparently standing on a small ledge about 30 feet in the air with only a narrow plank connecting him to the safety of a platform 15 feet away. Will he walk confidently across what he knows is only a virtual void? Or will he be unable to trust in the floor he knows is there, and drop to his knees in order to scramble cautiously across the virtual plank? Faced with the same challenge at a demonstration at the Tribeca Film Festival, the rapper Q-Tip crawled across the 'plank' on his hands and knees rather than take the chance of falling into a pit that at least one part of his

---

* Though this is not always the case with less sophisticated equipment than Bailenson's, and those with a tendency to motion sickness are advised to give headset-VR a wide berth.

brain knew could not possibly exist. He was not alone. Such is the power of 'presence' – the fundamental and visceral sense of 'being there' that is the hallmark of good VR – that when invited to step off the plank into a virtual abyss they know to be an actual floor, fully a third of Bailenson's subjects in the Stanford lab refused to do so.*

But you don't have to go to these lengths for immersive and transformative digital experiences. The big story of recent years has been the astonishing rise of virtual worlds that are simpler, cheaper, and easier to access, where we are spending increasingly important parts of our lives. No need to go to Stanford or suffer the indignities of an unwieldy helmet: there are plenty of cyberspaces accessible via your desktop, tablet, mobile, or console. Virtual worlds and video games combined already boast 2.5 billion users worldwide; in addition, there are an estimated 800 million users of Augmented Reality.† (Headset-VR, with fewer than 1.8 million active users globally, is a minnow by contrast.) Big money is being bet that these spaces, constituent parts of what is beginning to be known as the metaverse, the successor to the mobile internet, will be where we spend a great deal of our time in the future.‡

A virtual world is fundamentally an immersive computer simulation with which you interact via a digital incarnation

---

* 'Zuckerberg *does* walk the plank,' according to Bailenson, 'but it's not easy going.'

† Augmented Reality, as the name suggests, offers reality with an overlay rather than an immersive experience, either via your mobile, as with the phenomenally successful Pokémon series, or via so-called smart glasses.

‡ No one has yet come up with a wholly satisfactory definition of what the metaverse actually is; as the *New York Times* has pointed out, 'the biggest ideas in tech often lurch into the lexicon before they are truly coherent'.

known as an avatar, choosing your identity and donning your
'skin' on entry. Although virtual worlds and video games share
many features, they don't overlap completely. You play a game,
but you inhabit a world. A virtual world contains other people
(in the form of their avatars) and provides a form of social
communication that is absent from single-player games. The
other people are there for you to socialise, collaborate, or
compete with. (If they are simply there to give you something to
shoot at, then it's definitely a game, not a world.) Whereas a
game has an objective (saving kingdoms, defeating bosses, lining
up falling blocks, sequencing cards), participating in a virtual
world can often be an end in itself. Virtual worlds are designed
to share a number of characteristics with physical ones: they are
almost always 3-D, with a geography for you to explore and
inhabit; you go there as an individual and there are other individuals to interact and transact with. Most important of all, a
virtual world must be 'persistent' – it must carry on existing
while you are away from it. Whatever you build in the imaginary world must still be there when you return.

What fundamentally distinguishes virtual worlds from that
other great digital invention, social media, is that users of social
media are in the real – albeit often embellished – world, and
virtual worlds are imaginary. Social media applications were
invented to enable users to create and share content and to
participate in social networking. Compare, say, a social media
influencer with a user participating in a virtual world, such as
World of Warcraft, or Second Life, and some key differences
emerge. An influencer-inspired Instagram account is often
created in order to advertise an unrealistically perfect version
of a life. The creator knows it's not real, but others are
encouraged to believe that it is, often to the (potentially
harmful) point where their own lives are made to seem duller

by comparison.* Much of social media (sounding off on Twitter, showing off on Facebook) is about being seen and being heard, a performative bias that exerts a similar gravitational pull on users towards personal *in*authenticity.†

Though no generalisation will fit every one of the billions of social media and virtual world accounts, I find it telling that, whereas Instagram influencers are the apotheosis of 'cool', gamers and inhabitants of virtual worlds are often quite the opposite. But might the digital lives of these earnest nerds and electronic cosplayers be more vivid and authentic than those of the doyens of social media, their motivations more genuine? After all, there can be no question of deception in a world where imposture is a condition of entry. No one is going to think you actually are an elf, an orc, or a cartoon penguin. Social media is the shallow end of the pool to virtual worlds' deep and immersive end. Where social media offers a 'show and tell', or simply the chance to show off, virtual worlds make possible something more profound: the chance to live a new life.‡

It's hard to do justice to the sheer exuberant variety of virtual worlds on offer. There are cyberworlds for the intensely sociable and the socially engaged, for would-be farmers and budding builders, for aspirant sports managers to train their fantasy

---

* This kind of social media is often good for the individual, but bad for society as a whole. Have we learnt nothing from the elks?

† It also results in that strange pastime with which we have all become familiar: the recording of a life rather than the living of it. How often have you been in front of a magnificent view, or a historic masterpiece of art or architecture, and noticed others looking at it only through their camera phones?

‡ Though the fear is growing that the two may converge. In July 2021, plank-walker Mark Zuckerberg announced that his company's future lies in a virtual world. Facebook wants you to live, work, and play inside its metaverse, and to underline the point has changed its name to Meta.

teams. Some metaverses are geared to gritty explorers and survivalists, others devised for storytellers and creatives, and yet others (perhaps less surprisingly) designed with sci-fi enthusiasts and wannabe space-travellers in mind. Some worlds are so complex, long-lived, and player-driven that they have over time created treasure troves of data which economists are exploring for real-world insights. As one writer puts it, cyberworlds have a 'simplicity and intensity of purpose for an hour or two that's hard to find otherwise'. Virtual worlds offer life with more drama, more excitement, and sharper purpose than is to be found in your everyday office existence. Save a planet or prepare a PowerPoint presentation? It's no contest, really.

That we are spending so much time in them, and that they have already assumed such a central place in many of our lives, indicates that digital worlds are offering something more than gameplay.* It suggests they are in some important and fundamental sense *real*. Although one might be forgiven for regarding the life lived by an avatar as inauthentic (after all, your avatar is not really 'you'), that would be too hasty a conclusion. The discovery of self, the stripping-off of society's straitjackets and their replacement by new 'skins', the exploration of new relationships and different communities – these are things humans have always done in pursuit of a more authentic life. Users' experiences across cyberworlds as different as the prototypical Second Life, the massive multiplayer world of RuneScape, and Club Penguin (a snow-bound cartoon world with some distinctly un-cute aspects) attest to the truth of this. As the authors of the

---

* In a pioneering 2001 study by economist Edward Castronova, 20 per cent of participants attested to living their lives mostly in Everquest's Norrath, 22 per cent of respondents expressed the desire to spend all their time there, and 40 per cent indicated that if a sufficient wage were available in Norrath then they would quit their job or studies on Earth.

2004 *California Law Review* article 'The Laws of the Virtual Worlds' quoted at the top of this chapter observe, virtual worlds can be artificial, fictitious, imaginary and intangible, and yet still not fall entirely outside the ambit of reality.

Your World. Your Imagination

The aptly named Second Life is generally held to have been the first truly virtual world. Founded in 2003 by Linden Labs, it was exhilaratingly open-ended. Content was entirely user-generated: its original slogan was 'Your World. Your Imagination', empowering users to build to their own vision. Here was leisure computing with a different face to the geeky all-male province of Dungeons and Dragons, a metaverse that anybody might want to go to.

How you live and behave in cyberworlds highlights the difference between real life and virtual reality. The first thing you do as you enter a virtual world is the thing that is hardest to do in the real world: you choose a personality or identity other than your own. A lot of the early fun of Second Life came from choosing your avatar. Classic librarian or fantasy diva? Real-estate magnate or pole-dancer? The options seemed endless. And the bliss of being judged only on your virtual self! Identity tourism was rife – virtual worlds are fancy dress parties; almost no one comes as themselves. You could buy 'skins' for your avatar to make yourself younger or sexier (the basic free avatar came minus genitalia) and buy dance moves if you were planning to take in SL's nightclub scene. My first invitation to meet in Second Life came on a note slid surreptitiously across an office desk.

I wrote back. 'What's your name there?'

'It's Jeremy Newman. New. Man. Get it?' He looked pleased with himself.

'And what does your avatar look like?'

Another note. 'Like me, but without the paunch.'

You had to load up special software to visit, which could be a bore, but the 3-D graphics were extraordinary for the time. You could explore the 'grid', as the Second Life world was known, buy (virtual) islands, build (virtual) buildings, and earn (virtual) money. Excitingly, in-world profits realised in Linden Dollars, Second Life's proprietary currency, could be converted to real-world dollars. In 2006, a cheongsam-clad stunner named Anshe Chung, the avatar of a German schoolteacher, made the cover of *Business Week* when she reportedly became the first person to become a real-life millionaire from her Second Life real-estate business.

Everyone piled in. Entrepreneurs, broadcasters, and performers hosted events and concerts there. Churches held virtual

Fig. 14.1. Anshe Chung, Second Life's first real-life millionaire.

310

services, and even countries moved in. A 'diplomatic island' of embassies was created with Nigeria, Peru, Serbia, and Israel taking pitches. In just a few years, without any planning, a fully fledged capitalist system built out of bits and bytes rather than bricks and mortar evolved. But soon the gloss began to wear off. Second Life's virtual institutions grew real-life problems. There were bank crashes and credit card max-outs. Griefers,* gamblers, and porn merchants moved in. By 2007, Second Life was past its peak and teetering on the edge of irrelevance.

It's said that cyberworlds never die, they just depopulate. Virtual buildings can't crumble, nor digital gardens become weed-covered wildernesses. For as long as there is server space and some semblance of IT support, troops of die-hard loyalists can still camp out in pristine but deserted computer-generated citadels. Visiting Second Life in 2017, writer and academic Leslie Jamison found small but thriving communities. For some, their second lives were small miracles. A Middle Eastern woman whose avatar did not wear the hijab could move through life in a different way. A musician's career flourished as it had never done in the physical world.† These were not impossible dreams, just ones that had been out of reach in the real world. When Second Life launched with the slogan 'Your imagination is the limit', it spoke truer than it knew. Second Life founder Philip Rosedale had expected users to populate the world with the hyper-fantastic and the insane, incredible spaceships and

---

* Griefers are nihilist trolls who specialise in annoying and disrupting high-profile in-world residents and events. In 2006, a group of these digital jackasses hacked into a Second Life interview with Anshe Chung and attacked her cyber-character with an onslaught of flying pink penises.

† And in his case, playing virtual gigs ultimately led to a record deal in real life.

impossible topographies, and grumbled that what had emerged looked more like Malibu. But Malibu was what people wanted. They had found – and founded – communities in Second Life that were not a substitute, or a fantasy, but a restoratively complementary part of real life. Self-discovery, self-knowledge, and self-creation – locating the inner 'you' – are necessary steps towards what I've called 'personal' authenticity. But if there is something in real life that hinders those steps, and if you can take them elsewhere, somewhere virtual, does that make the 'you' any less authentic, or make the journey any less worthwhile?

Photographer Robbie Cook spent three years creating a series of intensely moving portraits of virtual world gamers (see Plates 11, 12, and 13). His pictures recorded the appearance of the real person alongside that of their avatar. Next to the portraits he gave biographical details of both: real name/avatar name, real-world job, average hours spent per week in game, character type, special powers, and so on. Unsurprisingly, almost everyone chose to be more muscular and high-cheekboned than they were in real life. But the details were eloquent. Some subjects changed gender but little else. One couple chose 'his & her' colour-coordinated superhero outfits to emphasise their togetherness. A wheelchair-bound, oxygen-masked young man, who spent 80 hours a week as an online rifleman in Star Wars Galaxies, was pictured next to his avatar, a supremely able-bodied marksman. These virtual worlds enabled their inhabitants to express not just how they wanted to live, but who they wanted to be. Digital technologies are not just a neat invention, they can also be a means of reinvention.

Blurring the Boundaries

Fast forward to now, and thanks to technological advances that could only have been dreamed of in the early 2000s – cloud gaming, triple-A quality graphics and storage, high-speed, low-latency internet* – virtual worlds are more popular than ever. The focus on human relationships has deepened. Industry pundits forecast that even the most hardcore video games will increasingly incorporate both online and real-world social experiences, and that the lines between virtual and real will blend and blur. Recent shoot 'em up game sensation Fortnite hosted its 2019 World Cup live in front of over 20,000 fans in New York's National Tennis Center, simultaneously livestreaming it to 2 million more. In 2020, a motion-captured avatar of Stetson-wearing rapper Lil Nas X performed to an audience of 33 million across two days and four shows on Roblox, a cutesy video game and creation platform.

Generations are growing up for whom dipping into and out of virtual worlds is a natural part of life. Language has absorbed gamer creole. In 2016, the *Oxford English Dictionary* added 'IRL' (In Real Life, the opposite of online or 'in game') to the lexicon, summing up a changing world where 'meeting' someone can mean we are connecting to them on Zoom, an internet friend can be somebody you've never met, an enemy is likely to be somebody you can't put a face or even a name to. There are even signs that changes in behaviour initiated in virtual reality may carry over to the physical world. Jeremy Bailenson, who we

---

* Latency is a measure of how 'laggy' the connection is. In the early days of Second Life avatars would repeatedly 'bump' into walls of buildings that hadn't loaded yet.

last met making the Facebook founder walk the plank, has carried out experiments centred on the Proteus Effect, the hypothesis that how you behave changes depending on the avatar you are wearing. He found that if their avatar was taller, people were more confident; given attractive avatars, people were more friendly and outgoing; those given progressively older avatars were more inclined to save money. Moreover, the changes persisted even after users left the virtual realm. We shape our avatars and then, it seems, they shape us.

Boundaries have also blurred between physical and virtual goods – goods whose ontological status is, at best, dicey. Global sales of the latter, such as digital Gucci trainers for your avatar to cut a dash in, extra moves in Candy Crush Saga, or (my favourite) the Unwither Ring from FarmVille (it may be just a GIF, but where else can you get a gift that simultaneously expresses love *and* protects crops from withering?), are worth trillions of dollars.

The conceptual troubles we have with virtual goods, products that are simultaneously real and unreal, were neatly satirised by

Fig. 14.2. At $40, the Unwither Ring from
Zynga's FarmVille is a generous if virtual gift.
The ring, launched for Valentine's Day, can be
bought by any player.

the popular nerdy American sitcom *The Big Bang Theory*. The episode 'The Zarnecki Incursion' opened with lead character Sheldon Cooper, a Caltech theoretical physicist of genius-level IQ and negligible personal and emotional development, describing to a policeman the nature of the robbery that has just taken place in his apartment. As Sheldon explains to the increasingly incredulous cop that his vicious gladiator armour, wand of untainted power, enchanted weapons, gold, and beloved battle ostrich have all been stolen, his roommate Leonard marvels, 'You called the police because someone hacked your World of Warcraft account?' Aghast that he is not being taken seriously, Sheldon attempts to prevent the officer from leaving, but the policeman, distinctly unimpressed, points out that the Pasadena Police Department has no jurisdiction in Azeroth.*

The policeman is only partially right. A similar case went all the way to the Supreme Court in Holland, to become something of a legal milestone. It concerned a robbery in Gielinor – a medieval fantasy virtual world which boasts a 'population' of over 200 million registered users – where RuneScape is played.† The real-life robbery in question took place in September 2007, when a 13-year-old schoolboy in the town of Leeuwarden was

---

* Sheldon – The Mighty Sheldor, a level-85 blood elf and hero of the Eastern Kingdoms – has spent three thousand hours clicking on his mouse collecting weapons and gold. After the robbery he comments, 'It's almost as if it was a huge waste of time.'

† RuneScape draws players in with a potent mix of combat, history, and mythology. 'Looking to slay evils that have long lurked in underground dungeons, sealed away by the gods for centuries?' it asks enticingly. The game's statistics boggle the mind. RuneScape claims that its players have racked up more than 443 billion minutes of gaming time since its launch, during which time they have mined a total of 28 trillion virtual gold coins, the equivalent of 58,000 times the gold in Fort Knox. On average, 27 RuneScape players meet their (virtual) doom every second.

beaten up and robbed of gold coins, a magic amulet, and an enchanted mask.* The schoolboy had become rich and powerful in RuneScape through a mixture of skills (combat, basic medieval crafts, monster-slaying) and luck (looting some valuable game items from a – virtual – dead man). Two slightly older boys asked to share his virtual swag, but the boy refused.

A couple of days later, jealous of the schoolboy's (in-game) success, the two older boys took him to their apartment (IRL) and demanded that the young gamer hand over his RuneScape fortune. When he refused to transfer his (in-game) riches to them, they started to punch him in the head and ribs (IRL – are you still with me?), and the bigger boy stood on his chest. The attackers picked up a (real) butcher's knife from the kitchen, and while one assailant held the schoolboy's neck in a stranglehold, the other swung the knife close to his throat, screaming, 'I'll kill you!' It was at this point that the schoolboy decided that he had no choice but to cooperate, and gave up his password and access details. His attackers logged into RuneScape, and while one kicked the schoolboy around the head and chest, the other dropped the (virtual) money and valuables, including the amulet and mask, into their accounts.

The attackers' lawyers advanced a slew of apparently contradictory arguments in their defence. They argued that since goods are made of paint and paper, wood and clay, or cloth and thread, a string of digits – the computer code that generated the coins, amulet, and mask – could not count as property. And if there was no property (drum roll …) there could not have been any

---

* The town of Leeuwarden has produced at least two people renowned for combining fantasy with reality: the artist M C Escher, famous for lithographs featuring impossible constructions, and Margaretha Zelle, who reinvented herself as exotic dancer Mata Hari and who was ultimately executed for espionage by the Germans in 1917.

theft. But theft, came the answer, had plainly occurred, and with considerable violence too. The defence lawyers tried again. Even if virtual goods are goods, they argued, they are goods with no value. But in that case, why did the older boys go to all the trouble of stealing them? With the kind of logical legerdemain we will have to get used to as virtuality increases, they then pointed out that stealing things was an accepted part of the game: the schoolboy's haul had included virtual valuables looted from a corpse. That being so, no crime could be said to have occurred 'in game' when those valuables were transferred to the attackers' accounts, and obviously a virtual amulet or mask can't be stolen *outside* of a game. So, if there was no offence committed in Gielinor, and no physical theft in Leeuwarden, then surely no crime had occurred at all?

At the heart of the case was the question: Are virtual goods in any sense *real* goods? Now, I'm not a lawyer, but it seems to me that if people are making fortunes from virtual goods and teenagers are pulling knives on each other for want of them, then in any sense that matters, they are real goods. Virtuality does not absolve us of responsibility. The court thought so too. It found that the virtual items qualified as goods under Dutch law, so that both defendants were guilty of robbery under Article 310 of the Dutch Criminal Code, and sentenced the two to 180 hours of community service and 'youth detention', thus setting a precedent for future judgements in the hybrid world that many of us increasingly find ourselves inhabiting. It was a recognition that the membrane separating the real and the imaginary is increasingly permeable and porous.

Whether you leave your real-world rights and responsibilities at the door as you enter a virtual world will become an increasingly important question. It will depend, in part, on how closely cyberworlds mirror reality. In 2013, the International Red Cross urged developers of games that convincingly portray real-war situations to punish in-game war crimes, such as torture and the killing of civilians or medical personnel. True-to-life, contemporary, and photo-realistic simulations plainly pose more of a risk than fantasy universes, but whether violence leaks from virtual worlds into real life is a highly contested question. Evidence making *causal* connections between the two seems shaky: researchers at the Oxford University Internet Institute have found no relationship between aggressive behaviour in teenagers and the amount of time spent playing violent video games. 'The idea that violent video games drive real-world aggression is a popular one, but it hasn't tested very well over time', says Professor Andrew Przybylski, Director of Research at the Institute. 'Despite interest in the topic by parents and policymakers, the research has not demonstrated that there is cause for concern.' We need to remain on the lookout for negative effects of virtual worlds on our real-world lives, but for the moment the jury is out. Those whose alter selves are more Middle Earth than Middle East can rest easy: if your orc kills my elf it's not going to count as murder any time soon.

Real Lives in Virtual Worlds

It's early days in cyberliving, but already there are virtual worlds for every age and stage, cyberhighways for every journey in life. For digital natives, the personal authenticity journey of self-discovery and self-expression will take place online as much as offline. They will work, play, make friends, and fall in love in both spaces, building lives, reputations, careers, and relationships in virtual as well as physical worlds. We've yet to see the lifetime effects on the first generation to have criss-crossed the boundaries between the real and the virtual throughout their lives. But there is plenty to learn from what we've seen so far. Perhaps the most poignant story is that of Club Penguin.

The vast majority of inhabitants of virtual worlds are children. And in the early decades of the twenty-first century, you would have found a great many of them in Club Penguin, which at its peak in 2013 had over 200 million registered users. Appealingly whimsical and immersive, Club Penguin was a virtual South Pole, your avatar a cute and customisable cartoon penguin. Intensely social, the Club would throw at least one party a week, and a lot of inhabitants' time was spent visiting other penguins' igloos, practising snow sports, and hanging out in virtual cafés.

Part polar Second Life, part social network, Club Penguin was where children (or at least their avian avatars) could learn to interact with others. For the shy or tongue-tied there was 'Ultimate Safe Chat', a list of pre-scripted messages on a drop-down toolbar. Children could earn their first money by 'mining' gold coins,* buy their first virtual consumer goods (penguin couture, igloo furnishings), have their first (virtual) animal companion in the form of the enchanting in-game pets known as Puffles.

Friendships formed; communities flourished. Penguin society even spawned homegrown mythologies. In one case a rumour spread that if enough penguins crowded onto the Iceberg – a chunk of ice to the north-east of the main island – it would tip over. As an MMO (Massively Multiplayer Online game) originally aimed at 6 to 14-year-olds, safety was a paramount concern. Around a hundred moderators, in penguin guise, would

---

* Coincidentally, you can earn Bitcoin and other virtual blockchain currencies by 'mining' too.

patrol the snows checking up on conversations. Swear or otherwise make trouble (racist, anti-Semitic, homophobic, and sexual messages were all a no-no, as was the giving out of personal details such as email addresses), and you would immediately see an automatic pop-up notice. The first said 'Oops! You used a rude or inappropriate word'; the second warned that you could be suspended from anything from '24 hours to forever', a salutary reminder, perhaps, of how easy it can be to root out bad behaviour if your business model is not based on stoking anger or outrage.*

In 2007, Club Penguin was bought from its creators by Disney for $350 million. For the next 11 years, life in Penguinland continued pretty much as normal. Sure, a few more Disney-themed items found their way into the ice-land's stores than previously, but the ice hockey, inner-tubing, and pizza-making fun continued.

On 30 January 2017, Disney announced that it was shutting down Club Penguin. The end would come at one minute past midnight on Thursday 30 March. Within days the internet was ablaze. Social media was loud with the cries of forlorn Antarctic bird lovers. Users did not hide their feelings:

2017 BE BAD ENOUGH ALREADY AND NOW THEY SHUTTIN DOWN CLUB PENGUIN I HAVE NO FAITH IN HUMANITY

tweeted pat@LOWKEYPAT in shouty capitals.

---

* In the last days of Club Penguin, speedrunners* began to compete to see who could get kicked off Club Penguin fastest. Twenty-nine seconds seems to be the record, a tribute both to them and to the site's safeguarding software. (*Speedrunner: a person who specialises in getting through a game fast.)

CLUB PENGUIN IS SHUTTING DOWN FOREVER NOT TO BE DRAMATIC BUT THIS IS LITERALLY THE WORST NEWS I'VE EVER GOTTEN EVER

yelled @ginapple_.

Disney announced that on the last day there would be the biggest virtual penguin party ever to celebrate and to say good-bye, and players across the world flocked to the online island for a final meet-up. The party, by turns ecstatic and emotional, was a riot. The clever Club Penguin coders in British Columbia had written new scripts, and the Iceberg finally did tip over – to reveal a disco floor complete with flashing lights and dance music blaring out.

Despite the flashy send-off, the closing down nevertheless left a bitter taste. For a while the Club Penguin website redirected users to a new mobile app, Club Penguin Island. But existing users would not, said Disney, be allowed to transfer over their virtual goods, coins, remaining subscriptions, or any other property built up in their former lives. The new mobile app boasted cheaper monthly membership charges, $4.99 rather than $7.95, but that didn't seem to cut much ice with the former penguins.*

For many it was not just a financial hit, but an emotional one – they were losing money and property, but also their memories of childhood. Parts of themselves were no longer their own. There were howls of outrage as people began to realise that virtual goods are just that, and that ideas of ownership, like ideas of identity, are very different in a digital world. A year later, Club Penguin Island closed down too. Its new mobile

---

* Nor indeed their parents, who in many cases would have been paying the subscriptions.

format – more video game than social hangout – had evidently not been the success its owners hoped for.

Have the millions of penguins who once roamed and partied in cyber-Antarctica learned to be careful who they entrust their money and their memories to? Realised that important parts of their lives may not belong to them, and may even be deleted? That no matter how cute the virtual world, in the end business is business? It would be good to think that they had.*

Recently, fragments of stolen code have been used by fans to create samizdat Club Penguin sites. Some of these illicit ice-lands, on so-called 'mature servers', disabled the content filters and, without moderators, became a haven for bad characters and even worse behaviour. Others, though, simply provided a haven for bird lovers missing their erstwhile homeland. In the surge of nostalgia that gripped people during the COVID-19 pandemic, many made their way to these fan sites, some of which garnered as many as 8 million visitors. To judge by the internet posts hailing the return of 'old school' Club Penguin, many may not have realised that these sites were not officially endorsed. Or maybe it was just people's overwhelming desire for 'self-continuity' of their virtual selves, and the chance to reconstruct their memories and to reconnect with their past, that led otherwise law-abiding folk to set aside any concerns they might have had about breaching intellectual property laws or acting illegally.

---

* Dispossessed penguins might be heartened to know that new block-chain-based platforms are emerging that claim to be addressing this issue. Users of Decentraland and The Sandbox, for example, can record ownership of their in-game items, land, and income on blockchain.

We've seen many times in this book that property can mean anything deemed to be valuable. What if parts of our digital selves become valuable to someone else? Virtual personal identity is more distributed and fragmented than the physical version. Our cyberworld adventures will leave more digital trails, more partial online identities and cyber crumbs* for digital profiteers to pick up and use at any time. At the moment, your virtual world provider (Second Life, RuneScape, Club Penguin) is likely to own the bits and bytes that go to make up your avatar in perpetuity. They own bits of you. They own your reputation, your virtual goods and chattels, even your business, no matter how long it took you and how much it cost you to build them up, and with a near-feudal dominion they can terminate them at will. And this is not just a financial issue. Just as e-commerce has become indistinguishable from commerce, before long virtual world identities will be as important as real identities. Control over digital footprints and avatar life is about more than money. Much of what is being collected, not just in virtual worlds but in social media – data about friends and lovers, photos and videos, journals and chat – also bears on our identity and our sense of self.

Just as personhood is fundamental to authenticity, so too is provenance. The tracing back, the chronology and history of a person or object, is key to our understanding of them. That in virtual worlds there may not be anything physical to trace back to plays havoc with our age-old notions of authenticity. For most of human history, the real has been inextricably linked to the physical and the durable. We take our abstract ideas and make them concrete; we turn the products of our imagination into property. Now, as we live increasingly virtual and intangi-

---

* Is it just a linguistic curiosity that cookies leave a crumb trail?

ble lives, producing short-lived and imperceptible digital records, we risk creating a culture that leaves few if any traces for future generations.* A gradual loss of substance both literal and metaphorical. Without a firm grip on the past, our future is anything but secure.

You don't have to take the troubles of cartoon penguins seriously to see that a sense of self is key to our concept of personal authenticity. Our inner storyteller chooses from experiences we have been through and fits them into a narrative that makes sense to us. But with more and more multi-stranded narratives to choose from as we live more and more of our lives online, what will it mean to be a person who lives in both real and virtual worlds? The word 'person' derives from the Latin *persona*, meaning a mask put on by an actor. The idea of 'personhood' treats life as a series of façades connected to a single, persistent physical identity. But as the components of 'personhood', continuity of looks, character, possessions, behaviour, beliefs, and reputation, are increasingly built up digitally, lived in many different incarnations, stored in different places, and owned by different people, will our sense of personhood begin to disintegrate? When personality is no longer identity, but duplicity, or multiplicity, will we be less 'our own person' and more someone else's? And how do you live in a world of serial digital impostures?

Perhaps it is a blessing in a series of disguises. Perhaps digital disembodiment is a dissolution that allows us to be and become

---

* 'It is very likely that in the long term the only traces of our present activities will be global warming, nuclear waste and Red Bull cans', says Martin Kunze, whose Memories of Mankind project seeks to record our civilisation on laser-cut ceramic tablets of up to 5 million characters each that will be buried deep under Austrian salt mines in the hope that, like the Sumerian clay tablets that inspired them, they will last for millennia and be re-discovered by future generations.

whoever we want to be, that gives us room to grow and spread, a licence to try on clothes and personalities until we find the ones that fit. But if we create a generation of electronic Weymans, testing different identities, discovering themselves through digital imposture with not just serial identities but multiple simultaneous identities, will they, like Stanley, eventually become what they pretend to be, or will they just live mayfly existences, forever trying on new personae? Living a more varied existence has the power to augment and enrich our lives, but we need to take care that it does not fragment them instead.

Designers have a word for games where the software creates landscapes on the fly as players explore them, rather than the features being pre-programmed; they describe them as 'emergent'. Minecraft – a 3-D sandbox game ostensibly about mining and placing blocks (and incidentally the world's bestselling game) – is, despite that less than exciting description, one of the most imaginative, creative, and engaging metaverses around. It's designed so that the game world is emergent and virtually infinite. Despite the blocky buildings and pixelated landscapes, it is deeply immersive because, like imagination, it is unbounded. In emergent realms, neither geography nor buildings are fixed before the game begins. As players travel through the game, a new world unfolds; mountains rear up, rivers uncurl beneath their feet. There is no saying what creatures will abruptly cross their path, and whether they will be friendly or hostile.

As we mingle our real with our virtual lives, a new form of authenticity is emerging too. Like players in Minecraft, we have only the vaguest idea of what shape it will take, although if human nature is anything to judge by we will always want to be able to demonstrate identity, sincerity, and consistency; to prove that we are who we say we are, that our actions match our words, and that there is a constancy and thread to our being. It is all a giant experiment, the first time in history that so many have been able to live such richly rendered fantasy lives. As Stanford's Jeremy Bailenson says of VR, 'the most psychologically powerful medium in history is getting an alpha test on the fly, not in an academic lab but in living rooms across the globe'. It seems to me that the same applies to all digitally simulated worlds, as yet unregulated and little understood: the impact of these imagined environments is being assessed in real time and in real lives. Digital wonderlands have conjured up for us imaginary communities and enabled a series of experiments in living that we have much to learn from, but whose side effects are not yet clear.

As I write, the latest multiplayer gaming sensation is a space-themed social deduction game called Among Us.* A game that makes digital Sherlocks of its players, it calls for ten participants: eight to act as authentic crewmembers, and two to play the impostors who will affect to carry out their duties while covertly sabotaging and killing their crewmates one by one. The aim is to identify the masqueraders and remove them before they wipe out the crew. Players can point a finger at those they suspect of imposture or murder. But equally the accused may come up with an alibi or point the finger at someone else.

A majority vote is required to eliminate an impostor, so if you are one, you will have to do what counterfeiters and conmen have always done: lie and dissemble as convincingly as possible. The genuine crewmembers' role, by contrast, is part investigator, part fact-checker. They will need to watch what their fellows are doing when they believe themselves to be unobserved, get wise to their lies, spot the 'tells' of repeat offenders, and not

---

* Winner of a Golden Joystick Award, for which the trophy looks very like a golden sink plunger.

believe anything they hear without questioning it first. Among Us calls for skills quite different to the keyboard or console dexterity required in more traditional games. Players need to be able to judge who is telling the truth and who, in the language of the game, is 'sus'.

Without reading too much into what is, after all, a video game of jellybean astronauts and space-capsule floorplans, is it too fanciful to think that at critical junctures we get the games we need? Cometh the hour, cometh the game? It may be a little far-fetched, but the game's recent success (it languished for a couple of years after release) seems to be particularly timely. As the lines between reality and illusion are increasingly blurred, and the need to distinguish between the two becomes an ever more urgent daily challenge, as we face a torrent of fabrications from deep fakes to demagogues, and as we struggle to determine what is and isn't true, we can do with all the help we can get.

It is undoubtedly getting harder to locate accurate, truthful accounts of the world. This chapter has been concerned with the consequences of new technology for the inner, self-actualising sense of personal authenticity I identified in the Introduction. But technology has also created new challenges for authenticity in its other sense, the outward-facing, fact-based one. There is a part of us that seeks out details and data, facts and figures, that needs reliable representations of the world, and that part has reason both to celebrate and to fear our increasingly online digital world. We have shaped the technology, but are we happy with how it is shaping us?

15

RECLAIMING REALITY

Armies of Truth

*'Under normal circumstances the liar is defeated by
reality, for which there is no substitute; no matter how
large the tissue of falsehood that an experienced liar has
to offer, it will never be large enough, even if he enlists
the help of computers, to cover the immensity of
factuality. The liar, who may get away with any
number of single falsehoods, will find it impossible
to get away with lying on principle.'*

Hannah Arendt, 'Lying in Politics:
Reflections on The Pentagon Papers'

There's never been a better time to be a liar, a faker, or an impostor. If you are the kind of person who likes to tell it how it *isn't* – a conman, a conspiracy theorist, a fantasist, or a fabulist – this is your time. So say the cyber-miserabilists, that gloomy fraternity who see technology as the enemy of authenticity and the internet as a digital blanket obscuring all reality beneath.

Do they have a point? Of course they do. Many of the things we associate with authenticity, the markers and the rules of thumb that have helped us over the first twelve chapters of this book to identify the genuine, such as the physical presence of an

author or authoriser, the artist's hand, uniqueness, intentional-
ity, indivisibility, traceability, provenance, even something as
simple as having a label that matches the contents, appear to be
undermined by digital technologies. But is the digital world
inherently inauthentic? I'm not so sure.

It's easy to paint a bleak picture of cyberspace. The author is
often absent, an invisible, unreliable, or even – increasingly –
artificial intelligence. In a world where everything starts with a
digital copy, can anything be truly original? When any number
of pixel-perfect copies are possible, is anything unique? If counterfeiting and proliferation are child's play, there's no need to
bother with creative improvement. If objects are reduced to bits
and bytes speeding across the globe in random, barely traceable
routes, establishing provenance is almost impossible. If moving
a business becomes nothing more than a cut-and-paste to servers in a more lawless jurisdiction, then borders are irrelevant
and geography collapses. On this view, the charlatan trades –
impostor, scammer, free rider, proliferator, multiplier, mythmaker
– are all made irreversibly easier by digital technologies. The
world we knew was physical, tangible, stable; the world digital
has brought us is virtual, ethereal, volatile. Have digital technologies contrived to alter the fabric of our world, tilting its axis
irretrievably away from reality? The cyber-miserabilists would
say they have.

'Everything has changed for the worse' is a sombre but
powerful diagnosis. But popular as it is, I'm not convinced this
view holds water, even though it sells newspapers in an age
when not much else does. Technologies as disruptive as these
take generations to work their way through. Transitions are
often difficult. Where the previous chapter looked at how we
find ourselves living in in-between places, this one explores our
in-between times.

Tracking authenticity, in all its various forms, is a tricky business at the best of times. Although there is no single universal litmus test – no Holden Caulfield index of phoneyness – that can tell us how authentic or fake the world is at any particular moment, the internet has unquestionably made a huge difference. At first, technology was the saviour. 'Information wants to be free', said countercultural environmentalist and online pioneer Stewart Brand in 1986, because it's so easy to transmit. In those heady days, the internet was hailed as a digital library of Alexandria: the web would bring about a new Gutenberg revolution; cyberspace would become a centre of knowledge and learning. But the other, much less quoted half of Brand's prediction was that information also wants to be expensive, because it's so valuable. The right information in the right place can change lives. And, as Brand prophesised, the two sides would fight each other. As more and more people got their news via social media, a sense of unease set in. The internet came to be seen as the villain. Online representations of reality drifted further and further away from the underlying facts. Bad information drove out good. From 2016, the dissemination of falsehood by rogue states was all but eclipsed by the irruption of false news from a single individual. Reproducing and distributing misleading information became a highly profitable business model. People retreated into their echo chambers.

And then … I fancied I saw a glimmer of hope. I was sure that the terrible scenes we witnessed every day during the COVID-19 pandemic would be the moment when people realised they could not do without an authentic picture of the world. Representation would have to match reality. After all, people – hundreds of thousands of them – were dying grim and lonely deaths. Why would anyone deny the existence of this disease, or turn their heads away from suffering on such an unprecedented scale? And yet they did. Doctors spoke of terminally ill patients who still clung to what they had been told: that the virus was a hoax; the pandemic a 'plandemic', a conspiracy involving Bill Gates, 5G masts, and who knows what else. It got worse. People for whom the polite term is the counterfactual community spread rumours that hospitals were empty, that vaccines would change your DNA. The reality-based community hung its head in despair.

Where we are now is not an easy question to answer. Are we 'post-truth'? Or post-'post-truth'? Innumerable surveys of authenticity-adjacent areas give a useful though necessarily fragmented picture. The surveys tend to ask questions about trust – which doesn't always correlate with authenticity – in political institutions (where it's going down) and in the financial sphere (where in parts of the sharing economy it's going up). Some studies are about confidence in representations of reality by the media (which splits along partisan lines), others look at media literacy across different countries.* Some are snapshots, capturing the moment but not the long view. Others tell us where we've been, but not where we're going. Nobody should downplay the challenges to authenticity posed by digital technologies and techniques, but we should bear in mind that these are, by their very nature, tools that are decentralised, egalitarian, and open to (almost) all. I could be a cyber-miserabilist, but I'm not. In a view from now that is very much a view from me, let me tell you why.

The cyber-miserabilists have a point, though it is not quite the one they think it is. Digital technologies have undoubtedly

---

* In pretty much all of them the conclusion seems to be: if you care about this stuff, move to Scandinavia.

amplified the existing forces favouring fakery. But that's the point: they are *existing* forces. Technology may have accelerated, heightened, spread, given colour and immediacy to, or multiplied many of the inauthenticities outlined in this book, but it didn't invent them.

The internet didn't invent aspiration, or our propensity to dream or to imagine a life more exciting than the one we were born to. But it has made aspiration accessible to all. Social media gives us an always-open window into other people's lives, through which we gaze enviously. It is, however, a window that cuts out context: every Instagram influencer's pose looks effortless, every styled-to-perfection food shot belies the hours of preparation, the shots that were discarded, and the often cold and unappetising meal that followed.* It creates a constant drip feed of apparent flawlessness, along with a pressure, as we've seen, to curate and showcase an Instagram-perfect life that forces people to pretend to be someone else, rather than living their own lives.

Nor did the internet invent scams, though it accelerates and disseminates them more widely. All the old favourites from the conman's playbook have turned up online, rebadged and reformatted for the digital age. Phishing emails are the new 'ropers', enticing unsuspecting members of the public into a con; celebrities who brazenly plug freebies ('am loving @brand-

---

* In February 2021, in a storm-in-a-teacup scandal nicknamed 'soufflégate', it was revealed that judges on the BBC's *Celebrity Best Home Cook* had been doing some of their judging on food that had gone cold. In Episode 1, 'Omelette Spectrum', contestant Ed Balls complained that he had been promised that his soufflés would be judged while they were still hot and puffy. In the event, the soufflés were judged after the camera team had done all the various 'packshots' of contestants' offerings, by which time the dishes were collapsed and leathery. Balls won the series anyway.

name's new energy drink/beauty serum/whatever') without an all-important #advert prefix are the new 'shills'. A fake website with some bought-in followers is a quick and easy version of the 'Big Store' and its 'boost'. More money than ever is lost to 'lonely hearts' scammers who post fake profiles on dating sites and apps. The newest digital twist on an old story is the robot romance scam. Around 11 million of the 31 million men who signed up for the Ashley Madison website (tagline: 'Life is short. Have an affair') failed to realise that they were chatting to 'automated engagers', or 'fembots', and not the eager and available women of their imaginations.

Nor did the internet invent complicity or conspiracy, though it certainly smooths their course. Technology has been a godsend to conspiracy theorists everywhere, particularly at times when self-esteem has been low. Although the essence of any conspiracy theory is that the conspiracy never actually happened, so that by rights the theory should die a natural death when it rocks up against the truth, such is the vastness of the web, with its plethora of rabbit holes to disappear into, that anyone exploring the tunnels and burrows beneath the surface will likely find fellow believers. Those inside the rabbit holes are themselves unlikely to talk or listen to anyone outside, preferring to find confirmation of their beliefs within their own ecosystems and echo-chambers. As Professor Kate Starbird of the University of Washington, who has mapped many of these alternative media ecologies (see Plate 14), observes: 'Your brain tells you, "Hey, I got this from three different sources". But you don't realize it all traces back to the same place and might have even reached you via bots posing as real people. If we think of this as a virus, I wouldn't know how to vaccinate for it.'

The world wide web is a giant pick 'n' mix of conspiracy theories, and the long tail of the internet allows everyone to find the ones that suit them. Some are relatively harmless. The 4 per cent of Americans who told a Gallup poll in 2000 that they believed Elvis was still alive may congregate in some virtual Graceland, but are unlikely to cause the rest of us much trouble. Less trouble, at any rate, than the much higher number of adherents to a theory that began in 2016 and maintains that Hillary Clinton and other Democratic Party members were connected to a paedophile ring run from the basement of a pizza parlour in Washington DC. In its many versions, the 'pizzagate' conspiracy illustrates the theorists' propensity to add their own embellishments to any dodgy narrative that is doing the rounds. Like the toppings on a pizza, speculative theories are easy to customise. 'Do you want Satanism, or Deep State, or a little bit of both?' 'How about a sprinkling of White Supremacy on that?' 'You can have extra Paedophilia for the same price ...' Take a seat in the nearest echo chamber and you will find a neat self-reinforcing bubble of people to share it with. People who will swear to things that never happened, for whom no set of facts will ever shake their beliefs or alter their behaviour. But technology didn't invent them, it just enabled and multiplied them. Conspiracy theories were happening long before the internet was ever thought of. The revisionist historians who re-wrote German history on the basis of Lothar Malskat's wall paintings of turkeys didn't need advanced technology to gain country-wide complicity; all they needed was a shared desire to make their country great again.

What's new is not that conspiracy theories have been weaponised as propaganda, nor that the more adherents a theory can acquire, the greater the incentive for others to hop aboard the tribal bandwagon. The seismic change has been the speed and reach of the network effect that the internet affords. Every tweet is potentially a tech-enabled information virus. The more it arouses readers' emotions, the higher its reproduction rate. A conspiracy theory shared with ten people, who share it with ten others, each of whom then shares it with ten more, means that the theory – no matter how bonkers – could be just three clicks away from being seen by a thousand people.* Two more 'power of ten' shares and you've filled Wembley Stadium. With a further four or five similar shares, all 4.9 billion active users of the internet globally are within reach. The old top-down 'broadcast' model no longer works to prevent this type of dissemination that may come from the bottom up, from the far left or the far right of the political spectrum, or simply from a single person's fevered imagination. What is clear is that to stop the spread of misleading information, we will have to use the tools in the same way that the spreaders are using them. If they are networked, we will have to be networked too. If they have online armies, so must we. If they are on social media, we had better be there too. Until we go where they are, the conspiracists will go on winning.

Back in the art world, it's more of the same. The internet has not created new challenges so much as magnified challenges already there. In the struggle for attention in an ever more crowded online world, many makers and sellers of art have reached for the Warhol playbook. Wherever ubiquity has replaced authenticity as a measure of value, wherever repetition enhances rather than diminishes reputation, the power of the internet can be used to maximum effect. Art works are created with an eye to immediacy and impact, with brash and Instagram-

---

* Before you shout at me, this illustrative calculation assumes that all ten shares are to people who have not encountered the claim before. In practice, of course, many people within a given counterfactual community will receive multiple versions of the same share.

friendly colours (neon brights are a frequent feature), and sold as multiples. Attention-grabbing tactics have filtered through to the formerly solemn moment of the sealing of a sale at auction. In October 2018, buyers at Sotheby's watched in horror as, the moment the hammer came down for *Girl with a Balloon* by street artist and prankster Banksy, the million-pound work began to slip down slowly through its frame, slicing into fragments as it did so. The artist had built a shredder into the frame in preparation for a supreme moment of art world theatre.*

I can only wonder what Andy Warhol, who loved to cock a snook at authentication, would have made of the latest craze for crypto-art, art with no physical existence, sold as a purely digital asset. I can't help thinking that he would have smiled to see a giant 300-million-byte work, Beeple's *Everydays: The First 5,000 Days*, become the third most expensive work by a living artist in March 2021, when it sold at Christie's for $69 million – the price of a top-end Warhol. In return for their $69 million, the lucky buyer received a blockchain non-fungible token (an NFT or 'Nifty') as a certificate of authenticity to 'prove' their ownership of the work. Niftys are an ingenious way to restore uniqueness in a world of multiples. Since digital art is infinitely reproducible, and countless perfect copies can be made, each as 'original' (in aesthetic terms) as the other, it has had some people scratching their heads as to the point of it. Or at least as to why people are paying quite so much for it.† Perhaps this is just the

---

* Three years later, the new work created by the stunt – now titled *Love is in the Bin* – was sold for an astonishing £18 million, eighteen times the price paid for the unshredded *Girl with a Balloon*.

† Others point out that digital art is no different to a digital video or music download that you don't physically own, but of course nobody on Spotify is claiming that they own an 'original' recording.

logical conclusion of the fashion for 'art as an asset class', where the fact of ownership so often counts for more than the artwork itself. It may help digital artists to have a form of authentication, however divorced from the work itself, but intangible art paid for in intangible currency is a phenomenon that is going to take some getting used to.

One development poses genuinely new technological challenges to authenticity, and cyber-miserabilists have seized on so-called 'deep-learning' artificial intelligence (AI) programs with glee. AI is a new and dangerous technology, they say excitedly. AI programs can imitate life in an uncanny manner, with mesmerising fidelity, and at superhuman speeds. Who knows what dastardly use hoaxers, tricksters, and even (heaven forfend!) authors might put these imitative and generative technologies to?

Set it a goal, and an artificial intelligence will adapt and learn from its surroundings without the need for explicit instruction – indeed, quite often even its operator won't understand why an algorithm has reached a particular conclusion. These computer systems, known as deep-learning neural networks, have revolutionised the way humans carry out daily tasks. They are essentially 'thinking' computers, based on artificial neural networks (ANNs), a type of computational system inspired by the structure of the brain. Researchers have made great advances in machine learning (ML) and neural networks over the last few years, enabling machines to recognise and learn from patterns in vast quantities of data.

In fact, AI programs are so good at pattern recognition that it is only fair to the reader to point out that only the first sentence in the paragraph above was written by me. The other three were generated automatically by a neural network using my first sentence as a prompt. So, while we recognise the many advantages AI can bring, should we really be frightened that it can do this? Or should we just say – as I am tempted to – that if you feed a machine technoblurb, it will give you technoblurb back?*

Perhaps the best way to look at AI is as a mirror rather than a threat. In 2016, Microsoft launched a chatbot named Tay on Twitter. Openly declaring that 'she' was intended as an 'experiment in conversational learning', Microsoft encouraged the public to interact with her, saying 'the more you chat with her, the more intelligent she gets'. But within twenty-four hours her algorithm, programmed to learn how to converse from other Twitter users, had turned Tay into a ranting misogynistic racist spouting unabashedly extremist views, and Microsoft rapidly withdrew her for 'adjustments'. The lesson – and I'm reminded of the eminent scientist who said that what he feared was not so much artificial intelligence as human stupidity – is that we cannot abdicate responsibility and blame the machine. No AI algorithm (after all, only a set of instructions given to a computer) is good or bad in itself. Like a child that takes its cues from its environment, AI can only learn from the 'reality' you feed it. As mathematician and writer Dr Hannah Fry puts it, 'In the age of the algorithm, humans have never been more important'.

Some of the more recent moral panics have been around AI-generated video and audio 'deepfakes'. There was a time when hardly a week went by without one of these astonishingly

---

* And it will keep doing so. Another iteration using the same prompt yielded different artificially generated but still human-sounding text: 'Do we trust AI? As brilliant and fascinating as AI might be, it also raises some thorny ethical issues that we need to start thinking about. With machine learning being used in sectors as diverse as medicine and crime-fighting, decisions are made based on data sets that could potentially be biased towards humans or even against it [sic].'

realistic pieces of fake media making the news.* Deepfakes are convincing representations of things that never happened. Faces are swapped onto other bodies, words spoken by people who never said them, and lifelike videos created of people who never existed. Deepfakes can be wonderful: a photograph of Einstein is animated so that he can give a lecture. Or deeply moving: in the ultimate in counterfactual history, a voice-to-text company uses speeches made by JFK in his lifetime to recreate him delivering the speech that he was meant to give in Dallas on 22 November 1963. Or they can even be satirical: a deepfake video of Mark Zuckerberg (posted on Facebook, naturally) intones solemnly, 'Imagine this for a second. One man with total control of billions of people's stolen data, all their secrets, their lives, their futures ...' Just *imagine*. The entirely valid fear is, of course, that a malicious fabrication – picture a deepfaked Kim Jong-un announcing that missiles are already speeding towards the West – might cause panic or, worse, retaliation.

AI's eerie ability to mimic can appear mysterious as well as disquieting, but on closer examination the technology doesn't look quite so inscrutable after all. Video deepfakes learn from the data they are fed, just like Microsoft's chatbot or the text-generating AI program that I used earlier, but with an ingenious twist. To create these hyper-realistic counterfeits, technology has taken a leaf out of nature's playbook. To create a deepfake video, AI programmers set up two neural networks in opposition to each other, one playing the part of the 'counterfeiter' and the other the 'detective'. The counterfeiter program

---

* Although the scare headlines are that a deepfake CEO might send share prices tumbling, or a deepfake president propel us into World War III, the less reported and more sobering truth is that 95 per cent of deepfakes are used for pornography, for face-swapping a female celebrity's face onto sexually explicit videos, or for 'revenge porn' to humiliate a former partner.

draws on as much footage as is available of, let's say, Kim Jong-un, studying the association between his mouth movements and the sounds they correspond to, so that the dictator's face can be affixed onto that of an actor mouthing words the dictator never uttered.* First attempts to merge the two are amateurish and unconvincing. As the 'counterfeiter' generates further videos, including its still imperfect deepfakes, the second, 'detective', program tries to spot the fake. Each time the 'counterfeiter' is caught by the 'detective' it improves the images it generates until one day, after hundreds or thousands of iterative generations, it finally creates one good enough to fool it.

Sounds familiar? It should ring a bell. Just as the battle between cuckoo finches perfecting their counterfeits and prinias improving their fake-spotting skills yielded astonishingly accurate imitations of the little warbler's eggs, so the duelling neural networks use a process of adaptation and selection to improve their counterfeiting. Neither the fakery nor the mechanism is new, but the speed at which it happens is staggering. Battles in nature play out over centuries, but a computer 'generation' may only take a matter of seconds; a realistic deepfake can be produced in a matter of hours. To watch a deepfake being made is to see evolution taking place at warp speed.

What we have not seen so far (touch wood) are the threats to public discourse we were warned to expect from deepfakery. There are a number of possible reasons. It may be that Big Tech's deepfake detector programs are already sifting out many

---

* As it happens, an uncannily accurate video of the North Korean dictator did circulate late in 2020. Produced by voting rights campaign group RepresentUs, it featured Kim Jong-un explaining how he didn't need to interfere with US elections as America was quite capable of ruining its democracy for itself. The video included a disclaimer at the end, stating: 'The footage is not real, but the threat is.'

of the fakes before we see them. Or it may be that we have already begun to read viral videos more as allegation than evidence, just as we have learned to do with other internet headlines. Or it may be that deepfakes are a great deal more bother than they are worth. 'The Pope endorses Trump' had the highest engagement of any news story, real or fake, in the run up to the 2016 US election. A scrappy little story, originating on an unknown website that has since disappeared, it took no time at all to disprove, and yet it had around a million likes, comments, and shares. It wasn't damaging because it was convincing; it was damaging because people wanted to believe it. Perhaps the point is that there is no need to bother with high-tech deepfakes when a simple article will do the trick.

Action and Reaction

Retaliation against new technologies happens quickest when either money or power is at stake. Take the example of cryptocurrencies such as Bitcoin and Ethereum that operate across borders with no allegiance to a particular country or governing body. Cryptos are not the same as counterfeit currency, but they too nibble away at state revenues and create back-channels to black-market payment mechanisms, thereby causing problems of authority and authorisation that would be familiar to Isaac Newton and King William III. The power to issue and multiply money, whether you are minting it or 'mining' it, is the ultimate act of commercial copyright. A number of governments, loath to cede control, are fighting back, and are already experimenting with creating their own central bank digital currencies.

Nor are businesses taking digital incursions lying down, if the publicity industry's experience is anything to go by. With the advent of sophisticated search engines, such as Google and Bing, advertisers believed they would finally be able to solve one of the most enduring conundrums of their trade. Legendary adman David Ogilvy famously wrote in 1963 that a client complained: 'Half the money I spend on advertising is wasted, and the trouble is I don't know which half.' By the end of the first decade of this century it looked as if the problem had been solved. Advances in search engine software meant that advertisers' spending could be accurately tailored to their consumers' preferences and profiles. Advertisers would no longer pay for the placing of an advert on a website (as in the old billboard or print model), only for its performance as measured by the number of clicks it attracted. But before long scammers spotted a tech-enabled opportunity. They realised that if they set up fraudulent websites displaying the pay-per-click adverts, a bot could click on the ads just as well as a human. In fact, bots could do a lot of things better than a human could: they could 'like' your social media accounts, 'share' your content, watch your videos, upvote your site, as well as clicking on your ads a great many times more than a person ever could. The client incurred the costs of paying for the clicks generated by the adverts on the bogus website but, since the bot clicks would never lead to a sale, they got nothing in return. The only benefit was to the scammers. It was a free rider's dream.

By 2017, by some measures, bot traffic on the internet had overtaken human, and more than half of all internet engagement was machine-to-machine, with harmful bots outweighing the helpful ones. At least 20 per cent of ad-bearing sites were visited exclusively by bots, raising the entertaining (though probably not *that* entertaining if you are an advertiser) prospect of a world of phoney pages, with automatically generated adverts clicked on by algorithmic software, and not a human being in sight. A robot ecology whirring away in a marketplace emptied of people, beating on ceaselessly, talking to itself with ever increasing circularity.

As you might expect, advertisers were distinctly unamused to find themselves spending a great deal of money for robots to click on their ads, and 'click fraud protection' software was rapidly developed that could automatically detect, block, and analyse clickbot attacks. The story of advertising's 'Ogilvy issue' is the now familiar story of the arms race. First digital was the solution (pay per click software). Then digital was the problem (scammers and bots). Then digital was the solution again (click fraud prevention software). Stop the clock at any particular point and you might miss the pattern. Take the longer view and you don't.

A static or 'snapshot' view misses both the fact that when representations cease to match reality, we can do something about it, and that there is a time lag while we assess the negative effects of a new technology and marshal the resources to counteract it. The consumer internet has only been with us for 30 years: the first webpage was in 1991 and the first banner ad in 1994. These are early days. It took 150 years for the effects of a comparable technological disruption – the printing press – to be felt in full.

First-Mover Advantage

What the online advertisers' story illustrates is what we instinctively know to be the case: that scammers move in first and fast. There are a number of reasons why villains are so often in the vanguard. The first is that charlatans are uniquely well placed to seize first-mover advantage. Technology often advances more quickly than our knowledge of what to do with it. The killer app (industry jargon for a compelling use for a new technology that will propel it into mainstream use) may take years to emerge after the hardware or platform has been developed for it, as the makers of headset-VR would ruefully tell you. Fakers, by contrast, already have their killer app: self-interest – how to get something for nothing.

Another reason is that there is often something just a little mysterious and beguiling about new technology, making us easy marks. Arthur C Clarke's famous third law – that any sufficiently advanced technology is indistinguishable from magic – allows us to indulge in the willing suspension of disbelief that we find so enjoyable. We have a fondness for attributing supernatural powers to new inventions. In October 1920, the great inventor Thomas Edison revealed that he was working on a new device, a 'spirit phone' that would allow the living to communicate with the dead, and the deceased to send messages back from the spirit world. To a world that had learned from the telephone that words could cross any distance, that you could hear people's voices without their being physically present, and that was at the time longing to communicate with loved ones lost in the Great War, the idea of a hotline to the recently departed did not seem implausible.

I doubt you would convince many people today that the internet could give them a direct line to the other side. And that highlights an important point: almost every deception, including tech-enabled ones, has a 'best before' date. We may be duped, but we are not duped for very long. History is littered with the red faces of those who fell for hoaxes that deceived many at the time, but would not deceive a ten-year-old today. A little hindsight is all that is needed to see what very short lives most deceptions have. Between 1917 and the early 1920s two young cousins, Elsie Wright and Frances Griffiths, took a series of photographs of fairies they had met while playing in the stream at the bottom of the garden. The 'Cottingley Fairies' convinced many, including Sir Arthur Conan Doyle, for whom they were clear proof of psychic phenomena. By the time, sixty years later, that Frances admitted that 'it was just Elsie and I having a bit of fun', and confessed to their embarrassment at having fooled the great creator of Sherlock Holmes, few still believed in the photographs' authenticity.

To modern eyes the fairy photographs are as implausible as the *Evening Graphic*'s 'composographs' of Valentino in his coffin, or of the movie star in heaven with opera singer and fellow Italian Enrico Caruso. It doesn't take long for us to get wise. Look at any mid-twentieth-century stop-motion movie monster that had audiences cowering under their seats back in the day, or even at early CGI from the 1980s, and you will wonder what on earth people were frightened by. Early examples of Photoshopped pictures and Auto-Tuned songs already look and sound unconvincing. Quite simply, we have learned in those cases how to spot the signs that separate apparent reality from ingenious forgery.

One of the most powerful contributors to the cyber-miserabilist view is the phenomenon known as 'bad news bias' – our collective hunger to read and remember bad news. On one hand it makes sense: we are wired to be alert to danger, and the potential costs of missing out on bad news outweigh the benefits of taking in good news. But it's a bias that can turn healthy scepticism into knee-jerk cynicism.* Bad news makes a bigger

---

* Rutger Bregman, historian and author of *Humankind: A Hopeful History* (2019), makes 'Avoid the News' one of his 'Ten Rules to Live By'. In his words, 'Watching the evening news may leave you feeling more attuned to reality, but the truth is that it skews your view of the world. The news tends to generalise people into groups like politicians, elites, racists and refugees. Worse, the news zooms in on the bad apples.'

splash: 'Fake fools millions!' is memorable, 'Fake no longer fools anybody much' may not be, and more often than not we register the scare stories but not the successes. The lack of follow-up is a problem, as is the rapid turnaround of 24/7 news which does not lend itself to multi-generational stories of counterfeiters versus detectives, or of arms races that are long-drawn-out narratives of moves and countermoves.

Fight Back Against Falsehood

Unless you are an evolutionary biologist, or you work in the art world, or in consumer brands, or pharmaceuticals, you may not have come across many of the types of inauthenticity that I have talked about in this book. Unless you have had an impostor in your life, questions of authenticity and aspiration may not have troubled you unduly. But there is one area of fakery that you will almost inevitably have come across by now, and that is the falsification of information. We live in a world where mis- and disinformation are rife; where the consensus on what constitutes a publicly verifiable representation of reality – what constitutes authenticity – is under threat.

The truth of the everyday information that is presented to us matters. We need to know how things *are*, not just how they appear to be, or how someone else wants them to be. In recent years we have seen an extraordinary mobilisation of those who care that what we see, hear, and read corresponds to objective reality, and are prepared to fight for it. Whether it is disinformation by state actors, unreliable material put into circulation by organisations and individuals, or the amplification and distribution of misinformation by platforms and publishers – look closely, and you will see the forces being marshalled against it.

347

The fightback against falsehood is happening, but it is not happening equally, at the same speed, or with the same enthusiasm at every level of society. At the top, governments are moving as cautiously as a giant tanker docking.* Further down, an army of organisations and individuals, which I'll come to shortly, is moving at a furious pace. And between them, where a great deal of the power lies, the behemoths of Big Tech – the platforms and the publishers – are beginning to move unhurriedly in the direction of authenticity too. Having suspended the instigator of the Capitol riots after four years of giving him free rein, some have felt emboldened to bring in a few more controls. But, reluctant (to put it mildly) to upset the business model that has been so good to them, Big Tech would prefer not to have to clamp down on all the user-generated misinformation that so successfully fuels clicks and brings in advertising revenue.

They have the tools, but not – yet – the will. But since this is not a policy proposal, let me leave to one side what Big Tech ought or ought not to be doing in the future, what legal provisions should or should not be revoked, and let me tell you instead what they are capable of doing *right now*.

They are developing AI that can identify deepfakes, doctored images and video, and are well advanced in their programmes to track, analyse, and report on what's happening with public content across social media. In short, they already have technology to ensure that what appears on their sites bears a

---

* Not all of them. Under fire from Russian 'troll farms' attempting to rewrite the country's history and undermine its independence, Finland has since 2014 been educating its population in countering misinformation. From kindergarten classes where children watch videos of a teddy bear critiquing the news to training state officials to spot and hit back against fake news, in less than a decade Finland has created perhaps the most misinformation-resilient population in the world.

better-than-approximate relation to reality. Facebook, for example, can take any post, video, or image that makes a factual assertion, have it checked out and, if it is false, track down every instance of its publication on their platform. Take, for example, a dangerous rumour that did the rounds recently, that if you are suffering a heart attack, you should cough repeatedly in order to keep your heart beating (not true). Facebook is able to flag that content as false, and to ensure that the originator and every other user who has posted or shared it receives an automatic notice saying that it is false.

Some will ignore the notice, of course, but others – and it may take a few automated reminders to chivvy them along – will take it down. Nudging people to think about accuracy is a simple but potentially powerful way to improve their choices about what to share on social media. A recent study suggests that people may actually prefer to share only accurate information, but that the social media context distracts them from giving effect to their preference. One experiment asked participants to consider whether a headline was accurate before they decided whether to share it; the sharing of false headlines decreased by 51 per cent as a result. Another large-scale experiment on Twitter asked users who had recently shared links to misinformation sites to rate the accuracy of a politically neutral news headline, a prompt that caused the users to be almost three times as careful about the truthfulness of the information that they subsequently shared.

Platforms can further nudge (or shame) the misinformation spreaders by telling them how many other users have already removed the false information. And, if they choose to, they can of course block the accounts of persistently guilty parties. The social media giants already know how many people respond by taking down falsehoods (currently around 30–50 per cent of them do so), and they know exactly who the laggards and who the repeat offenders are. They also know that a small proportion of users is responsible for the vast majority of falsehoods – and they know who those users are.*

Let me say that again. *They already know who they are, and they know where to find them.* We're so used to digital omniscience as a worry, we forget both how amazing and what a power for good it can be. But just think: if these companies know who your friends are, where you live, what you listen to, what you buy, even how you vote, then *of course* they know what you're posting and sharing. They know where the bad stuff is happening and who is doing it. Just think how happy my friends at REACT would be if they actually knew who the counterfeiters were and where to find them. Or if burglars were considerate enough to leave their details at the local police station before going to do a job, so the cops could root them out. Well, the behemoths of Big Tech *do* know.

In fairness to the tech giants, the reason I can write about this is that some of it is already happening. Not enough of it, but enough for the world to see how technologically straightforward it would be to clean the Augean stables. The roadblocks are no great mystery either. It's well known that the platforms have a business model that is too slanted towards stoking outrage and cultivating anger. They also stand to lose a lot financially in the transition from toxic to authentic. They can't

---

* In one extreme case, a 2020 study by Cornell University of 38 million articles found that a single person was responsible for almost 40 per cent of coronavirus misinformation in the USA. (Go on, guess who.) In early 2021, at the height of the COVID-19 pandemic, the Center for Countering Digital Hate identified *by name* what they called 'The Disinformation Dozen', twelve individuals responsible for up to 65 per cent of the anti-vaccine misinformation on social media platforms at the time.

afford to transition; we can't afford for them not to.

Armies of Truth

Many are not waiting around for Big Tech to take the lead. The real action – and here I should say that I am privileged to have a ringside seat – is happening away from the spotlight. The number of fact-checking projects has grown from fewer than 50 worldwide in 2014 to around 300 today. Open-source intelligence outfits have mushroomed. Extraordinary collective action has taken the fight against pandemic falsehoods from a national to an international scale at record speed. In a massive fast-responder project, run under the #CoronaVirusFacts Alliance banner, over a hundred organisations got together to fight the (mis)infodemic globally. More than 9,000 coronavirus claims, in 70+ languages and 40+ countries, were fact-checked, and the results disseminated via social media, custom-created chatbots, Alexa (in a number of languages), viral infographics, Instagram influencers, video, animations … you name it. The claims they dealt with ranged from the frighteningly misleading ('masks make it more likely that you will catch COVID') to the daft and dangerous ('using a sauna or aiming a hairdryer at your nose will kill the virus'). Some were culturally revealing (one rumour was that Russia had released hundreds of lions from zoos in order to keep people at home during lockdown – you can just hear Putin thumping his chest, can't you?). Others were pure wish fulfilment (that Heineken were giving out free kegs of beer to encourage people to stay locked down at home), and some were so surreal that you could only wish that they did not need to be debunked (just in case you were in any doubt, COVID-19 vaccines do *not* contain nano-particles that will allow you to be tracked via 5G networks). The Alliance went a long way towards restoring my faith in humanity.

The truth-finders are out there. Unless you're in the fact-checking business, you are unlikely to have heard of CrowdTangle or Trendolizer, but you may have come across the BBC's Reality Check, or the Poynter Institute's PolitiFact with its 'Truth-O-Meter', or the *Washington Post* Fact Checker, which ranks statements by politicians on a range of one to four Pinocchios, or even the venerable (since 1994) Snopes. You may have heard of First Draft or The Ferret – the Scottish media co-operative that runs Ferret Fact Service (FFS) – or any of the very many others that have sprung up across the world: Fatos (who trialled a rapid rebuttal Twitter bot called Fatima); Factly (India); Fatnameh (Iran); Ellinika Hoaxes (Greece); Chequeado (Argentina); Forensia (specialists in fact-checking and debunking audio files). And if you haven't, you will soon.

Another approach to authentication at scale is the automation of fact-checking, or 'robo-checking', as it is sometimes known. It is the one that has been adopted by Full Fact, a UK-based outfit whose aim, according to COO Mevan Babakar, is to get as near as possible to a 'Shazam for facts'. The logic is simple: the more they automate fact-checking work – and a recently built tool has increased the identification of checkable claims a thousandfold – the more they free up checkers to work on more complex claims. But Full Fact are not just scrutinising claims. Once a statement has been shown to be false, Full Fact's software will find who is repeating it and send out corrections to the publishers. The service is a godsend to those journalists, academics, and policymakers who currently make up their core market, but Full Fact's ultimate ambition, says Babakar, is to produce an app that everyone can use.

Fig. 15.1. PolitiFact's 'Truth-O-Meter' scores representations of reality on a scale from True to False with an extra category – 'Pants on Fire' – for extreme falsehoods.

The newest model army is the community-powered fact-checking organisation. It harnesses the power of the internet and offers the opportunity to scale up. Again, the logic is sound: if the most-used encyclopaedia is an internet-based and crowd-sourced one – Wikipedia* – then why wouldn't you use that in pursuit of a more authentic world? Spanish outfit Maldita has attracted 45,000 volunteers and supporters of all ages and from all walks of life who have offered expertise, creative skills, time, and money in support of Maldita's fact-checking efforts. Co-founder Carla Jiménez Cruz calls them her 'disinformation warriors', and the volunteers work alongside a small core team debunking falsehoods already out there, 'prebunking' the next wave, and producing the rebuttals as shareable content – TikTok-style videos and memes are favourites

---

* Popular, much used, but not always wholly reliable, Wikipedia does at least have an entry entitled 'Reliability of Wikipedia'.

– that is both more appealing and more authentic than the fakes.

If conversations about authentic portrayals of the world tend to start with journalism, it is because responsible journalists, people who think deeply about how to give an accurate portrayal of the facts, have traditionally been our frontline defence against falsehood. But similar thinking is taking place in other sectors too. Digital technologies have enabled people to take fake-spotting and countering falsehoods into their own hands. I came across many of them while writing this book. Dr Bahijja Raimi-Abraham, of Fight the Fakes, puts out videos on how to tell fake pharmaceuticals from the real thing (top tip: look for spelling mistakes and poor-quality colour printing on the packaging, and avoid any unexpectedly gritty-looking tablets). An art authenticator has written an article entitled 'How Can I Tell if My Keith Haring Is Fake?' (clue: if the vendor says they bought it from a boyfriend of Haring's, and that 'boyfriend' is conveniently dead, it's probably fake). Then there was the dating site entrepreneur who was so incensed by fake profiles that he devised automated software for weeding them out; his company, Scamalytics, now has 10 million images of dating site scammers on its website, to help other match-making sites clean up their act. Or take fashion watchdog Diet Prada, founded in 2014 as a fun way to document suspicious similarities in fashion design, which has attracted 2.5 million Instagram followers since morphing into a more serious campaigning organisation. When it recently called out a mass-market retailer for designing a top that looked suspiciously like one created by a small and indigenous-owned sustainable brand (see Plate 15), the retailer rapidly removed the item from its site.

Perhaps the most extraordinary example of the power of collective action is that of Bellingcat. By now you will likely have heard of its founder Eliot Higgins and his online community of self-taught supersleuths, who used publicly available material to solve the mystery of who was behind the MH17 Malaysia Airlines flight crash in eastern Ukraine, identify and name the Skripal poisoners, prove that illegal cluster munitions were being used in Syria, and much more. Bellingcat's open-source intelligence tools and techniques have included satellite and aerial imagery (used to identify bloodstains at the site of extrajudicial executions in Benghazi), the shadow-measuring app SunCalc (to help trace a missile launcher), geolocation (confirming atrocities carried out by the military in Cameroon), and – every beginner's favourite – the reverse image search. But Higgins tells me that he believes that the key to a more authentic world is not more and whizzier tools, but communities. He points out that when the Russians put up what they claimed was irrefutable evidence of collusion between the USA and ISIS, it was Bellingcat's community of active and participatory Twitter followers who called it out as a screenshot from mobile phone game AC-130. The tracking of the Buk missile that downed MH17 was achieved by crowd-sourced intelligence; it was the coming together online of munitions experts that proved what was happening in Syria.

Higgins's vision of people power is intoxicating, and Higgins – who has described how he used to play online video games obsessively, organising players across several countries – has a more profound understanding than most of the workings of the internet: how online communities grow and coalesce, how networks of misinformation originate and how they spread, and how to root out the distortions and lies that flourish in dark corners of chatrooms. In his book *We are Bellingcat: An*

Intelligence Agency for the People (2021), a manifesto in all but name, he signals his intention to build ever larger communities of online detectives to hunt down publicly available information. Higgins has no truck with 'cyber-miserabilists' (a term I have borrowed from him); he argues that the digital era should not be viewed as a 'wrecking ball', and hails the internet as 'an extraordinary gift' that can help us all to seek out the truth and hold the purveyors of falsehood to account. In Higgins's words: 'At Bellingcat, we do not accept this cyber-miserabilism. The marvels of the internet can still have an impact for the better. However, guarding society and upholding truth are not the exclusive domain of institutions anymore. It is for all of us.'

Higgins is right: it is for all and each of us to fight back. The effect of the great digital democratisation is that almost anyone can play a part. In the summer of 2019 a protestor called Mohamed Hashim Mattar was killed by the authorities in Khartoum, Sudan. His online avatar at the time was a simple circle of his favourite colour blue. Thousands of supporters started using the hashtag #BlueForSudan and changing their avatars to blue dots. Celebrities joined the movement, urging their followers to do the same. Naomi Campbell changed her avatar, as did Rihanna and Cardi B. It was at this point that scammers got in on the act. They set up a series of accounts with names like @SudanMealProject (which racked up nearly 400,000 followers in less than a week), @Sudan-MealProjectOfficial, and @SudanMealOfficial, claiming that a 'like', 'share', or 'follow' would trigger a charitable donation and provide food and shelter for Sudanese in need. As the bogus sites multiplied, one of the most energetic accounts taking them down went by the name @ExposingInstaScams. It was so effective that some of the scammers tried to bribe the account holder to stop. But he refused. What was interesting was that he wasn't from law enforcement or any fact-checking agency, and he had nothing to do with Sudan: he was simply a 14-year-old from California on his summer holiday, disgusted by fraudsters using a crisis to turn a buck and using the internet to fight back. He wasn't a journalist, an intelligence professional, or even a citizen sleuth. He was just someone who believed in authenticity for the people, by the people.

It's also you. Everything you do moves the pendulum ever so slightly. You are already playing your part. Every time you 'block sender' on another Viagra-seller or 'Nigerian Letter' email, you are teaching an AI-powered spam filter a little bit more about reality. If you reverse image search that girl on Tinder who looked just too good to be true, or use Fakespot before you buy on Amazon, or if you are one of the bloggers affectionately correcting Snapple's inaccurate 'Real Facts', you are setting yourself and everyone else a little straighter. Every time you praise someone on LinkedIn or give a well-deserved star rating on Glassdoor, or report an issue, or call the fact-checking chatbot from inside WhatsApp (did you know that you could do that?), you are adding to a store of knowledge that improves the authenticity of our daily picture of the world. If, instead of the usual Google 'letterbox' screen, you use Google's Fact Check Explorer page, where a search will return all the fact-checked results available globally about almost any topic or person and in almost every language (and where in 2019 its 60,000 fact checks were seen over 4 billion times), you are playing an increasingly important part in defeating the enemies of authenticity. Remember: there are more of you than there are of them. You are not bowling alone. Even if you do nothing more than keep what you post more or less honest, truthful, and fair, you are doing something – a lot, in fact – because you are the data that artificial intelligence programs are learning from.

So no, despite the torrent of mis- and disinformation, I don't share the gloom of those who believe that technology has permanently put distance between us and reality. I am whatever the opposite of a cyber-miserabilist is – a cyber-optimist perhaps. We will never successfully disabuse those who want to believe in a big lie (and we know that even if they budge on their beliefs, they rarely change their actions to match). And yes, in the digital age fakers have won the first round yet again. 'Falsehood flies, and truth comes limping after it', wrote Jonathan Swift in 1710. Nothing new there. But it's always a story of move and counter-move. Although we are still in the early years of the digital era, truth has already got its boots on. There are forces out there fighting against fakery in every form. You will have encountered some examples already in your daily life, and a few more, I hope, in this book, but you may not have known the depth and breadth of the fightback. What you may not have accounted for is the human spirit in the age of the machine, a spirit that sees people at every level taking matters into their own hands.

Clara Jiménez Cruz, co-founder and CEO of Maldita, calls them her 'armies of truth'. I like to imagine them as big-hearted keyboard warriors, their faces shining in the blue light of their laptops, searching for authenticity in a world that seems ever more inauthentic. Unpicking the vast tissues of falsehoods we seem to have woven for ourselves. Disappearing down rabbit holes to recover the immensity of factuality.

Representing our better angels.

Reclaiming reality.

ON AVERAGE – SOURCES

To the 99 per cent of perfectly sensible souls who chose not to turn to page 359 from page 2 but read the book first instead – glad to see you. To the 1 per cent who flicked straight to this page – you are statistically unusual, but I'm glad to see you too.

Statistics, or at least the uses they are put to, can be famously slippery. Data can't speak for itself. It can't tell you how or why it was collected, or what its significance is. Nor can it tell you the motives of those who collected it.* Statistical pronouncements need to be authenticated. Here, then, are the sources and context for the statistics at the start of the book.

On average, you will be lied to three times within the first ten minutes of meeting someone.

The first ten minutes are when you are most trying to impress someone new. See Robert Feldman, *Liar: The Truth About Lying* (2010), p. 14. Feldman is Associate Dean of the College

---

* *How to Lie with Statistics*, written by Darrell Huff in 1954, sold more copies than any other general book on statistics. In 1965, Huff testified in front of Congress, ridiculing statistics that linked cigarette smoking with lung cancer and other diseases. It turned out later that he was in the pay of tobacco lobbyists.

of Social and Behavioural Sciences and Professor of Psychology at the University of Massachusetts, Amherst.

When asked by researchers, you will admit to lying one and a half times a day, unless you are the 45th President of the United States, in which case you will lie twenty-one times a day, but not admit to it.

See Bella M DePaulo, Deborah A Kashy, Susan E Kirkendol, Melissa M Wyer, Jennifer A Epstein, 'Lying in Everyday Life,' *Journal of Personality and Social Psychology*, vol. 70, no. 5 (May 1996), pp. 979–95. There were only 147 participants in the survey, so the study is too small to extrapolate to the population at large. Seventy-seven college students said they told two lies a day, and seventy community members said they told one lie per day. Participants said that they did not regard their lies as serious and did not plan them much or worry about being caught.

The *Washington Post* (among others) kept a running daily tally of the 45th President's lies, calculating that he told 30,573 untruths over the course of his presidency, or about 21 a day. He started slowly, telling an average of 6 lies per day in his first year in office; the rate grew to 16 per day in the second year, and 22 per day in the third. In his fourth year, in the run up to the election, he put on a spurt, reaching an average of 39 lies a day: https://www.washingtonpost.com/politics/2021/01/24/trumps-false-or-misleading-claims-total-30573-over-four-years/.

One in ten of you may not have the father you think you have. Best not to give DNA kits as Christmas presents.

This is a controversial statistic. Speaking at the Hay Festival of Literature on 30 May 2019, the Chief Executive of Health Education England, Ian Cumming, claimed that a Manchester University study of 220,000 people who had had genetic tests within families for reasons other than trying to work out paternity – if they were being tested *because* they had suspicions about paternity, you would expect a skewed sample – suggested that 'for one in ten people, your dad isn't who you think it is'. Other surveys put the figure much lower, at around 2–4 per cent, although R Robin Baker and Mark A Bellis, in *Human Sperm Competition: Copulation, Masturbation and Infidelity* (1995), put it at 9 per cent. A pair of socks, or one of those jumpers with reindeer on it, would probably make for a safer Yuletide gift.

In nature, as in life, there are the copiers and the copied. 'If you want honesty,' says the biologist, 'try physics instead.'

See Steve Jones, *Evolution (A Ladybird Expert Book)* (2017), p. 28.

'There are nine levels of authenticity for an Old Master', according to the auctioneer. Depending on how much of the picture the artist painted, and other factors. But what does it say about authenticity when the Andy Warhol Authentication Board says that a Warhol silkscreen signed, dedicated and dated by him is 'NOT the work of Andy Warhol'?

At the back of an auction house's catalogue, you will find their classifications of authenticity. If the entry in the catalogue gives the artist's full name, then it is in their opinion a work by that artist. Any other description ('Attributed to …', 'Studio of …',

'Workshop of …') means they are less sure of the artist's hands-on involvement in creating the work. 'Circle of …' or 'Follower of …' mean the work is in the artist's style (although 'not necessarily by a pupil'), but with no hands-on involvement by the artist. 'Manner of …' or 'After …' mean it is a later imitation or copy. The lowest level of authenticity, 'Bears signature', indicates that the work has been signed with the artist's name by someone other than the artist – i.e. it is an attempt to deceive. You have been warned.

For Andy Warhol, see Chapter 9. Warhol's 1965 Red Series self-portraits were once worth millions. And then they weren't.

By this point, on average, 16 per cent of you have started to wonder whether these are facts or wild assertions.

Results from author survey. I asked pre-publication readers to stick a Post-it note at the point where they started to wonder whether I was making it all up. Results should be treated with caution, since framing the survey in this way sets up behavioural biases in the form of 'anchoring'.

Protestant reformer John Calvin observed that there were enough pieces of the True Cross in existence by 1543 to make 300 crosses.

See John Calvin, *A Treatise on Relics* (1543). Calvin went on to say that the relic-mongers 'have invented the tale, that whatever quantity of wood may be cut off this true cross, its size never decreases'.

True Cross relics available on eBay today! Click to view details.

Plenty to choose from on eBay, where they have their own category, 'True Cross Relic', and often come with certificates of authenticity included.

It is said that in some places you will find 99 fake Louis Vuittons for every genuine one sold. The famous design was introduced in 1896 as an anti-counterfeiting measure. In a customs raid in France a hundred years later, police recovered enough fake Louis Vuitton fabric to cover 54 tennis courts.

The internet lore that there are places where 99 per cent of Louis Vuittons sold are fake is not verifiable. But one of the places might be South Korea, where Louis Vuittons are known as 'three-second bags', as they are seen in the street every three seconds; 90 per cent of the fakes are smuggled into South Korea from China.

Louis Vuitton introduced a series of fabric designs to try to distinguish his flat-top travel trunks from counterfeit imitations; the iconic monogram design was created by his son Georges four years after Louis's death. The French customs raid was in January 2005: http://news.bbc.co.uk/1/hi/world/europe/4378537.stm.

40 per cent of what doctors prescribe will be placebos. 'Do no harm' is the physician's first injunction. On the other hand, a million people worldwide (including 250,000 children) will die this year because the medicines they take are not what they think they are.

For placebos, see Ann Helm, 'Truth Telling, Placebos, and Deception: Ethical and Legal Issues in Practice,' *Aviation,*

Space, and Environmental Medicine, vol. 56, no. 1 (January 1985), pp. 69–72.

For fake medicines, see Chapter 13. The figure of one million deaths worldwide derives from World Health Organisation research into substandard and falsified medical products: https://www.openaccessgovernment.org/why-are-illegal-pharma-markets-still-prevalent-today/105600/.

Over two hundred million people – more than the population of Brazil – live, love, do battle, and grow crops in Gielinor, a world that doesn't exist.

See Chapter 14. RuneScape hit a peak of 200 million users in 2012, making the number of inhabitants of Gielinor greater than the number of inhabitants of Brazil: https://www.gamesindustry.biz/articles/2012-07-19-runescape-hits-200-million-player-mark.

Many chatbots are good enough to convince you they are real people. Around 11 million of the 31 million men who signed up for a 'dating' website (tagline: 'Life is short. Have an affair') didn't realise they were chatting to 'fembots', and not to the eager, available women they imagined.

See the cracking analyses by Annalee Newitz: https://gizmodo.com/almost-none-of-the-women-in-the-ashley-madison-database-1725558944; https://gizmodo.com/ashley-madison-code-shows-more-women-and-more-bots-1727613924. 'What I discovered was that the world of Ashley Madison was a far more dystopian place than anyone had realized. This isn't a debauched wonderland of men cheating on their wives. It isn't even a sadscape of 31 million men competing to attract those 5.5 million women in the database. Instead, it's like a science fictional future where every woman on Earth is dead, and some Dilbert-like engineer has replaced them with badly-designed robots.'

Only 1 per cent of you have turned to page 359 so far.

Actually, no one I gave this book to turned to page 359 at all. So 1 per cent is the figure rounded to the nearest positive integer.

Over 3,500 people come every year from all over the world to Blackpool, Lancashire, to learn to get better at deceiving others. With your patter, sleights of hand, distractions and multiplications, you are my favourite people. You are partly why I started writing this book.

Blackpool is the world's biggest and – they would claim – best magic convention. However much we search for authenticity, however much we love the data, let's not lose the magic.

SELECT BIBLIOGRAPHY

The sources I've consulted while writing this book include books on subjects that range from the psychology of pretenders to the economics of collective action, academic papers on topics as varied as avian egg mimicry and the problems of quantum money, and the tweets of big game hunters and the inhabitants of virtual worlds. Rather than list them all, I have selected those that I found particularly illuminating for the aspect of authenticity explored in each chapter, as well as those that inspired, entertained, or provoked me. I have also included the occasional suggestion for further reading.

INTRODUCTION

Considering the importance of the subject, there have been relatively few serious studies of authenticity. Three books have been particularly important to me: Lionel Trilling's *Sincerity and Authenticity* (1972), which charts the shift from earlier ideas of authenticity to our present-day concept, Charles Taylor's *The Ethics of Authenticity* (1992), which attempts to reconcile the notion of authenticity as self-fulfilment with the needs of society as a whole, and Charles B Guignon's *On Being Authentic* (2004), which explores authenticity as the modern project of becoming the person you truly are. J L Austin's *Sense and*

Sensibilia (1962) and Theodor W Adorno's *Jargon of Authenticity* (1973) helped me to make sense of our often contradictory notions of what 'authenticity' means. My interest in using magicians' deceptions as a lens through which to examine the topic was sharpened by reading *Hiding the Elephant: How Magicians Invented the Impossible and Learned to Disappear* (2006) by Jim Steinmeyer and *Sleights of Mind: What the Neuroscience of Magic Reveals about Your Brain* (2011) by Stephen Macknik and Susana Martinez-Conde with Sandra Blakeslee. Lewis Hyde's *Trickster Makes This World: Mischief, Myth, and Art* (1998) is an absorbing enquiry into the part played by deceit in our cultural life, and David Shields's *Reality Hunger: A Manifesto* (2010) an intriguing take on our modern obsession with reality. Of the books I've enjoyed while reading around the subject, I would particularly recommend the following: John D'Agata's *The Lifespan of a Fact* (2012), an entertaining chronicle of the author's battle with his fact-checker as to what counts as non-fiction, Sarah Bakewell's *At the Existentialist Café: Freedom, Being, and Apricot Cocktails* (2016), a wonderful account of the philosophy and philosophers that have contributed so much to our modern idea of authenticity, and Kurt Andersen's *Fantasyland: How America Went Haywire: A 500-Year History* (2017), on his countrymen's 'promiscuous devotion to the untrue'.

PART I – BASIC INSTINCTS

1 ASPIRATION: The Impostor Who Became What He Pretended to Be

For the details of Stanley Weyman's life, I relied on newspaper accounts of the time, and on St Clair McKelway's two engrossing long-form pieces for the *New Yorker*, 'The Big Little Man from Brooklyn' (8 and 23 November 1968). Woody Allen's mockumentary film *Zelig* (1983), about a little guy with a 'chameleon disorder' who can transform his appearance to match those around him and becomes a celebrity in 1920s and 1930s America, is interesting for its parallels with Stanley's story, while *Catch Me If You Can* by Frank W Abagnale, Jr. with Stan Redding (1980) is a colourful account of another impostor's career. A particularly insightful exploration of the issues around imposture is Sarah Burton's *Impostors: Six Kinds of Liar* (2000).

2 DECEPTION: The Anatomy of a Con

Everyone who has written about conmen owes a debt of gratitude to David W Maurer's classic account of their techniques in *The Big Con: The Story of the Confidence Man and the Confidence Game* (1940). Also indispensable for this chapter were Kid Weil's highly enjoyable, if self-serving, *'Yellow Kid' Weil – Con Man* (1960) (republished in 2011 as *'Yellow Kid' Weil: The Autobiography of America's Master Swindler*) and John Carreyrou's masterly *Bad Blood: Secrets and Lies in a Silicon Valley Startup* (2018). Saul Bellow's perceptive 1956 profile of the older, more reflective Kid Weil is reprinted in *It All Adds Up: From the Dim Past to the Uncertain Future* (1994). Particular mention should be made of Daniel Kahneman's

Thinking, Fast and Slow (2011) for insights into the behavioural biases that make us susceptible to deception, as well as Ian Leslie's highly readable *Born Liars: Why We Can't Live without Deceit* (2011), which makes the case that lying is part of human intelligence, and Maria Konnikova's *The Confidence Game: The Psychology of the Con and Why We Fall for It Every Time* (2016). Julie Wheelwright's *Amazons and Military Maids: Women Who Dressed as Men in the Pursuit of Life, Liberty and Happiness* (1989) offers intriguing histories of women who lived and worked as men.

3 COMPLICITY: Lothar and the Turkeys

I first came across Lothar Malskat, and the fascinating story of a country's complicity in a psychologically necessary lie, in Frank Arnau's *Three Thousand Years of Deception in Art and Antiques* (1961). More recently, Lothar's story has been used as part of the provocative argument made in *Forged: Why Fakes Are the Great Art of Our Age* by Jonathon Keats (2013). For background to the bombing of Lübeck, I have drawn on A C Grayling's *Among the Dead Cities: Is the Targeting of Civilians in War Ever Justified?* (2011), and for the effects of the devastation of war on culture and memory, on Stephen Spender's *European Witness* (1946), Ian Buruma's *The Wages of Guilt: Memories of War in Germany and Japan* (1994), and W G Sebald's *On the Natural History of Destruction* (2003). Alfred Stange's propagandist account of Lothar's murals in Schleswig Cathedral, *Der Schleswiger Dom und seine Wandmalereien* (1940), makes for an interesting study. Sarah Churchwell's *Behold, America: A History of America First and the American Dream* (2018) is a timely reminder that bigotry, like history, is apt to repeat itself.

PART 2 – NATURAL-BORN FAKERS

4 MIMICS: Nature's Impostors

At the core of this chapter is Henry Walter Bates's paper 'Contributions to an Insect Fauna of the Amazon Valley. Lepidoptera: Heliconidæ', presented to the Linnean Society in 1862, which contained his scientific account of the evolution of mimicry by natural selection. Other works from the period which helped to set the scene were Bates's rollicking *The Naturalist on the River Amazons. A Record of the Adventures, Habits of Animals, Sketches of Brazilian and Indian Life, and Aspects of Nature under the Equator, during Eleven Years of Travel* (1863) and Edward Bagnall Poulton's *The Colours of Animals, Their Meaning and Use, Especially Considered in the Case of Insects* (1890), which, despite the breadth of the title, is almost all about mimicry and, as Poulton frankly admits, mainly about butterflies. Peter Forbes's *Dazzled and Deceived: Mimicry and Camouflage* (2009) gives wonderfully clear accounts of both. For anyone interested in evolution, Charles Darwin's *On the Origin of Species by Means of Natural Selection; or, The Preservation of Favoured Races in the Struggle for Life*, first published in 1859, is not only a key text (obviously) but also a great read, as is Steve Jones's *Almost Like a Whale: The Origin of Species Updated* (1999).

5 FREE RIDERS: The Great Egg Race

The genesis of this chapter was Claire Spottiswoode's extraordinary work on egg mimicry and the cuckoo finch–prinia arms race. I've mainly referred to two papers, 'Host-Parasite Arms Races and Rapid Changes in Bird Egg Appearance' by Claire N

Spottiswoode and Martin Stevens (2012) and 'Repeated Targeting of the Same Hosts by a Brood Parasite Compromises Host Egg Rejection' by Martin Stevens, Jolyon Troscianko, and Claire N Spottiswoode (2013), and you can find a wealth of other material, including photographs and videos, on african-cuckoos.com. I also found Nick Davies's *Cuckoo: Cheating by Nature* (2015) extremely useful and informative. Mimicry and counterfeiting are just one subset of the much larger category of parasitic lifestyles, and Carl Zimmer's *Parasite Rex: Inside the Bizarre World of Nature's Most Dangerous Creatures* (2000) explores this most successful, if frequently gruesome, evolutionary strategy. Ed Yong's *I Contain Multitudes: The Microbes Within Us and a Grander View of Life* (2016) asks whether it is fair to divide the natural world, as we do our own, into 'bad' parasites and 'good' mutualists. When looking more broadly into our contradictory attitudes to animals I found Henry Mance's *How to Love Animals in a Human-Shaped World* (2021) a fascinating and thought-provoking read.

6 COMPETITORS: The Hunter's Dilemma

The story of Ryan's record-breaking rack can be found on hunting, wildlife management, and local news sites across the internet. With articles ranging from 'Fair Chase' to '7 Tips for Ethical Field Photographs', the Boone and Crockett Club's website is a source of rich and thoughtful information about the history of hunting and its practice today. The arguments about the effects of runaway competition made by Robert H Frank in *The Darwin Economy: Liberty, Competition, and the Common Good* (2011) are central to this chapter. I would steer anyone interested in delving deeper into competition for survival at individual rather than group level towards *The Selfish Gene* by

Richard Dawkins (1976). In the unlikely event that the reader becomes as obsessed by 'camo' as I did while writing this chapter, I highly recommend sourcing a library copy of the encyclopaedic, magnificently illustrated, and magnificently expensive *DPM: Disruptive Pattern Material*, compiled and edited by Hardy Blechman and Alex Newman (2004).

PART 3 – ON THE AUTHENTICITY OF THINGS

7 MULTIPLIERS: Death of a Counterfeiter

For a contemporary account of William Chaloner's death, I have relied on *Guzman Redivivus. A Short View of the Life of Will. Chaloner. The Notorious Coyner, Who Was Executed at Tyburn on Wednesday the 22d. of March, 1698/9: With a Brief Account of His Tryal, Behaviour, and Last Speech* (1699). For Chaloner's battle with the Warden of the Mint I have drawn on Thomas Levenson's masterly *Newton and the Counterfeiter: The Unknown Detective Career of the World's Greatest Scientist* (2009), as well as John Craig's 'Isaac Newton – Crime Investigator' (1958), Carl Wennerlind's 'The Death Penalty as Monetary Policy: The Practice and Punishment of Monetary Crime, 1690–1830' (2004), and Richard S Westfall's authoritative *The Life of Isaac Newton* (2015). Ben Tarnoff's *Moneymakers: The Wicked Lives and Surprising Adventures of Three Notorious Counterfeiters* (2011) is full of fascinating detail about America's rich history of counterfeiting, and Lawrence Weschler's *Boggs: A Comedy of Values* (1999) is a perceptive account of one artist's unusual and thought-provoking views on value and money. Specialist discussion of quantum money can be found in Scott Aaronson's entertaining if occasionally impenetrable 'The No-Cloning Theorem and the

Human Condition: My After-Dinner Talk at QCRYPT' (2016), available on Shtetl-Optimized (scottaaronson.blog), and more accessibly in Michael Brooks's 'Quantum Cash and the End of Counterfeiting' (2012).

8 ATTENTION SEEKERS: The Authentication Game

The source for Sir Dudley Carleton's fascinating correspondence with Rubens is *The Letters of Peter Paul Rubens*, edited by Ruth Saunders Magurn (1955). Everything else I learned about Rubens was lifted from Simon Schama's *Rembrandt's Eyes* (1999). Almost everyone who worked with Andy Warhol seems to have written about him, so there is a rich seam to mine. I have drawn intriguing snippets as well as insights into Warhol's attitude towards authenticity from Gerard Malanga's *Archiving Warhol: An Illustrated History* (2002), Blake Gopnik's magisterial *Warhol: A Life as Art* (2020), and the artist's own words in *The Andy Warhol Diaries*, edited by Pat Hackett (1989). The unhappy saga of Joe Simon-Whelan's 'Warhol' has been the subject of many articles, most notably by Richard Dorment. For background to the art market, I recommend Robert Wraight's classic account in *The Art Game* (1965). On the subject of the attention economy, Richard A Lanham's *The Economics of Attention: Style and Substance in the Age of Information* (2006) and Tim Wu's *The Attention Merchants: The Epic Struggle to Get Inside Our Heads* (2017) have been particularly valuable.

9 ABUNDANCE: The Battle for Tuxedoland, or Why We Overrate Originality

This chapter originated in a 1994 news item about the copyright infringement case between Yves Saint Laurent and Ralph Lauren, which led me to wonder what we mean when we call a design 'original', and what the relationship between creativity and originality might be. Olivier Meyrou's film *Yves Saint Laurent: The Last Collections* (2019), about the legendary designer's final show, was instructive on the creative process of fashion design as well as being intensely moving. Michael Gross's gossipy and fact-filled biography *Genuine Authentic: The Real Life of Ralph Lauren* (2003) and the filmic Festschrift *Very Ralph* (2019) were two useful sources on Ralph Lauren. Richard A Posner's *The Little Book of Plagiarism* (2007) and Lawrence Lessig's *Free Culture: How Big Media Uses Technology and the Law to Lock Down Culture and Control Creativity* (2004), on the uses and abuses of intellectual property law, were invaluable, as was Eric D Beinhocker's reshaping of economics as an evolutionary process in *The Origin of Wealth: Evolution, Complexity, and the Radical Remaking of Economics* (2004). Daniel C Dennett's *Darwin's Dangerous Idea: Evolution and the Meanings of Life* (1996), with its view that everything can be explained by the Darwinian algorithm, was a useful counterpoint to the 'designer' version of originality. For an unusual, eclectic, and unashamedly personal look at how our culture leads us to overrate the original, *The Culture of the Copy: Striking Likenesses, Unreasonable Facsimiles* by Hillel Schwartz (1996) is hard to beat.

PART 4 – SELLING AUTHENTICITY

10 INTANGIBLES: A Visit to the Fake-Hunters

Visits to the fake-hunters in Paris and Amsterdam first opened my eyes to the scale of counterfeiting of branded goods. Peggy Chaudhry and Alan Zimmerman's *Protecting Your Intellectual Property Rights: Understanding the Role of Management, Governments, Consumers and Pirates* (2013) is a useful primer on the problems caused by copyists, and Frank Trentmann's *Empire of Things: How We Became a World of Consumers, from the Fifteenth Century to the Twenty-First* (2016) a helpful guide to the history of the consumer society. Articles in *Brands and Branding* by Rita Clifton and others (2009) on methods of calculating brand value and the increasing contribution made to stock prices by intangibles helped me to flesh out my ideas on the weightless economy. The challenge of reconciling authenticity and advertising is a tricky one; *Authenticity: What Consumers Really Want* by James H Gilmore and B Joseph Pine II handles the issue thoughtfully, and, by framing the question as how to manage consumers' perceptions of authenticity, stays on the right side of the celebrated (if unattributable) dictum about sincerity and success. For other sides to the argument, I found Naomi Klein's classic anti-brand polemic *No Logo: Taking Aim at the Brand Bullies* (1999) well worth revisiting. A newer strand of anti-brand thinking, arguing that companies are packaging authenticity as a new form of conspicuous consumption, is well represented by Andrew Potter's *The Authenticity Hoax: How We Get Lost Finding Ourselves* (2009).

11 MYTHMAKERS: How Snapple Lost Its Juice

Snapple's first appearance in the annals of marketing mythology, and my jumping-off point for this chapter, was John A Deighton's famous Harvard Business School case study 'Snapple' (1999) – still a very relevant read. Douglas B Holt's *How Brands Become Icons: The Principles of Cultural Branding* (2004), which analyses how iconic brands address our collective anxieties and desires, was a great help in unpicking the constituents of Snapple's potent identity myth. Eric Schlosser's *Fast Food Nation: What the All-American Meal Is Doing to the World* (2001), on the harm done to us by what we eat and drink, is still as powerful and persuasive as it was twenty years ago. April L Farris's paper 'The "Natural" Aversion: The FDA's Reluctance to Define a Leading Food-Industry Marketing Claim, and the Pressing Need for a Workable Rule' (2010) made a great contribution to my thinking. For anyone interested in a deeper understanding of American soft drink marketing and mythologising, I heartily recommend Mark Pendergrast's *For God, Country and Coca-Cola: The Unauthorized History of the Great American Soft Drink and the Company That Makes It* (1993).

12 EXTERNALITIES: China's Gift to the World

It's hard not to be moved by the plight of the victims of counterfeit pharmaceuticals. Kathleen McLaughlin's 2013 on-the-ground reporting on 'China's Problem with Fake Drugs in Africa', funded by the Pulitzer Center, was my starting point for this chapter. The WHO and the WorldWide Antimalarial Resistance Network provided the statistical backdrop and information on the rise of drug-resistant malarial strains. Tim

Harford's *The Undercover Economist* (2006) was invaluable for its notably clear exposition of the concept of negative externalities. Tu Youyou's 2015 Nobel Prize acceptance lecture 'Artemisinin – A Gift from Traditional Chinese Medicine to the World' is well worth reading as a reminder that the country that counterfeits can also cure. Dr David H Gorski's 'In the Tradition of Chairman Mao, Traditional Chinese Medicine Gets a New Boost by the Chinese Government' (2017), available on science-basedmedicine.org, is a sobering account of the problems caused by the integration of Traditional Chinese Medicine into the mainstream. For background, I recommend Timothy C Winegard's *The Mosquito: A Human History of Our Deadliest Predator* (2019), and for a pertinent – though fictional – insight into the mind of a counterfeiter, Harry Lime's famous speech, quoted in the epigraph to this chapter, in either the film (1949) or the book (1950) of Graham Greene's *The Third Man*.

PART 5 – A VIEW FROM NOW

13 THE IMPOSTOR I KNEW: A True Story

For insights into the hold a certain sort of grand country house fantasy had – and still has – on many people, read Evelyn Waugh's *Brideshead Revisited* (1945).

14 REAL LIVES: Virtual Worlds

In an era when we can meet each other on Zoom, in the metaverse, or IRL, it is perhaps not surprising that I started to wonder what separates our real life from our virtual life. I was greatly helped when writing this chapter by Samuel Greengard's *Virtual Reality* (2019), an account of the history of virtual and augmented realities and the technologies underlying them, as well as by Jaron Lanier's amazing and very personal *Dawn of the New Everything: A Journey Through Virtual Reality* (2017). Both helped me to future-gaze without falling for the hype. Cyberworlds often get a bad press, so it was salutary to read Jeremy Bailenson's *Experience on Demand: What Virtual Reality Is, How It Works, and What It Can Do* (2018), and also his paper with Nick Yee, 'The Proteus Effect: The Effect of Transformed Self-Representation on Behavior' (2007), to see how they might help us shape lives for the better. Andrew K Przybylski, Niklas Johannes, and Matti Vuorre's paper 'Video Game Play Is Positively Correlated with Well-Being' (2020) is a welcome corrective to the moral panic that so often accompanies new digital developments, as are Karen Hao's articles on AI in the *MIT Technology Review*.

15 RECLAIMING REALITY: Armies of Truth

I first came across the idea of a society that chooses fiction over fact and prefers appearance to reality some years ago in Guy Debord's *The Society of the Spectacle*, first published in 1967. Many of his insights, though not necessarily his solutions, still seem relevant today. I'm grateful to Michael Shermer's *Why People Believe Weird Things: Pseudoscience, Superstition and Other Confusions of Our Time* (1998) for introducing me to sceptical thinking with a moral dimension, and to David Aaronovitch's *Voodoo Histories: The Role of the Conspiracy Theory in Shaping Modern History* (2009) for a historical perspective on people who like to hold peculiar and irrational beliefs. Matthew d'Ancona's *Post-Truth: The New War on Truth and How to Fight Back* (2017) captures the moment when we began to realise what we had created. His fighting spirit helped to shape this chapter, as did Bobby Duffy's expert dissection of human fallibility and his practical solutions in *The Perils of Perception: Why We're Wrong About Nearly Everything* (2018). My understanding of the new information ecosystem and its consequences was greatly enhanced by Martin Moore's *Democracy Hacked: Political Turmoil and Information Warfare in the Digital Age* (2018). Eliot Higgins's *We Are Bellingcat: An Intelligence Agency for the People* (2021), with its 'David versus Goliath' narratives and its repudiation of cyber-miserabilism, was a real inspiration, as was Rutger Bregman's *Humankind: A New History of Human Nature* (2020), with its belief in the better angels of our nature. Many of the organisations I mention, such as Full Fact and PolitiFact, have websites offering fact-checking services, online courses, toolkits, trust ratings, and fake-spotting browser extensions, as well as opportunities for the public to participate in fact-checking and fact-finding.

ACKNOWLEDGEMENTS

This book has been a long time in gestation, and I owe many debts of gratitude.

First and foremost, to the Policy Institute at King's College London for the visiting research fellowship which gave me the time and space I needed to develop my thinking. My thanks to its director, Professor Bobby Duffy, and to everyone at the Institute.

I'm enormously grateful to Fiona St Aubyn, Martha Stenhouse, and all at the Royal Society of Literature. Winning an RSL Giles St Aubyn Award in 2020 was a crucial source of encouragement, a bright moment in a dark pandemic.

My gratitude, as always, to the staff at the London Library. You have been a lifeline, not just helping to find books, but letting me keep them for an indecently long time.

Thanks to Julie Wheelwright and Sarah Bakewell, as well as to my coursemates, for making my time on the Narrative Non-Fiction course at City University such a rewarding one.

Heartfelt thanks to all at CP+R, especially Sam Howells – the one-man book club.

As ever, a big shout-out to the Rising Tide network. The friendship and support of the members is a total joy, and the speakers at its events arm, the Kit Cat Club, provide inspiration at every turn.

The academics and specialists I interviewed have been as generous with their time as with their knowledge, and have made a significant contribution to the writing of this book. I hope they recognise something of themselves in what I've written. For help in all matters zoological, my thanks go to Dr Claire Spottiswoode and Dr Gabriel A Jamie of Cambridge University's Department of Zoology; Will Beharrell, Librarian at the Linnean Society of London; Dr Blanca Huertas, Senior Curator, Lepidoptera, at the Natural History Museum, and the staff at the NHM's Reading Room; Professor Tom Sherratt at Carleton University's Department of Biology; Dr Luke Tilley of the Royal Entomological Society; Professor Francis Gilbert, Professor of Ecology at the University of Nottingham. For much-appreciated help on the principles underlying quantum money, my thanks to Professor Scott Aaronson, director of the Quantum Information Center at the University of Texas at Austin, and Michael Brooks, science writer, broadcaster, and journalist. Closer to home, many thanks to Dr Martin Moore, Director of the Centre for the Study of Media, Communication and Power at KCL, Nicholas Gruen, Visiting Professor at KCL and CEO of Lateral Economics, and Bobby Duffy (again) for sharing their insights and expertise with me. It goes without saying that any and all errors are my own.

I'm indebted to Sophie Yin, director of the Musée de la Contrefaçon, for an education in counterfeit-spotting, and to Bjorn Grootswagers, formerly regional director of REACT, for the chance to see fake-hunters in action. Also to those dogged seekers after truth, Bellingcat founder Eliot Higgins and Mevan Babakar of Full Fact, who took time to share their knowledge with me. Thanks as well to Chris Westcott, Adina Pintilie, and my other friends and colleagues at Ridgeway Information, whose research skills and professional ethos always inspire me.

I've had the great good fortune to be able to chat with beverage expert Mike Weinstein, to shoot the breeze with expert storyteller Sean Stewart of Endless Adventures Incorporated (thanks to Gaby Darbyshire for introducing us), and to be briefed on brands by advertising supremo Axel Chaldecott. Thanks too to Peter York for entertaining exchanges on authenticity, Matt Bosworth for guidance on libel law, Maria Alvarez for a philosophical steer, and Joe Simon-Whelan for talking me through his extraordinary story. Particular thanks to Richard Dorment, who took a real interest and was a great help with this book at an early stage. I never left our conversations without feeling I had learned something.

I'm grateful to all those who have given me the opportunity to develop my ideas in front of an audience: Professors Tamar Garb and Anthony Julius, for the chance to speak at the Institute of Advanced Studies at University College London on 'The Business of Lies and the Lies of Business'; Tara Rastrick, for inviting me to talk to the Augusta Group at Christie's; and Julia Hobsbawm, not only for the invitation to speak on 'Judging Authenticity' as part of her 'pithy polemics' series at Names Not Numbers in Oxford, but also for her unfailing friendship and support.

I feel extraordinarily lucky to be published by HarperCollins. My sincere thanks to all the Mudlark team: my editor, the energetic and unfailingly positive Joel Simons; Fiona Greenway and Ameena Ghori-Khan, who worked hard on picture research and permissions; the talented Orlando Mowbray and Simon Armstrong for marketing and publicity respectively, and special thanks to Jessica Jackson for her great and timely help. I'm particularly grateful to Claire Ward for the stylish and clever cover design. My warmest thanks to the production team: the incomparable Simon Gerratt, Alan Cracknell, Tom 'Wowser' Whiting, typesetter extraordinaire Graham Holmes, eagle-eyed

Steve Burdett, designer Mark Rowland, and studio manager Dean Russell, whose work immeasurably improved the manuscript I gave them.

This book simply could not have happened without my agent, the wise and irresistible Zoë Waldie, whose support, advice, and editorial counsel have been invaluable throughout. I'm eternally grateful to Sarah Churchwell for introducing me to her. Thanks also to Natasia Patel and all at RCW.

I have been lucky enough to have close friends who've supported, encouraged, and inspired me at various times during the writing of this book. Thanks are due above all to Simon Schama, who has been an enthusiastic and generous supporter of the book from its earliest incarnation, as well as, when necessary, an incisive critic. Also to Mary Ann Sieghart, whose wise words, both in person and in her book *The Authority Gap*, came at just the right time; to Fiona Macpherson for twenty years of illustrations and friendship; to Emma Bleasdale for walks and talks in Hyde Park; and to Allyson Stewart-Allen for sound advice. Lucy Taylor, always calm and supportive, has lived with this book for as long as I have – thank you for your patience. Thanks also to my wingmen: Guido, who took time out from his doctoral research to fact-check my manuscript, and Godfrey, the best comma-and-colon man in the business. And I'd like to pay tribute to two absent friends, the luminous Kate Power and the irrepressible Peter Clayton, both very much missed.

Lastly, it's been a long haul and there are three people I could not have done this without. My undying gratitude and affection go out to my sons, who have grown up with this book and, in their different ways, enormously improved it: Ben, gifted editor and nascent philosopher, whose literary sensibilities are second to none; Archie, endlessly and wisely supportive and thoughtful.

Most of all, thanks to Guy – the Real Thing.

PICTURE CREDITS

While every effort has been made to trace the owners of copyright material reproduced herein and secure permissions, the publishers would like to apologise for any omissions and will be pleased to incorporate missing acknowledgements in any future edition of this book.

All images are courtesy of the author, with the following exceptions.

Fig. 9.2: © Fiona Macpherson
Figs 10.1 and 10.2: The Advertising Archives
Fig. 14.1: anshechung.com
Fig. 14.2: © Zynga
Fig. 15.1: Politifact/Poynter Institute

Plate 1: Darrell Gullin/Getty Images
Plate 2: Leekris/Getty Images
Plate 3: Trustees of the Natural History Museum, London
Plate 4: © Andreas Kay
Plate 5: Shutterstock.com (signs) and Getty Images (butterflies)
Plate 6: © Claire Spottiswoode
Plate 7: © Mitch Haaby
Plate 8: Bridgeman Images
Plate 9: Joe Simon-Whelan
Plate 10: © Fiona Macpherson
Plates 11,12,13: © Robbie Cooper
Plate 14: © Kate Starbird

Author photo: © Sandi Friend

INDEX

ABOUT THE AUTHOR

Currently a Senior Visiting Research Fellow at the Policy Institute at King's College London and a director of an open-source intelligence company, Alice Sherwood has undergraduate degrees in philosophy and in chemistry, an MBA from INSEAD, and an MA in literary criticism and narrative non-fiction. She has worked in business, in television documentary production, and as an education and multimedia producer at the BBC. She is chair of the Rising Tide women's network and has served as a trustee of the Hay Festival Foundation and the London Library. She lives in London and Wales.

Authenticity is Alice's first book. It won a Royal Society of Literature Giles St Aubyn Award for Non-Fiction.